Cybersecurity Leadership Demystified

A comprehensive guide to becoming a world-class
modern cybersecurity leader and global CISO

Dr. Erdal Ozkaya

BIRMINGHAM—MUMBAI

Cybersecurity Leadership Demystified

Copyright © 2022 Packt Publishing

Group Product Manager: Vijin Boricha

Publishing Product Manager: Mohd Riyan Khan

Senior Editor: Shazeen Iqbal

Content Development Editor: Romy Dias

Technical Editor: Shruthi Shetty

Copy Editor: Safis Editing

Project Coordinator: Shagun Saini

Proofreader: Safis Editing

Indexer: Sejal Dsilva

Production Designer: Shankar Kalbhor

Marketing Coordinator: Hemangi Lotlikar

First published: January 2022

Production reference: 1040122

Published by Packt Publishing Ltd.
Livery Place
35 Livery Street
Birmingham
B3 2PB, UK.

ISBN 978-1-80181-928-2

www.packt.com

This is my sixteenth book with my name on the cover and, like its predecessors, this book represents several years of in-depth research, analysis, and real-life work experience.

Each book takes a lot of time to come into your hands, and each book means I am stealing time from my most loved ones. Like all my other books, I would like to dedicate this book to my wife, Arzu, my son, Jemre, and my daughter, Azra. Their endless love and support are motivating me to do even more.

In this book, I have a special "Ask The Expert" section, like in some of my other books, and I'm honored to welcome Dr. Timothy Summers, Dr. Suleyman Özarslan, Dr. Mike Jankowski, and my very close friends Marcus Murray, Raymond Comvalius, Sukru Durmaz, Raif Sarica, Vladimir Meloski, Paula Januszkiewicz, and Mert Sarica. They shared their time, insight, and experiences freely and without reservation. I am thankful for the contribution of their expertise and wisdom in this book.

Additionally, I thank the Packt team for their support.

Foreword

The **Chief Information Security Officer (CISO)** executive plays one of the most critical roles in today's business environment. Together with their team, they evaluate all possible security risks that face an organization, and subsequently develop and put in place measures that will minimize these risks and the impact of these risks if a security incident occurs.

The CISO communicates all the identified risks to all the stakeholders of an organization and makes decisions on the best means to achieve higher levels of security while considering all the business repercussions of their decisions. This book focuses on the role of the CISO and how they go about playing their role to ensure heightened security for the organizations they work for. In a world of increased cyber dangers, which are continually evolving, every business now needs to have an individual who will play the role of the CISO in an organization to help keep the business more secure from cyber-attacks.

The cyber-world presents many dangers to the modern business landscape, especially with the increased integration of technology into all parts of modern businesses. Some of these dangers manifest in the form of hacks leading to loss of data, access to systems, disruption of business operations, and loss of finances, especially when the attackers corrupt systems and/or steal data and ask for a ransom to return the stolen data. CISOs need to coordinate with all the business departments to ensure that all the business operations are conducted securely and that cyber attackers do not find loopholes in the system to exploit. This book addresses all cybersecurity issues that relate to the CISO role including laws and policies that an organization needs to comply with to enhance the cybersecurity aspects of its business operations.

The book will immensely benefit CISOs as it highlights how critical their role is, how their role has been evolving in the recent past, and what they can do to improve their effectiveness in the CISO role. The CISO executive's role in HR by helping with the hiring of the right personnel, their contribution to optimal budgeting functions, and their increased importance to long-term strategic decision-making for organizations are some of the roles that are discussed in detail throughout the book.

The current cybersecurity posture

As you all know, malware/ransomware is legitimate code (within the context of the CPU instructions) that is doing illegitimate things. The code is legitimate because the CPU understands and executes the code in this executable file that we call malware/ransomware. However, what this code does is bad for us…so why are we allowing this malware/ransomware to execute?

Today, the vast majority of the cybersecurity world works with *allow everything, deny the bad*. They try to deny the bad by trying to detect it by using AI, machine learning, heuristics, behavior analysis, and **Endpoint Detection and Response** (**EDR**). I must say, the results speak for themselves! Breach after breach, damage after damage!

The amount of money spent on cybersecurity compared to the damage sustained is unacceptable, all because of a poor posture choice.

This posture is not a posture you can achieve. It's an impossible posture! You cannot deny the bad if you don't know that it's bad! It's mathematically impossible. Detection cannot be, should *NOT* be, the first of the *ONLY* method for protection! 100% detection does not exist. It's a scientific fact! No cybersecurity product can detect 100%!

The bottom line is that allowing everything while denying the bad means when you fail to detect something, you get breached! This posture gives you a guaranteed breach, mathematically speaking. Yep, it's guaranteed that you will be breached!

Ask yourself this question: *"How will you prevent damage when your cybersecurity product fails to detect?"* No matter what the detection method may be (AI, machine learning, heuristics, behavior, signature, and so on), they all are trying to detect something bad…and they can never be 100% accurate.

Coming back to posture, *allow the good, deny the rest* is a posture you can achieve, but it's not user friendly. Why? Because people don't want to be restricted and want to run applications.

We need a new cybersecurity posture that can give us the best of both worlds: *allow the good but also allow the rest with Attack Surface Reduction (ASR)*.

Here is a brand-new security posture, where you allow the good, but you also allow the rest, but in an environment with an ASR.

This way, you are not restricting users by denying any application from running on their computer, but you are denying any unknown ransomware and malware from causing damage because they run in a restricted (ASR) mode in which they are not allowed to cause damage.

A takeaway thought: If you were the guy creating the ransomware, would you be stupid enough to release it knowing that it will be detected right off the bat, or would you first make sure it can't be detected, before you unleash it?

- IF you still wonder why all cybersecurity breaches are happening

- THEN go to the beginning of this section and read again!

- REPEAT UNTIL you understand

Empowering and protecting your end users

We have one goal: to empower and protect our end users. My motto is "look after our users, money will follow." It works, and it always has. We put our users first. We know that our users empower our business with their business. It's a beautiful relationship that works.

Everything we do is designed to either empower or protect the end users. It's as simple as that, and I highly recommend that CISOs follow this approach. You are the protectors of your organization, customers, co-workers, and shareholders. You need to ensure your users are empowered and protected at the same time. Throughout this book, you will learn many different ways to do so. Erdal did a great job. I believe you will learn a lot. I encourage you to seriously consider the lessons in this book, and I wish you all the best in your journey.

Melih Abdulhayoglu

CEO at MAVeCap

Innovator, engineer, entrepreneur, and cybersecurity leader

Contributors

About the author

Dr. Erdal Ozkaya is a passionate, solutions-focused professional with a comprehensive global background in information technology and cybersecurity.

He worked at Standard Chartered, where he was regional CISO and managing director of the Middle East, Africa, and Pakistan. Before working at Standard Chartered, he was a trusted security advisor and cybersecurity architect at Microsoft, where he perfected the art of mapping customer business problems to technology solutions. He remains committed to delivering accurate, accessible resources to inform individuals and organizations of cybersecurity and privacy matters in the internet age.

Dr. Ozkaya is a collaborative team leader with expertise spanning end-to-end IT solutions, management, communications, and innovation. He is a well-known public speaker, an award-winning technical expert, an author, and a creator of certifications (courseware and exams) for prestigious organizations such as Microsoft, EC Council, and other expert-level vendors with an esteemed list of credits to his name. Dr. Ozkaya is a graduate of Charles Sturt University in Australia.

About the reviewers

Dr. Deepak D. Kalambkar is an IT professional/author with a doctorate in cyber law, a certified ISO 27001 auditor, and a CISO with over 20 years of experience in designing and managing IT infrastructure and creating policies. His experience includes installing and managing Windows/Linux servers, IT policy management, and managing teams of engineers both in-house and outsourced to generate optimum infrastructure efficiency. He works with Safexpay as VP Infosec with the vision to build a digital platform infrastructure that will transform the payment and banking needs of every business globally. Its robust and seamless payment products allow businesses to transact securely and the company is committed to the digital future. He has been honored with several awards and certifications.

Nikolaos (Nick) Thymianis is an information security professional with over 4 years of experience in IT, currently working in Infosec for one of the biggest pharmaceutical companies in the world. Nick has broad knowledge in securing enterprises through incident response, penetration testing, threat hunting, table-top exercises, enterprise architecture, and IT operations. He holds a degree in information security. He is an advisor at the University of Piraeus and has spoken at multiple events as an information security expert.

Table of Contents

Preface

1

A CISO's Role in Security Leadership

Defining a CISO and their
responsibilities   2
Definition of a CISO   2
Responsibilities of a CISO   3
What exactly is a CISO?   4

Understanding the similarities
and differences between a CISO
and a CSO   5
Distinguishing between a CIO,
a CTO, and a CISO   6
Designing a security leadership
role   7

Expanding the role of a CISO   8
The changing role of a CISO   8
How to become a CISO   9
CISO responsibilities   11
Who should not become a CISO?   11

Learning about CISO certification 12
EC-Council CISO program   12
CCISO program   13
Other certifications   13

Summary   14
Further reading   14

2

End-to-End Security Operations

Evaluating the IT threat
landscape   16
Knowledge of company operations   16
Assessment tools   16
Trends in cyber threats   17

Devising policies and controls
to reduce risk   17

Internal staff policies   18
Other company policies   18

Leading auditing and
compliance initiatives   19
Anti-malware and anti-spyware software 19
Compliance with international
regulations   20

Examples of regulations and
regulatory bodies   20

**Managing information security
initiatives**   **21**
Strategic security planning   21
The hiring of a security team   22

**Establishing partnerships with
vendors and security experts**   **22**
Establishing partnerships   23

Security experts as a knowledge
resource   23
System security evaluation tools   24
Creating long-term working
relationships with vendors   24
Establishing clear communication
channels   25
Customer advisory groups   25

Summary   **26**
Further reading   **26**

3

Compliance and Regulations

Defining data compliance   **30**
Understanding GDPR   **32**
The history of GDPR   32
GDPR key definitions   33
GDRP data protection principles   34
The CISO role in GDPR   35

Learning about HIPAA   **36**
Privacy rule   36
Right to access PHI   37
Potential risks   38
The three HIPAA rules   38

Introducing the CCPA   **40**
What does the CCPA entail?   41
The CCPA rights   41
Personal information   42
Failure to comply with the CCPA   42

Understanding the HITECH Act   **43**
Important HITECH amendments and
provisions   44
Goals of the HITECH Act   45

Getting to know the EFTA   **46**
History of the EFTA   47
The EFTA requirements for service
providers   47

Introducing COPPA   **48**
COPPA violations   49
COPPA compliance   50

Learning about Sarbanes-Oxley   **51**
History of the Sarbanes-Oxley Act   51
Key provisions of the Sarbanes-Oxley Act 52

Understanding FISMA   **53**
Reasons for creating FISMA   53
FISMA compliance   53
FISMA non-compliance penalties   54

Finding out about PIPEDA   **55**
**Understanding IT compliance
and the CISO's role**   **56**
Summary   **56**
Further reading   **57**

4

Role of HR in Security

Understanding security posture **60**
Security posture features 60
IT assets inventory 61
Security controls 61
Attack vectors 61
Attack surface 62
Automating the security posture 62
Ways of improving an organization's
security posture 62
Assessing an organization's security
posture 63
Important steps in security posture
assessment 63

**Exploring human error and its
impact on organizations** **65**
Preventing insider security threats 66

Hiring procedures **67**

Performing verification checks for job
candidates 68
Security education and training 68
Security risk awareness 69
Organizational culture 69
Policies for IAM 70
General safety procedures 72
Employment procedures 73
Vendors, contractors, and consultants
– procedures 74
Tight hiring practices 74
Using strong authentication mechanisms 75
Securing internet access 75
Investigating anomalous activities 75
Refocusing perimeter strategies and
tools 76
Monitoring misuse of assets 76

Summary **76**
Further reading **77**

5

How Documentation Contributes to Security

**Why information system
documentation for security is
important** **80**
What is information security
documentation? 80
Why document? 82
Approving the security documentation 84
Maintaining the security documentation 84
Communicating the security
documentation 84

**Understanding compliance with
documentation** **85**

ISO 27001 85

**Describing some examples of
cybersecurity documents** **86**
Information security policy (ISP) 86
Incident management plan (IMP) 87
Risk management 87
Disaster recovery (DR) and the
business continuity plan (BCP) 90

Tips for better security **92**
Building a cyber strategy plan **93**

Why do we need to build a cyber
strategy?   94
How to build a cyber strategy   95
Best cyber-attack strategies   98

Best cyber defense strategies   99

Summary   **102**
Further reading   **103**

6

Disaster Recovery and Business Continuity

**Integrating cybersecurity
with a DPP**   **107**
BIA   **107**
Classification of data   108

DRaaS   **109**
Developing a communication plan   109
Automated testing processes   110
Immutable data backups   110
Data reuse   111
Continuous updates   111
Long-term planning   112

**Understanding the relationship
between cybersecurity and BC** **112**
Planning for ransomware and DoS
attacks   114
Using quality backups   114

User training and education   115
**Learning about supply chain
continuity**   **116**
**Introducing the key
components of a BC plan**   **116**
How to identify BC risks   117
Types of DR   118
Using AI for DR and BC processes   119
Emerging technologies in the DR and
BC landscape   120
Tips on building a strong and effective
DR plan   120
Importance of a certified and skilled
cybersecurity workforce   121

Summary   **121**
Further reading   **122**

7

Bringing Stakeholders On Board

**Evaluating business
opportunities versus security
risks**   **124**
The role of a CISO in risk management 125

Optimal budgeting   **126**
Communication   127
Corporate governance   127
Duties of top management in an
organization   128

Reporting to the board of directors   129
Getting employees on board   130
Getting customers on board   131
Getting shareholders on board   132
Getting the community on board   133

Summary   **134**
Further reading   **134**

8
Other CISO Tasks

Contributing to technical projects   136

Partnering with internal and external providers   137

Security policies implementation   137
Security planning needs resources   138
Role in recruitment   138
Partnering with security tool providers and consultants   139

Evaluating employee behavior   140

Employee motivation   141

The remuneration and rewarding systems   141
Employee skill level   141
User and entity behavior analytics (UEBA)   142

Financial reporting   143

Addressing cybersecurity as a business problem   144

Summary   145
Further reading   145

9
Congratulations! You Are Hired

How to get hired as a CISO   148

Qualifications for a CISO job   148
Job experience   149
Communication ability   149
Leadership skills   149
Steps to follow to become a CISO   150

The top skills required to succeed as a CISO   151

Your first 90 days as a CISO   153

List of dos in the first 90 days   155

Summary   158
Further reading   158

10
Security Leadership

Developing suitable security policies   163
Communicating cybersecurity issues clearly   163
Getting a bigger budget   164
Leading by example   165
Having training conferences and seminars for employees   165

Building a cybersecurity strategy   166

Telling your story   167
Presenting to the board   168
Leadership and team   169
Summary   169
Further reading   170

11

Conclusion

Defining the CISO role and what the role entails 172

How a CISO ensures E2E security operations are in place in an organization 172

The compliance factor and how a CISO addresses the issue 173

The role of HR management in cybersecurity issues 173

How documentation plays a huge role in effective security leadership 174

DR and BC factors in cybersecurity 174

Understanding the role of various stakeholders in an organization 175

Other CISO roles in an organization 175

Getting hired as a CISO executive 176

What security leadership entails 176

Summary 176

12

Ask the Experts

Protecting and defending your organization from cyberattacks – by Marcus Murray 178

Path to becoming a successful CISO – by Adel Abdel Moneim 185

Recommendations for cybersecurity professionals who want to be CISOs – by Mert Sarica 200

How a modern CISO could work on improving security within their organizations and maintain a good cybersecurity posture – by Dr. Mike Jankowski-Lorek and Paula Januszkiewicz 203

Advice for a CISO – by Raif Sarica and Şükrü Durmaz 211

Cybersecurity leadership demystified – Pave your way to becoming a world-class modern-day cybersecurity expert and a global CISO – by Dr. Timothy C. Summers 216

The future of cybersecurity leadership – by Timothy C. Summers, Ph.D. 217

Working with security experts – by Vladimir Meloski 223

A CISO's communication with
the board on three critical
subjects – by Dr. Süleyman
Özarslan   229

Crush the triangle – by
Raymond Comvalius   232

Index

Another Book You May Enjoy

Preface

Being in an industry that has all the spotlights sounds great. Advising board members on the importance of cybersecurity, being in touch with departments from finance to HR, working closely but separately with IT, overviewing even physical security, and, depending on your organization, traveling and seeing the world as well as having a nice paycheck is perfect.

But be aware that every medallion has two sides to it. You will have countless nights calculating the budget, unrelenting and unforgiving deadlines, trying to sync with a globally distributed team, fighting daily cybersecurity threats, dealing with company politics…it's a list that can quickly make you fear the job, and if it does, then this book and being a **Chief Information Security Officer** (**CISO**) might not be right for you.

So, you are a new CISO or want to become a CISO/cybersecurity leader. This means you're interested in having a growth mindset, being mentored while mentoring, and, of course, honing your skills to help take you into the CISO role.

Are you not sure where to start? Then this book is right for you. You will read text from a global CISO who has served CISOs as an advisor in his own company in the Asia Pacific, then at Microsoft in the Middle East, Africa, and Europe region. He holds the CISO title at a global bank, and finally, works in one of the most successful cybersecurity firms in the world as CISO.

Who this book is for

The CISO is responsible for an organization's information and data security. The CISO's role is challenging as it demands a solid technical foundation as well as effective communication skills. This book is for busy cybersecurity leaders and executives looking to gain deep insights into the domains important for becoming a competent cybersecurity leader.

The book begins by introducing you to the CISO's role, where you'll learn key definitions, explore the responsibilities involved, and understand how you can become an efficient CISO. You'll then be taken through end-to-end security operations and compliance standards to help you get to grips with the security landscape. In order to be a good leader, you'll need a good team. This book guides you in building your dream team by familiarizing you with HR management, documentation, and stakeholder onboarding. Despite taking all due care, you might still fall prey to cyber-attacks; this book will show you how to quickly respond to an incident to help your organization minimize losses, decrease vulnerabilities, and rebuild services and processes. Finally, you'll explore other key CISO skills that'll help you communicate at both senior and operational levels.

By the end of this book, you'll have gained a complete understanding of the CISO's role and be ready to advance your career.

What this book covers

Chapter 1, A CISO's Role in Security Leadership, explains who and what a CISO is, the requirements of the CISO role, the differences between other technology leadership roles, and what is required in the role for you to be successful. The chapter also covers how to develop the core components needed to be a good CISO for your organization.

Chapter 2, End-to-End Security Operations, covers a day of a CISO and their end-to-end security operations and presents CISO activities that make up this strategy.

Chapter 3, Compliance and Regulations, highlights the issues of data management, data protection, as well as various laws and regulations that have been developed to protect user data. The role of the CISO in data management is to ensure that firms are compliant with regulations to prevent fines, as well as safeguarding companies' reputations.

Chapter 4, Role of HR in Security, addresses the role of CISOs in HR management and intends to show how the HR department is critical to the security of an organization and how CISOs use HR management to improve organizational security.

Chapter 5, How Documentation Contributes to Security, handles the role of documentation in security and the sectors that need to be documented. Documentation helps keep all security processes in check and aids in the evaluation of the current security situation to determine whether updating is required.

Chapter 6, Disaster Recovery and Business Continuity, covers cyber-attacks, data breaches, and how you can build a cyber response and disaster recovery plan based on risk management.

Chapter 7, Bringing Stakeholders On Board, evaluates the CISO's task of security onboarding by evaluating business opportunities versus security risks as well as how a CISO can budget optimally.

Chapter 8, Other CISO Tasks, looks at other important roles CISOs play in an organization, which include such roles as contributing to technical projects, partnering with internal and external providers, evaluating employee behavior, financial reporting, and addressing cybersecurity as a business problem.

Chapter 9, Congratulations! You Are Hired, shows the practical application of what we have learned about the duties of the CISO in an organization and the CISO's first 90 days on the job.

Chapter 10, Security Leadership, provides insights into your role as a security leader in an organization and how to offer security leadership in the most effective manner.

Chapter 11, Conclusion, highlights the dos and don'ts of the CISO role.

Chapter 12, Ask the Expert, is where experts explain their tips and recommendations for CISOs and everyone who wants to be a CISO.

Download the color images

We also provide a PDF file that has color images of the screenshots and diagrams used in this book. You can download it here: `https://static.packt-cdn.com/downloads/9781801819282_ColorImages.pdf`.

Get in touch

Feedback from our readers is always welcome.

General feedback: If you have questions about any aspect of this book, email us at `customercare@packtpub.com` and mention the book title in the subject of your message.

Errata: Although we have taken every care to ensure the accuracy of our content, mistakes do happen. If you have found a mistake in this book, we would be grateful if you would report this to us. Please visit `www.packtpub.com/support/errata` and fill in the form.

Piracy: If you come across any illegal copies of our works in any form on the internet, we would be grateful if you would provide us with the location address or website name. Please contact us at `copyright@packt.com` with a link to the material.

If you are interested in becoming an author: If there is a topic that you have expertise in and you are interested in either writing or contributing to a book, please visit `authors.packtpub.com`.

Share Your Thoughts

Once you've read *Cybersecurity Leadership Demystified*, we'd love to hear your thoughts! Scan the QR code below to go straight to the Amazon review page for this book and share your feedback.

`https://packt.link/r/1801819289`

Your review is important to us and the tech community and will help us make sure we're delivering excellent quality content.

1
A CISO's Role in Security Leadership

In this day and age, the security of internet-connected devices and applications has increasingly become critical to the success of firms operating in the internet space. While the internet has provided numerous opportunities for businesses to conduct business, expand their operations, and reach their customers more easily, it has also introduced cybersecurity risks to both the businesses and the customers that interact with these businesses via digital platforms.

Cybercrime has been on the rise in recent years, and data breaches continue to wreak havoc among many companies globally. It has become essential for all businesses that deal with financial and other important data from customers to implement security measures in their organizations to ensure their organizations remain secure. Organizations now have departments that exclusively tackle security issues that affect an organization resulting from interactions with the digital world.

One of the key positions in modern organizations is the **chief information and security officer** (**CISO**), who is generally tasked with security-related duties.

In this chapter, you will learn who and what a CISO is, the requirements of the CISO role, the differences between other technology leadership roles, and what is required in the role for you to be successful. The chapter will also cover how to develop the core components needed to be a good CISO for your organization.

You can expect the following topics to be covered in this chapter:

- Defining a CISO and their responsibilities
- Understanding similarities and differences between a CISO and a **chief security officer** (**CSO**)
- Distinguishing between a **chief information officer** (**CIO**), a **chief technology officer** (**CTO**), and a CISO
- Designing a security leadership role
- Expanding the role of a CISO
- The changing role of a CISO
- How to become a CISO
- Learning about CISO certification

Defining a CISO and their responsibilities

In this section, we provide a definitive description of the term *CISO*, the role of a CISO in a firm, and the importance of this position in any modern organization. The section attempts to provide readers with an introduction to the world of digital platforms, the role they play in organizations, and the integral role that CISO executives play in making all this happen.

Definition of a CISO

A CISO has an executive-level position within an organization and is tasked with establishing and maintaining various mechanisms and structures that safeguard the informational and technological assets of the organization. CISOs are technologists who can participate in high-level initiatives as business strategists. CISOs ensure that **information technology** (**IT**) systems comply with security and regulatory requirements. In summary, a CISO is the top *cyber executive* of an organization.

The following screenshot shows a man interacting with a digital device that bears the name **CISO** and depicts a lock. It confers a message of the core role of CISO executives, keeping digital platforms safe from external threats:

Figure 1.1 – A CISO executive keeping digital platforms safe from external threats

In the next section, you will discover the responsibilities of a CISO.

Responsibilities of a CISO

The main responsibilities that a CISO performs in an organization include the following:

- Determining and establishing the right governance and security practices for the organization

- Creating and enabling a framework that ensures risk-free scalability of business operations

- Helping executives at a C-suite level understand cyber risks

These three items are the overarching responsibilities that define the main responsibilities of a CISO in any organization. On the other hand, some of the more minor responsibilities include the following:

- Evaluating the IT landscape and determining all the necessary factors that affect the security of the organization concerning digital platforms.

- Devising policies that impact the digital landscape affecting the organization's operations.

- Quantifying security risks and determining the level of risk they pose to the organization and taking necessary steps to curb the threat.

- Communicating effectively with the rest of the team regarding any updates and changes to a system as well as during the aftermath of a security breach, to ensure a united front when facing challenges posed by security breaches.

- Recruiting a capable team that is responsible for mitigating threats. As a CISO, it is important to have an informed team that can identify threats and take the necessary action against such threats.

- Keeping updated on the IT landscape to remain informed of evolving threats and the resources to help in mitigation against these threats. Adversaries stand little to no chance against a CISO who invests in studying new threats and is proactive against evolving threats.
- Auditing security measures that have been put in place to safeguard the organization and ensuring that these measures are not only up to date but also capable of protecting the company from security risks and threats.

The next section will clarify what a CISO executive does in an organization.

What exactly is a CISO?

Before we dive deep into the nuances of cyber chiefs' career paths, it is important to understand the nature of the role. Six critical responsibilities underpin a CISO's success, and we'll look at these roles in the following sections.

Trusted security advisor

As a CISO, you need to translate technical matters into the language of the business. In other words, you will be helping non-technological executives and boards understand technical matters and help them make risk-informed decisions confidently.

Strategist

As a CISO, you need to get involved in setting goals, determining actions to achieve the goals, and mobilizing resources to execute *prioritized* actions that need to be tightly linked to the business strategy.

Leader

As a CISO, you need to have leadership skills not just to build an inspired and bonded diverse team, but also set an example as a role model to create a culture of constant learning, innovation, and active collaboration.

Modern marketer

Modern marketing is the ability to harness the full capabilities of a business to provide the best experience for the customer and thereby drive growth. As a CISO, you need to evangelize cybersecurity capabilities to regulators, client prospects, insurers, and business partners—helping win new business, lower the cost of capital, and maintain a license to operate.

Change agent

CISOs should be able to create a cyberculture whereby everyone in the organization understands cyber risks and helps to mitigate them.

Influencer

CISOs should be able to influence critical stakeholders to support the cybersecurity transformation.

This section has shown what a CISO does in an organization and the various core roles they play within an organization. However, there are other similar roles in an organization, and the next section seeks to clarify the distinct role of a CISO in relation to roles played by other officers in an organization.

Understanding the similarities and differences between a CISO and a CSO

In some organizations, the roles of a CISO and a CSO may be synonymous. If an organization has a position for both individuals, it is most likely that they will have redundancy of roles. Both executive positions in an organization have similar roles, with subtle differences between the two. Both executives are responsible for securing information and assets such as information in an organization. A CSO is normally tasked with the security of people, processes, and products, while a CISO is tasked with specific security issues that ensure that people, processes, and products are protected. In many organizations, however, these two roles are used interchangeably, or one individual may perform both functions.

However, it is important to note that having two individuals playing these two roles in an organization can lead to conflicting scenarios due to the overlapping roles of the two executives and the ever-evolving nature of the challenges that could be classified under both roles. A CISO is tasked with supervising a company's cybersecurity by designing and implementing an organization's security program to deter and curb any security threats that may face the organization. A CSO also plays a similar role in an organization and ensures that the organization is safe from cyber threats and that all organizational assets, processes, and people are safe from both internal and external threats.

With the digital landscape continuously evolving, both a CSO and a CISO are required to keep up to date with current technological advances and changes. This requirement ensures that they keep abreast of any current changes in the digital sphere and evolving threats as well. Without continuous updates, adversaries will have an upper hand, and these two executives will have failed in their roles. Therefore, both executives are similar in their need to continually update their knowledge base to carry out their roles effectively.

This section has differentiated the CISO role from that of a CSO. Next, we will look at what differentiates the role of a CISO from those played by CIO and CTO executives in an organization.

Distinguishing between a CIO, a CTO, and a CISO

In many organizations, CIOs are the foremost leaders of IT departments, answerable directly to the **chief executive officer** (**CEO**) or the board of directors. They oversee strategic IT investments, manage IT operations, and lead digital transformations within an organization. If an organization is planning on making huge infrastructural changes that will affect the digital space, the CIO will be tasked with overseeing such projects, ensuring that all organizational information goals are met through the project and that the project meets the long-term mission and vision statements of the organization.

A CTO is an individual in an organization tasked with the integration of new technologies. The role typically requires long-term planning and is concerned with technological infrastructural changes that organizations perform when taking on board new technology or when upgrading to new technology that will see major changes in information flow within the company. A CTO typically reports to the CIO.

Both a CTO and a CIO play roles that are similar to the role of a CISO. Some of their roles may overlap with those of a CISO. The CIO role, in particular, presents the highest similarity level. Having both CIO and CISO executive positions in an organization may prove problematic due to many overlapping roles. A CTO, however, typically works under both individuals and works hand in hand with these two executives in an organization. A CIO mainly deals with the management side of an organization and will usually focus on the internal operations of the organization and how technological changes affect the informational needs of the organization. They are also tasked with coming up with ideal operational changes that can maximize the information available and leverage the information potential of available resources to the benefit of the company.

Now that we have differentiated the roles played by a CTO and a CIO and how they are similar in some respects to those of a CISO, we are going to see what defines the various security aspects in an organization and how the CISO role fits into the **security leadership** dimension.

Designing a security leadership role

Business organizations are increasingly suffering from digital threats in the form of cyber-attacks that have become a top concern for businesses globally. Some of these cyber-attacks have led to the destruction of business entities. To make matters worse, the ever-changing IT landscape has led to increased threats for businesses. This has increased a need for businesses to invest in the *security* of informational and technological resources within their business enterprises, hence the establishment of the role of a CISO. Organizations must have a department within their organization that deals in security and safeguarding an organization's assets. A failure to adequately protect an organization from both internal and external threats will put the business at risk, resulting in successful data breaches, reduced trust in the company from stakeholders and customers, and threats to the continuity of the business.

To design a **security leadership role** in a company, all factors affecting a business need to be put into consideration. Both internal and external factors will be used in designing the role of a security leader in a business setup. Internal factors include such things as the available resources of a company, the digital space in which a business operates, and the informational needs and plans of an organization. These various factors will help determine the kind of plans an organization needs to put in place to define the position of the security leader—in this case, the CISO. The external landscape that affects business operations is also crucial to the designing of a CISO role. The business operations and the digital environment it requires to operate will determine the kind of threats facing a company and the kind of responses a business will initiate to handle security risks and threats to their business operations.

After understanding the security leadership requirements in an organization and how a CISO fits into this description, we will next define how the CISO role has been evolving.

Expanding the role of a CISO

The role of a CISO has been expanding with the changing needs of many business operations. Technology has been changing quickly, leading to businesses having to adapt to their new environment. Many businesses are adopting the internet space and are utilizing this to expand their businesses. Within the internet space, businesses are interacting with other businesses and conducting many transactions on the internet platform. Customers interacting in the digital space provide businesses with personal data, as well as financial information that can be targeted by attackers. A CISO has become a necessity, with more businesses going online not only to promote and advertise their business but also as a means to carry out their business. The online space has become an important channel for business transactions, with thousands of online e-commerce sites sprouting up by the day.

The CISO role has traditionally only dealt with keeping information and systems secure from both outside and inside threats. However, more responsibilities are being added to the portfolio of CISO executives, and the expanding role sees CISOs taking an integral role in the long-term planning and strategic planning of an organization. The very things that introduce information and security risks into a business are the things that are required for the strategic growth of the business—for instance, a business may need to perform an overhaul of its business operations to digitalize and automate many aspects of the business. Such an operation would intend to automate the system to make it more effective and introduce competitive advantage and efficiency into business operations.

However, since a strategic plan introduces new information and security risks, a CISO needs to be included in such plans. Therefore, the expanded role of a CISO requires the executive to be integrally involved in the long-term strategic planning of a business enterprise.

You now have a good idea of how the role of a CISO has been expanding and continues to expand. Next, we'll go over the evolving nature of the CISO role.

The changing role of a CISO

The role of a CISO is not what it was 5 or 10 years ago. According to those who find themselves in the role today, that's not necessarily a bad thing.

In the past, it used to be that CSOs were over-glorified IT security administrators, babysitting the firewalls, arguing with software vendors over botched antivirus signature updates, and cleaning spyware off of infected laptops and desktop PCs. True—that's still the role some CSOs find themselves in, but for the majority, the responsibility has shifted to looking at the big picture and designing a program that balances acceptable risks against unacceptable ones.

In an ideal world, today's CISO hires someone else to handle all those technical security tasks. Of course, a question remains as to whether you can inspire them to do what you once had to do or if you'll turn them off with an attitude of superiority.

The role of the CISO is ever-evolving due to the ever-changing IT landscape. Every day, new threats arise that a business needs to be wary of. Cybercriminals are always finding new ways to attack the new system, using such means as new viruses and intrusion systems. The changing environment means that a CISO cannot have a fixed role; the role of a CISO will keep changing as the information needs of a company change and the operations of a business change to reflect new informational needs. Also, when a business invests in new technological infrastructure, business operations will change to accommodate the new technology, along with the new security challenges that come with these changes to business operations. A CISO role will therefore change with the evolving needs of an organization.

A business is always in competition with other businesses in its respective industry. One of the ways a business beats the competition is through the introduction of new business applications and technology that processes data and business transactions more efficiently. The introduction of new technology into business operations is a common means of achieving an edge over the competition. However, the introduction of new technology and implementation of the same into a business introduces new processes that come with unique challenges.

A CISO role is, therefore, flexible and needs to adapt to the changing environment to remain effective. In a multi-department business, security risks may arise from operations affecting particular departments. Because of this, a CISO executive needs to have unparalleled access to all departments within a business to be most effective.

How to become a CISO

There is no direct path to the CISO role. While this is true, it's really important to hire the *right talent*. Being a CISO used to be a hardcore cybersecurity role; however, the function of a CISO involves much more business leadership and risk management.

Today, a CISO must be able to help executives at a *C-suite* level to understand risk. CISOs in any enterprise organization must have skills to be able to explain security for *non-techies*, build and maintain critical relationships, and communicate at both senior and operational levels. Soft skills are critical to evangelizing security initiatives and celebrating wins, which need to be expressed as business outcomes.

CISOs who can develop those skills can *sell security* to their peers and other business-line executives. So, who can become a CISO? Let's find out who the contenders are here:

- Experienced techies, such as cybersecurity architects, network security engineers, or IT security managers

- An experienced technology risk manager

- A CIO or technology leader with extensive experience building high-performing teams, driving digital transformation, and sitting on executive committees

Becoming a CISO requires both theoretical and practical knowledge of information security. Practical experience of information security qualifies one insecurity—presently, there are no formal requirements to becoming a CISO executive in organizations globally. However, with the intricate nature of the field and the ever-evolving demands of the role, more expertise may be required for effective CISO experts going forward. The many key responsibilities of a CISO expert may not require someone who has practical experience of information security. However, they may require at least theoretical knowledge in the field of information security to effectively carry out the mandate required of CISO experts.

It is a common misconception that a CISO, given the role they need to execute, must come from a technical background to be an effective executive. However, this need not be the case. A CISO expert often works with other experts as part of a team. The team can have people with practical knowledge in various fields, from data management to data security, as well as networking knowledge. In some cases, all that is required is a good manager to manage the team well to ensure that they perform effective work with the right motivation and direction.

However, with the introduction of certified **CISO programs**, it is now possible for an individual to have qualifications and certification to prove they can handle the various aspects of the role of a CISO. The program will test a candidate on various skills that are critical to the core roles of a CISO expert in any organization. To become a CISO expert, you thus need to learn the theoretical background regarding the management of data and how information requirements are central to an organization's business operations.

A CISO expert needs to at least understand the IT landscape to enable them to make informed decisions regarding the impact of the changing landscape on the organization. It is critical for individuals pursuing a career in information security to continually update their knowledge base regarding the information security industry. Other fields of knowledge include learning about the tools necessary to carry out some of the tests and security implementations for a business entity. A CISO expert needs to understand the tools available and the kind of threats that can face their entity, as well as the best ways to avert those threats.

In the next section, we will look at some areas of focus of a CISO.

CISO responsibilities

Some of the daily tasks of CISOs are outlined in the following list. Please keep in mind that we will cover a CISO's day, end-to-end, in *Chapter 2, End-to-End Security Operations*:

- **Security operations**: Real-time analysis of immediate threats, and triage when something goes wrong

- **Cyber risk and cyber intelligence**: Keeping abreast of developing security threats, and helping the board understand potential security problems that might arise from acquisitions or other big business moves

- **Data loss and fraud prevention**: Making sure internal staff don't misuse or steal data

- **Security architecture**: Planning, buying, and rolling out security hardware and software, and making sure IT and network infrastructure are designed with best security practices in mind

- **Identity and access management (IAM)**: Ensuring that only authorized people have access to restricted data and systems

- **Program management**: Keeping ahead of security needs by implementing programs or projects that mitigate risks—regular system patches, for instance

- **Investigations and forensics**: Determining what went wrong in a breach, dealing with those responsible if they're internal, and planning to prevent repeats of the same crisis

- **Governance**: Making sure all of the preceding initiatives run smoothly and get the funding they need—and that corporate leadership understands their importance

Let's now have a look at a comparative viewpoint—who should not become a CISO—in the next section.

Who should not become a CISO?

As a trusted security advisor in the past, I met many CISOs who had no clue about cybersecurity, and unfortunately, those CISOs needed the most help. CISOs should not be just hired based on experience in the company or for just being a program delivery manager. CISOs are much more than just a delivery manager, politician, or someone who has networked well to get the *hot seat*, which pays well.

Mark my words— organizations that follow this path will have ex-CEOs who blame interns for using weak passwords. (Read the news article here: `https://edition.cnn.com/2021/02/26/politics/solarwinds123-password-intern/index.html`.)

I met many CISOs depending on our *advisory*, or they were great leaders but had no clue of *what was exactly happening in the cyber landscape*. In summary, anyone who is not cyber literate should not think of being a CISO unless they are happy to learn.

In the last section of this introductory chapter, we are going to explore how to become qualified as a CISO.

Learning about CISO certification

To effectively play the role of a CISO executive, you need to be qualified in the *information and security* aspects of technology alongside other critical skills that are integral to the role of a CISO in an organization.

Not too many organizations focus on CISO training, but we will discuss some of them in the next sections.

EC-Council CISO program

The **International Council of Electronic Commerce Consultants (EC-Council) CISO program** is one of the globally leading bodies that offer certification to CISO experts to qualify them to carry out various roles that are integral to a CISO executive. The body provides a qualified individual with a **Certified CISO (CCISO) certificate**. The body focuses on practical experience and recognizes the experience of people in the world of information security in awarding the certification. The body was created by high-level executives that formed a foundation on which the program was built to offer some form of training and recognition to people who were qualified in the field of information security. The body identified an increasing need to recognize the increasingly important role of CISO experts in the modern digital world.

CCISO program

The **CCISO program** is one of the first such programs in the world and offers both training and certification opportunities to already practically qualified people globally. The founders of the program were both aspiring CISOs and other renowned sitting CISOs in various capacities in world-leading technology firms. Before certification, candidates must sit an exam that will test their knowledge in the information security realm. The aim of the exam is not just to test the candidate's practical skills in data management and security, but also to test their theoretical knowledge in principles that guide information security principles. Both the theoretical aspects and practical aspects of the exam are important to the qualification of CISO experts. Theoretical knowledge in matters of information security requires theoretical underpinning for a better and holistic outcome.

Other certifications

Besides EC Council, the **SysAdmin, Audit, Network, and Security Institute (SANS Institute)** has some cybersecurity management courses, such as *Leading Cybersecurity Change: Building a Security-Based Culture*, *Security Leadership Essentials for Managers*, and more.

Based on a study by *Digital Guardian*, 53 of the *Fortune 100* CISOs held the **Certified Information Systems Security Professional (CISSP)** certification from the **International Information System Security Certification Consortium (ISC²)**, and 22 held the **Certified Information Security Manager (CISM)** certification from ISC². The top five certifications held by *Fortune 100* CISOs include the CISSP, CISM, **Information Technology Infrastructure Library (ITIL)**, **Certified Information Systems Auditor (CISA)** from **Information Systems Audit and Control Association (ISACA)**, and **Certified in Risk and Information Systems Control (CRISC)** certifications.

While certifications are good to show what you know, keep in mind that they don't necessarily make you a stronger professional. Certifications won't turn a CISO candidate from analyst to a C-suite dweller overnight, but what they can do is offer expertise across the many areas CISOs must have basic knowledge of, if not in-depth expertise.

Summary

In this chapter, we have learned that a CISO is the guardian of an organization, building a cyber strategy, acting as an advisor to the board, and still being a technical executive. A CISO is also known as a CSO and **vice president** (**VP**) of security.

The demand for business-centered technical CISOs will continue to grow, as having the right CISO will provide assurance to companies, their strategic business partners, regulators, and customers that their cybersecurity capabilities are robust and fit for purpose. Being a CISO can be rewarding; as data breaches soar, so will a CISO's paychecks.

In the next chapter, we will cover a CISO's operations, end to end.

Further reading

Here are some resources that can be used to gain more knowledge on this subject:

* All about CISOs: `https://www.erdalozkaya.com/tag/global-ciso/`
* *Understanding CISO Roles and Responsibilities*: `https://www.deepwatch.com/blog/understanding-ciso-roles-responsibilities/`
* *Global CISO Forum:* `https://www.globalcisoforum.com/`
* *EC-Council CCISO Certification:* `https://ciso.eccouncil.org/cciso-certification/`
* *The changing role of the CISO:* `https://www.securitymagazine.com/articles/91653-the-changing-role-of-the-ciso`
* *CIO Vs. CSO Vs. CSIO – How Are These Roles Evolving?:* `https://www.digital-adoption.com/cio-vs-cso/`
* *How to become a CISO:* `https://portswigger.net/daily-swig/how-to-become-a-ciso-your-guide-to-climbing-to-the-top-of-the-enterprise-security-ladder`
* *Hacker Combat* CISO posts: `https://hackercombat.com/?s=CISO`
* SANS security leadership courses: `https://www.sans.org/cyber-security-courses/?&focus-area=security-management-legal-audit&training-format=`
* ISACA training: `https://www.isaca.org/training-and-events`

2
End-to-End Security Operations

The **chief information security officer (CISO)** ensures the **end-to-end (E2E) security operations** of an organization. Together with their security team, they handle all security operations, enforce policies, and evaluate and address system vulnerabilities to ensure that a company's information assets are safe from both internal and external threats.

This chapter will cover a typical day of a CISO and their E2E security operations and present the CISO activities that make up this security strategy. By the end of the chapter, you should be able to understand the reasons behind all the CISO and team's security activities and why they need to address all sectors of an organization without neglecting any.

We will cover the following topics in this chapter, which also form a list of the main CISO roles in an organization:

- Evaluating the **information technology (IT)** threat landscape
- Devising policies and controls to reduce risk
- Leading auditing and compliance initiatives
- Managing information security initiatives
- Establishing partnerships with vendors and security experts

Evaluating the IT threat landscape

A CISO is responsible for company security, and the entire process begins with an evaluation of the threat landscape before implementing any tangible solutions. Evaluating the **IT landscape** helps reveal the various vulnerabilities present in a system and the various attack surfaces present in information assets that can be exploited by attackers. Threats to a company's information assets may come from users who are authorized to use the system or from external attackers. The evaluation process needs to determine all the threats facing a company before it can determine avenues to address these vulnerabilities.

We have now addressed the need for CISOs to evaluate the threat landscape before they can brainstorm solutions to address identified issues. In the next section, we will look into the importance of CISOs gaining in-depth knowledge of company operations to create effective solutions.

Knowledge of company operations

An evaluation of the IT landscape of a company requires in-depth knowledge of the company's operations. With the evolving nature of modern businesses, the duties of a CISO are also evolving, requiring them to have unrestricted access to all departments of a company. Accessing all sections of a company allows a CISO to thoroughly understand all company operations and enables them to perform an effective evaluation of all internal processes. Attackers perform an exhaustive evaluation of a company's system to find vulnerabilities. For CISOs to effectively counter such efforts, they also need to have a full view of a company's systems and operations to determine all avenues and attack surfaces an attacker may use to infiltrate the company's system.

Assessment tools

A CISO also needs specialized tools to conduct a thorough evaluation of a company's systems. These specialized tools should be sourced from proven vendors who trade in network tools for system evaluation purposes. These tools aid a CISO in the assessment of a system including penetration testing and other ethical hacking processes. The result of penetration testing is a report that establishes all attack surfaces as well as revealing all possible vulnerabilities that can be exploited by attackers.

Internal evaluation of the threat landscape also encompasses an evaluation of a company's own internal control mechanisms in place to protect a company's information assets. A CISO needs to objectively evaluate a company's internal controls that are meant to safeguard the company's system from attacks. These controls apply to both external threats and internal threats. To ensure the effectiveness of the threat landscape evaluation, the internal processes should be evaluated with the standards of external vulnerability assessments. In many cases, companies tend to be complacent about internal systems where company employees are involved. However, reports continue to show that disgruntled employees are one of the leading causes of cyber threats to organizations.

Trends in cyber threats

Understanding trends in cyber threats is an important skill for all CISOs. The IT sector is ever evolving. New **attack vectors** keep coming up, and CISOs need to be updated about current trends in the IT sector as this will enable them to have an understanding of all the threats they are likely to face and take measures to mitigate such threats. An organization needs to be safeguarded from all common attack vectors as a minimum requirement. Since security mechanisms get outdated quickly, CISOs must keep abreast of changes in the threat landscape. Continuous improvement of skills and knowledge are key traits of an effective CISO in the current times.

This section has addressed the important role of evaluating the cyber threat landscape. The next section will address the role of devising policies and security controls as measures to keep a company safe from threats.

Devising policies and controls to reduce risk

To ensure E2E security in an organization, a CISO is tasked with devising **policies** and setting up **security controls** to help mitigate any threats facing a company. The CISO role is an executive role in the management sphere and should have the influence to create policies that safeguard a company's operations. These policies affect a company's internal operations and mainly focus on the company's staff members. A CISO also reviews all interactions of all users within a system and the threat level from all these users. These users also include vendors of all software used within an organization. Some vendors may not be trustworthy and may provide an organization with software that is insecure or that has unaddressed security patches unknown to buyers.

We now have an idea of how security leaders devise security policies and controls in the implementation of their security functions. The next section highlights some of the internal staff policies developed by the security team.

Internal staff policies

Internal staff can be supportive in helping a company address internal threats. Staff members should be subjected to security controls that ensure that they do not have unlimited access to information assets within an organization. Access to information should be on a need-to-know basis to allow them to perform their functions effectively. Database administrators, who are part of the team that works directly under the CISO in an organization, are tasked with assigning privileges in the accessing of information within a company. These restrictions should be strictly reinforced. If an employee is terminated from an organization, their access privileges should be revoked immediately. Disgruntled employees are a known source of internal threats to an organization and have the capability to do major damage to a company's information assets.

Internal policies should be printed and pinned on a board where all employees can access them for reference to remind them of all the security policies. This should include the consequences of failing to adhere to these security policies. Consequences should be in the form of termination, fines, suspension, or legal action against employees violating these policies. These policies should be reviewed regularly to ensure that they continue to effectively safeguard internal operations and ultimately safeguard the company's information assets. In addition, the security team should ensure that employees respect these security policies and thus develop a culture of security. Employee culture is an integral factor in the implementation of security policies. While internal policies should be meant to safeguard company operations, they should not make staff members' execution of their duties unnecessarily difficult.

Other company policies

Aside from internal staff policies, CISOs also create policies that affect customers and other people that interact with the company, such as vendors. The main security policies that safeguard a company's information assets from non-staff members come in the form of **physical security controls**. Organizations will restrict sections of the company from customers and other non-staff members as a form of basic security control to limit the access of unauthorized people to sensitive information assets or simple theft. These are usually implemented through the use of security cards to access some rooms meant for staff only. These security cards can also have privilege access controls to limit even junior staff members from accessing rooms meant for only senior or authorized personnel. The security team is tasked with devising these security policies and continually reviewing them to ensure that they are effective in enforcing security measures within a company's premises.

We have addressed how a CISO devises policies and security controls to keep a company safe. The next section handles the role of auditing a company and ensuring it is compliant with laws and regulations, as the security controls must be able to enforce compliance.

Leading auditing and compliance initiatives

A CISO and an organization's security team are tasked with leading auditing efforts of the company's security systems and ensuring that a company complies with all the security *standards* and *regulations* that govern its operations. Auditing efforts include a thorough review of a company's assets to ensure that they perform as they should. It also includes taking an inventory of all the company's infrastructure and information assets to determine all possible attack surfaces. Evaluation efforts also ensure that all software is up to date with the latest security patches to reduce a company's exposure to risk and exploitation of vulnerabilities.

We've touched on how CISOs lead in the auditing and compliance initiatives. The next section addresses examples of some of the IT components that CISOs seek to confirm whether they are functioning properly in enhancing a company's security posture.

Anti-malware and anti-spyware software

These series of software, in addition to firewalls, are critical components of securing a system from cyber-attacks. These series of software are not foolproof on their own but need additional security features. However, they are effective in helping protect an organization against simple and common attacks. *Malware* is among the most common attack vectors that attackers will use against a system to help gain access. **Anti-malware programs** and **anti-spyware software** help organizations in protecting their systems and information assets from many external threats. For internet-facing information assets, these types of software will help in the mitigation of risks and possible malware getting into the system.

An **auditing** process carried by the security team ensures that these anti-malware programs, as well as firewall programs, are working as intended and that they are up to date. Updating the software ensures that new malware definitions have been included in a database to help a system fight off newer forms of malicious programs that attackers may use.

After understanding the role of anti-malware in an IT system, the next section seeks to address how CISOs ensure compliance with international regulations.

Compliance with international regulations

Modern companies are regulated by many organizations that have been created to protect consumers, as well as firms, from malicious attacks. Many firms engage in the collection of data from their consumers that they use in the dissemination of their services, as well as to improve their products. However, without management, firms have been known to misuse this information. Therefore, governments have been forced to step in to ensure that firms engage in data-collection exercises in a regulated manner that ensures that the data collected is only used for the purposes it was collected and that users are aware of all the purposes. In addition, these users need to provide their consent to these firms before they can use their data. Most of the regulations involve the collection and use of consumer data.

Examples of regulations and regulatory bodies

Some of the bodies whose regulations affect many operations include **GDPR** and **HIPAA**. GDPR is an acronym standing for **General Data Protection Regulation**. These are statutes created by the **European Union** (**EU**) to protect European citizens from exploitation by companies that engage in the collection, use, and storage of their data. Any company, regardless of whether they operate within the EU or not that collects information from an EU citizen, is required to adhere to these rules. HIPAA, on the other hand, is an acronym that stands for the **Health Insurance Portability and Accountability Act**. This is a statute that was created to ensure that health and insurance information was protected within the **United States** (**US**), and its laws and regulations affect all companies that directly or indirectly through business association deal with such information. These two are some of the many regulations that affect company operations globally, and modern firms need to ensure that they comply with these laws, which the CISO and their team are tasked with.

Consequences of non-compliance

A failure to comply with these laws and regulations jeopardizes a company's existence, and it may be suspended or fined heavily. For instance, all federal firms that deal in health information are governed by the HIPAA statute, and a failure to comply will deny them subsequent federal funding. For other firms, such as those governed by GDPR laws, a failure to comply may lead to heavy fines that could lead to millions of **US dollars'** (**USDs'**) loss to the company. Adherence to some of the laws is possible through the implementation of various security measures, such as the secure storage of data to keep it safe from possible breaches. While ensuring compliance, a firm also benefits from such actions by protecting itself from successful attacks that could threaten the continuity of operations.

We have now addressed the role of a CISO in terms of auditing the company to ensure safety and compliance with laws and regulations. The following section handles their role in managing various information security initiatives.

Managing information security initiatives

A CISO and their security team are tasked with managing a company's **security initiatives** to ensure that the firm is safe from threats and that attackers fail in their endeavors to infiltrate the company's systems. Security initiatives come in the form of an evaluation of the threat landscape, taking the necessary measures to address identified vulnerabilities and implementing policies and security controls to ensure information assets are fully protected.

This section has introduced a major CISO role in managing information security initiatives in an organization. The next section will show how CISOs manage these initiatives.

Strategic security planning

A company has a **strategic plan** that addresses its long-term plans of continuity and business direction. A company's information assets and system infrastructure are critical components to the success of a company's operations. Therefore, planning for *information assets* and the infrastructure that safeguards these assets is part and parcel of the long-term planning of any company. The CISO is an integral component in the management of a company due to their critical role in the management of information assets and any plans relating to these assets. Both long-term information asset planning and long-term strategic business planning have to go hand in hand. While strategizing for long-term business operations, the CISO is tasked with determining how long-term plans will affect information assets and any changes to security requirements resulting from those plans. These determinations will then be included in the discussion to decide on the direction of the business.

While engaging in strategic planning for security operations within a company, the CISO needs to ensure that security plans fit the business's strategic plans, both in the short term and the long term. If a business wants to perform a full overhaul of its IT or introduce a new system as a means of improving its business operations, it needs the CISO's input in the strategic planning. This shows that the CISO, in this day and age, plays a critical role in business operations and is poised to play core roles in most businesses' long-term strategic planning.

After learning how CISOs manage information security initiatives through strategic security planning, we will next address the hiring of security team members and how this affects information security initiatives.

The hiring of a security team

The hiring of a security team is a direct responsibility of the CISO. The critical nature of the responsibilities of the CISO and the impact of the security team's work on the business risk calls for direct involvement of the CISO in hiring their team members. The CISO often has to delegate responsibilities to various team members to handle various facets of security operations. The security team members need to be individuals with both the integrity to perform this sensitive job without compromise and the technical skills to implement various security responsibilities within the company.

We have addressed the CISO's role in handling various security initiatives within a company by showing how the hiring of security team members is an important security initiative. The next section will provide more insight into their relationships with vendors and the importance of this relationship.

Establishing partnerships with vendors and security experts

CISOs need to establish **partnerships** with **vendors** and **security experts**. A CISO is the overall head of the IT security docket in any organization and is tasked with creating a network with possible vendors and security experts that can help in situations where security expertise and implementation are required.

The following sections will show how to establish these partnerships and how beneficial these partnerships are from a security perspective.

Establishing partnerships

Creating partnerships with vendors of software tools is a critical component that helps a CISO in offering effective security to their organization. With good partnerships, the CISO can purchase tools and software from vendors at friendly prices. These friendly prices enable an organization to make cost savings on issues such as purchasing antivirus programs that are necessary for safeguarding the networks in an organization. Other tools that come in handy in CISO security operations are the testing tools and software that an ethical hacker needs to attempt to gain access into a firm. Ethical hackers are hired by the CISO to attempt hacking into the system. The tools used for such exercises may legally be available on the market. Access to these tools is a basic requirement for CISO executives' work, so getting access to these tools is crucial. Partnerships with such vendors ensure that CISO executives have access to such tools so that they can use them to conduct tests on the internal system to identify any system vulnerabilities.

Security experts as a knowledge resource

Security experts are an important resource for CISO executives who need to update their knowledge of the latest trends in the market. Partnerships with security experts will benefit an organization immensely, ensuring that any updates to the current systems will easily be communicated to the CISO, who can then subsequently make the required changes to update their systems. Security experts can also help in informing a company of the weaknesses of using a specific system and possible solutions to a problem. Security experts are informed people who are normally tasked with providing the security field with research and information regarding changes to the security market, and possible ways of adopting changes to the security requirements of any business. Partnerships with such a team can only help an organization in its quest for better security initiatives. These experts can also help a CISO in educating the team of experts working under them on the best way to complete their work in that current environment.

One way for experts to help the CISO is for the CISO to organize refresher courses with security experts, helping give the security team guidance on matters to do with security. Security experts are likely to know more about security aspects in the market and can offer guidance to the CISO on trends in the market, how an organization can benefit from various resources, and where to get these resources. A partnership with security experts is therefore important and ensures that CISO executives can continue to carry out their role effectively amidst a challenging environment that is filled with hackers and malicious individuals.

System security evaluation tools

CISO executives need software tools that are critical in the offering of their services. Vendors develop and sell tools that CISO executives need to carry out their normal routines. **Penetration testing** is an important exercise for CISO executives. With penetration testing, CISO executives hack into their systems as a means of determining weaknesses inherent in the systems. This exercise is normally done by ethical hackers who perform hacking voluntarily under the permission of the security team as a means of identifying vulnerabilities in the system and subsequently tweaking the system to correct any errors that the system has.

To perform effective penetration testing, a CISO and their team rely on specialized tools that are not readily available on the market. Partnering with such vendors and experts in the market offers a CISO a chance to access these tools easily and at affordable prices. This helps security departments keep their budgets low. Renting or subscribing to some of these tools offers cost advantages to CISO executives. However, pricing is favorable for firms that develop partnerships with these vendors. Budgeting is an important aspect of any business, and the opportunity to get tools that are necessary for business functions at competitive prices helps lower the costs of managing the business and increases profitability levels.

Creating long-term working relationships with vendors

Selecting vendors to work with is a critical part of vendor choice. In general terms, choosing a popular vendor and a market leader is often the best way to go about choosing vendors. Market leaders ensure CISOs will have proven tools that can help them in effectively carrying out their duties. On the other hand, choosing vendors based on marketing gimmicks is likely to backfire. A CISO needs to choose a vendor that can assure them that their tools can meet the demands of the organization. In this case, it is advisable for the CISO team to meet with the actual vendors and not with the sales team, who are more interested in making a sale for the commission than the actual work of the product in question. Meeting the actual team also helps the CISO to explain their organizational needs. Explaining these needs helps get the best response from vendors on whether their tools can meet the demands of the organization. It is also important to factor in the growth potential of the company in question. If an organization is expected to grow soon, a CISO must choose a vendor that has tools that can also meet its increasing demands. Consistently using the same vendors helps a CISO establish trust with vendors and establish a long-term working relationship and partnership that is mutually beneficial.

Establishing clear communication channels

The establishment of clear **communication channels** is an essential part of building an effective vendor relationship for CISOs. A CISO should anticipate situations where they need to urgently get hold of vendors in case of emergencies. In such cases, the CISO must have a clear system of communication with the vendor. This is not the point where the CISO is supposed to figure out how to get in touch with the vendor and stress about whether the vendor will be reachable or respond in time. Good and effective vendors have customer liaisons on their payroll that are tasked with solving emergency problems quickly. These staff members are also tasked with developing customer rapport, hence increasing customer success and loyalty. In most cases, these customer liaisons are responsible for creating strategic partnerships with clients to boost sales and retain customers in the long term. One way of obtaining customer loyalty is the ability to quickly fix a customer's problem. A CISO develops long-term strategic partnerships with vendors through these customer liaisons. The goals of the company should be clearly and transparently communicated by the CISO to the vendors. This clarity ensures that the customer liaison can make the best decisions and give the best fixes for problems that may arise during their mutual partnership.

This section explained the importance of creating a clear communication channel with vendors and other security experts. The next section will address the importance of CISOs joining customer advisory groups.

Customer advisory groups

Customer advisory groups are a great way to build long-term partnerships and relationships with vendors. Vendors often develop these customer advisory groups as a means to acquire feedback from their trusted customers on features and system updates. These groups offer vendors feedback on features they have already developed and also allow vendors to solicit suggestions from customers. These groups are an important route for a CISO to develop a long-term partnership with a vendor. The CISO can use these advisory groups to gain valuable information regarding the use of the tools from their vendor. They can also learn about challenges facing other customers and use that information to avoid those challenges or be better prepared to face them.

Cybersecurity challenges are risks that need all the information a CISO can gather from the security industry, and arming themselves with this information can only help in improving the perspectives of the CISO. Investing time in creating effective partnerships with the right vendor and having the right resources is worthwhile as this can immensely benefit an organization, in terms of both the short-term and long-term strategic plans.

This section provided insights into the important roles of CISOs that is rarely given much thought, and into how they help enhance the security initiatives in an organization. Creating partnerships with vendors and other security experts helps improve CISOs' knowledge of current trends as well as helping them get the best out of their vendors' software, hence improving the security posture of an organization.

Summary

This chapter has addressed five important roles of a CISO executive. Firstly, we evaluated the IT threat landscape, which entails assessing both the internal and external aspects of the company to identify potential risks and take measures to mitigate them. Secondly, we looked at devising various policies and controls, such as granting various security privileges to users to reduce risk. Thirdly, we considered leading auditing and compliance initiatives whereby the CISO assesses all security aspects of an organization and ensures they comply with regulations and international standards. Then, we touched on how CISOs manage an organization's information security initiatives, such as securing servers and purchasing up-to-date anti-malware programs; and lastly, we explored establishing partnerships with vendors and security experts to enable a CISO to obtain effective software tools for threat identification and mitigation of threats, as well as keeping abreast of current threats in the IT threat landscape.

The next chapter will address various regulations and laws that govern the IT industry that CISOs need to comply with to enable the effective dissemination of their duties. The focus will be on international standards that govern the security of stored data, the transmission of data, and ensuring the privacy of user data.

Further reading

Here are some resources that can be used to gain more knowledge about the topics discussed in this chapter:

- *The Overlooked Key to CISO Success: Maximizing Effective Security Partnerships*: `https://www.tenable.com/blog/the-overlooked-key-to-ciso-success-maximizing-effective-security-partnerships`

- *What CISOs really want from security vendors*: `https://www.csoonline.com/article/3617809/what-cisos-really-want-from-security-vendors.html`

- *The Chief Information Security (CISO) Role Explained*: `https://www.bmc.com/blogs/ciso-chief-information-security-officer/`

- *Three Cyber Security Issues Organizations Face*: https://online.maryville.edu/blog/three-cyber-security-issues-organizations-face/

- *10 Common IT Security Risks in the Workplace*: https://www.ccsinet.com/blog/common-security-risks-workplace/

- *GDPR Compliance: Should CISO serve as DPO?*: https://www.bankinfosecurity.com/gdpr-compliance-should-ciso-serve-as-dpo-a-13722

- The CISO's resource: https://www.youtube.com/c/erdalozkaya

3
Compliance and Regulations

The modern business landscape is increasingly being influenced by big data held in servers at business premises or in the cloud. These huge amounts of data have led to increased scrutiny for businesses to ensure that they collect, share, protect, and use these huge amounts of data in the required manner that protects user privacy. In the recent past, Facebook and Cambridge Analytica have been involved in a global data scandal that involved the misuse of user data for business gain. This scandal helped highlight the growing concerns about data collection and the use of this data on digital platforms.

Businesses are increasingly at risk of reputational damage if they engage in activities that result in carelessly handling consumer data. Apart from this reputational risk, businesses also face penalties in the form of fines, as well as serious regulatory measures regarding the collection, storage, and use of data from both online and offline sources. The number of **regulations** and laws continues to increase by the day as the use of technology and the amounts of data in the hands of businesses continues to increase. These huge fines are meant to ensure that businesses adhere to the basic principles of handling user data and that they take the necessary precautions to protect the data they obtain from their business engagements.

These regulations and laws aim to ensure that users across the globe are protected from exploitation by firms that can potentially misuse the data they collect. The values of fines that firms are subjected to have also been on the increase. Increasing the value of fines has the likelihood of deterring firms from mishandling user data.

This chapter seeks to highlight the issue of **data management** and **data protection**, as well as various laws and regulations that have been developed to protect user data. The role of the **CISO** in data management is to ensure that their firms are compliant with regulations to prevent fines, as well as safeguard companies' reputations.

We are going to cover the following main topics in this chapter:

- Defining data compliance
- Understanding GDPR
- Learning about HIPAA
- Introducing the CCPA
- Understanding the HITECH Act
- Getting to know EFTA
- Introducing COPPA
- Learning about Sarbanes-Oxley
- Understanding FISMA
- Finding out about PIPEDA
- Understanding IT compliance and the CISO's role

Defining data compliance

Data compliance is a term that is used to refer to any laws and regulations that a business must follow to ensure that it adequately protects the digital assets at its disposal. In most cases, these regulations seek to protect and govern how personally identifiable information is handled, as well as financial information. Any business that handles personally identifiable information, as well as financial information relating to its clients, needs to follow certain regulations that have been created to protect these users from the theft, loss, and misuse of their information.

The regulations that businesses need to follow come in various forms and jurisdictions. They may be state, federal, or industry standards. In some cases, the laws may be supra-national and apply to citizens of a given region, regardless of where these citizens reside. For instance, the GDPR is supra-national and protects **European Union** (**EU**) citizens wherever they are. It applies to any business online, wherever it may be located, if they are doing business and interacting with EU citizens where personally identifiable information or financial information may be exchanged.

Data compliance is different from *data security*. While these two terms may be used interchangeably on some occasions, they only have the same goals but refer to different aspects of data management and protection. With data compliance, a business only needs to keep the minimum standards and requirements, as mandated by the law. If technology changes and the law's minimum requirements are no longer sufficient, a business cannot be held legally responsible. Therefore, a business can be said to be data compliant but still insufficient as far as data protection is concerned. On the other hand, data security refers to business-specific measures that are crafted to ensure that the data at the business's disposal is kept safe from malicious individuals.

Data security encompasses all procedures, as well as technologies, that help a business safeguard data, especially against potential data breaches. Therefore, a business ideally aims to achieve data security, not data compliance. Data compliance only saves a business from run-ins with the law and governments. However, data security safeguards a business's assets, as well as its reputation, by keeping malicious individuals away, hence ensuring business continuity. A CISO is tasked with ensuring both are met. In addition to ensuring the business is compliant with the laws and regulations of the land, a CISO also ensures that all business procedures and technological processes are adequate in terms of how the business safeguards its digital assets.

The following topics in this chapter describe the various statutes in the United States and across the globe that regulate *information technology* applications on the internet and how they approach the issue of data management and enhancing data privacy. Let's start with GDPR.

Understanding GDPR

GDPR is an acronym that stands for **General Data Protection Regulation**. These are regulations that are developed and overseen by the *European Union*. These are wide-reaching regulations that seek to address many aspects of data management by firms dealing with data obtained from EU citizens. These regulations target users' knowledge of the data being collected, the processes of collecting the data, and the rules for reporting data breaches in case they occur. GDPR aims to tighten business processes in the wake of the increasing supply of user information to the cloud and other online services. It is a privacy and security policy that enumerates obligations that businesses ought to follow and affects businesses across the globe, so long as they conduct business that affects citizens of the EU. So far, GDPR is the toughest set of laws in matters of *security* and *privacy*. They enumerate a list of regulations that touch on many aspects of global business processes and how they can be implemented based on the industry a business operates in.

Data breaches have become a daily occurrence. This problem occurs at a time when more people are increasingly entrusting online businesses with their information. Regulations aim to protect EU citizens globally from their data being misused and force businesses to engage in business processes that will protect the data they collect and process. The GDPR laws are tight on many specifics, and this makes their implementation a nightmare, especially for medium- and small-sized businesses.

The CISO is tasked with the role of understanding how GDPR impacts a business's operations and ensuring that a business implements all the regulations set out by GDPR. This is critical, especially when a business deals with global clients and has a high likelihood of dealing with EU clients on their platform. In these modern times, more businesses are engaging online as a means of expanding their sales and business, which increases their likelihood of dealing with EU clients. Therefore, most businesses will need to be **GDPR compliant**.

Let's take a walk down history lane and understand how GDPR came about.

The history of GDPR

GDPR has its roots in the **1950 European Convention on Human Rights**. The convention declared that the right to privacy is part and parcel of each European's rights. The convention espoused that each human being has a right to their privacy, which included their family life, their home, and their correspondences. All these three aspects define the personally identifiable information, as well as financial information, that forms the basis that many of the data management laws and regulations are based on. From this 1950 convention, the EU has sought to ensure that the right to privacy is implemented through legislative processes.

Implementing privacy laws regarding individuals' physical rights was easy. However, the digital landscape has been evolving over the years. The internet was invented as this landscape grew, which led to increased privacy concerns highlighting the need to have legislative measures that guaranteed that users were protected when interacting on this digital platform.

In 1995, the EU passed the **European Data Protection Directive**, which offered minimum standards and regulations that sought to protect the privacy and security of data on the internet. However, after that directive, the internet saw tremendous growth over the last 3 decades and has seen unprecedented data sharing and collection on digital platforms. By 2011, it was clear that the EU needed to revise the 1995 directive to develop a more comprehensive legal framework that could address the increase, as well as new challenges, that the internet had introduced and that threatened the right to privacy for EU citizens. A few years down the line, in 2016, the GDPR was passed by the EU parliament into law, taking effect from 2018.

GDPR key definitions

The following is a list of data term definitions, as per the GDPR statute:

- **Personal data**: The GDPR defines personal data as any information that relates to an individual and that can be used to identify the individual either directly or indirectly. This includes names, email addresses, ethnicity, gender, biometric data, web cookies, political opinions, and biometric information. In some cases, pseudonymous information can also be categorized as personal data if it can be used to positively identify someone.

- **Data processing**: This includes any action that's performed on a given set of data, whether these actions are manual or automated. These actions include collecting, recording, organizing, storing, structuring, editing, deleting, and using data.

- **Data subject**: A data subject is any individual whose data is being processed. In most cases, it will refer to customers or site visitors who provide their information to a business.

- **Data controller**: This is an individual in a business that makes the decisions on how data will be processed. This individual may either be the owner of a business or an employee with the power to decide on data processing matters.

- **Data processor**: This is a third party or an individual that engages in processing data on behalf of the data controller. This third party could be a service firm such as an email service provider or a cloud service provider.

Now that we've learned about the GDPR key data definitions, in the next section, we will introduce the GDPR data protection principles that the various laws are based on.

GDRP data protection principles

GDPR can be summarized into a set of seven *principles* that can help us understand the concepts that inspire the regulations. These principles are as follows:

- **Lawfulness, transparency, and fairness**: Data processing must be done as per the law, it must be transparent, and it should be fair to the data subject.

- **Purpose limitation**: Data must only be processed for the purposes that were explicitly specified to the data subject during the data collection exercise. Using data for any other purpose fails to meet the GDPR principles.

- **Data minimization**: A business should only collect data that it needs and no more. Therefore, it should not engage in collecting data that it may only possibly use.

- **Accuracy**: The data that's collected from a data subject must be accurate while it is needed for processing. Therefore, the data must be up to date for it to retain its accuracy. Outdated information should not be stored or processed.

- **Storage limitation**: Data cannot be stored for unlimited periods. Collected data can only be stored by a business for the period it requires to use the data. If the purpose that the data was collected for has been completed, then the business should not keep the data any longer.

- **Integrity and confidentiality**: Data processing must be done in such a way that the data remains secure during the processing period. Technologies such as encryption should be used to keep data safe from eavesdropping or unauthorized changes to the data.

- **Accountability**: The data controller (the owner or employee responsible for data processing activities) has the responsibility of demonstrating GDPR compliance. The CISO plays this role in an organization.

Now that you have learned about the GDPR data protection principles that the laws are founded on, in the next section, we will offer insight into the role of the CISO concerning GDPR requirements.

The CISO role in GDPR

The accountability requirement of GDPR defines the *roles* and *responsibilities* that fit part of the job description of the CISO executive, and are to be carried out by the data controller of a business to ensure accountability. According to GDPR, the data controller must be able to demonstrate that the business is GDPR compliant. This demonstration of GDPR compliance is possible through several actions:

- Designating data protection responsibilities to the team members.

- Maintaining detailed documentation of all the data that's collected, how the data is collected, how the data collected is used, where the data is stored, how the data is stored, and the employee that's responsible for the data.

- Training employees and other staff members on various privacy and security measures that are consistent with GDPR requirements and demands.

- Ensuring that the business has legal data processing contracts with the third parties that they sub-contract to process data on their behalf.

- Appointing an officer in charge of data protection, also referred to as a **Data Protection Officer** (**DPO**). This role is useful in large organizations. For medium- and small-sized organizations, this role may be played by the owner or the person in charge of the IT aspects of the business.

Through these activities, a business can demonstrate its GDPR compliance. If a business claims that it is GDPR compliance is unable to demonstrate this through the aforementioned actions, then it is deemed not to be GDPR compliance. The CISO is tasked with this role in an organization that has a CISO executive. Their team members may include the DPO, as necessitated by GDPR.

The section offered insight into the GDPR statute, which is one of the major data protection laws in the world that governs EU residents and impacts all firms that may collect, store, and use data concerning EU citizens, regardless of the location of the company. The next section addresses another important statute in the United States called HIPAA.

Learning about HIPAA

HIPAA is an acronym that stands for **Health Insurance Portability and Accountability Act**. It is a statute that was enacted in 1996 and is also referred to as the **Kennedy-Kassebaum Act**.

HIPAA, a unified federal statute, is meant to address the healthcare and healthcare insurance industries regarding data management, as well as safeguard sensitive data managed in these two industries from possible theft and fraud. The act is categorized into five titles. The second title is of particular interest as it deals with data management. **HIPAA title II** provides requirements and provisions that guide the establishment of national standards for electronic transactions, as well as identifiers for health and insurance providers, health plans, and employers. It also targets user privacy and the security of healthcare information.

With the technology and integral nature of electronic transactions, healthcare and insurance industries oversee huge amounts of personally identifiable information, as well as financial information, through their platforms. Without proper care and procedures, fraud and theft cases would negatively impact the delivery of healthcare in the United States. The act outlines several offenses that relate to using and handling personally identifiable information and establishes various criminal, as well civil, penalties and violations for people that do not adhere to these regulations. The second title's main provisions focus on the administrative guidelines it provides, which seek to help the *Department of Health and Human Services* in creating an efficient healthcare system. In this case, an efficient system is characterized by proper use and dissemination of sensitive healthcare information.

Privacy rule

HIPAA seeks to ensure that the privacy of individuals seeking to use healthcare health insurance systems is guaranteed to prevent the misuse of sensitive information that is transmitted between people and systems in the healthcare network. The HIPAA regulations provide guidelines that attempt to regulate the national use and disclosure of **Protected Healthcare Information** (**PHI**). The act establishes authority over several institutions that operate in the healthcare industry, such as healthcare clearinghouses, health insurers, medical service providers, employer-sponsored health plans, and more. The regulations also extend and cover other institutions that do not exclusively operate within the health and health insurance industries. These institutions are considered *business associates*. Institutions such as banks fall under this category and often work in unison with the healthcare and healthcare insurance industries to make provisioning healthcare possible. Any institution that gets in contact with the PHI is considered an institution of interest and, therefore, governed by the HIPAA federal statute.

These entities can only disclose personal information to selected institutions or people that the patient/client consents to. HIPAA is a statute that ensures that patients' rights to privacy are protected and that all institutions of interest and that operate within the healthcare and healthcare insurance industries take reasonable steps to protect the PHI under their care. So, the electronic systems should be safe from malicious individuals and servers, along with the networks that these institutions use, which should use proper safety features. The CISO's role in any of these institutions of interest is to ensure that the systems are safe from fraudulent schemes and actions that are either performed by internal staff or external hackers.

Right to access PHI

Individuals with information within the healthcare and healthcare insurance industry have a right, as per the HIPAA regulations, to access their information whenever they want to do so. These institutions are mandated by the regulations to provide the information that's requested by the owner of the PHI and should do so expeditiously. The owner of the PHI, however, needs to request the institutions holding the information by writing about their need to access their information. The owners of the PHI can request to access their information either in writing or via electronic means. If the owner requests the institutions to provide them with healthcare records in a given format, the suppliers of the information must supply them with the information in the requested format, not any other.

For electronic formats, this information should be provided much quicker, considering the ease of transmission. However, safeguards should be put in place to ensure that the transmitted information does not get into the wrong hands. For instance, the information that's kept within the systems should be up to date. The information should be accurate to ensure that the written information is not sent to the wrong address. For electronic records, the issue is similar and information such as the email addresses of the recipient should be kept accurate to ensure that, when dispatched, it gets to the right party.

A CISO working in these institutions is tasked with ensuring that the stored information is safe from any unauthorized access or tampering. The systems that transmit, process, and receive this PHI should be safeguarded from potential breaches and fraud and a CISO executive is responsible for ensuring that is the case.

Potential risks

The healthcare industry has been rapidly growing and the adoption of technology has been enormous. Recent times have seen increased adoption of self-service digital applications, wearable devices, and the use of the internet of things, to name but a few technologies. All these systems are meant to ensure that healthcare practitioners can access patient information from many parts of the world, allowing them to be more mobile and offer better care, even from a distance. However, the risks of PHI getting into the wrong hands have also increased with the increased adoption of technology.

The major goal of the security rule of HIPAA is to protect PHI while allowing the covered entities to adopt new technologies. The adoption of new technologies by these institutions is a CISO role where the CISO executive needs to ensure that the adoption process improves the security aspects of PHI while remaining compliant with all the regulatory requirements. The HIPAA's security measures seek to ensure the following data protection principles are adhered to. These include **integrity**, where unauthorized alterations to PHI are prevented; **confidentiality**, where the acquired PHI should be kept secure and not be accessed by unauthorized individuals; and the **availability** of the information, where the stored information can be accessed whenever the need to access the information arises. HIPAA provides administrative, technical, and physical guidelines that entities that deal with PHI ought to follow to ensure the safety of PHI. The CISO executive in these institutions ensures this compliance and hence the safety of the information.

The three HIPAA rules

HIPAA regulations have three golden rules that all organizations affected by the HIPAA regulations must abide by. These three rules are largely categorized as follows:

- The **privacy rule**
- The **security rule**
- The **breach notification rule**

The privacy rule outlines various provisions that offer guidelines regarding organizations that must follow the HIPAA standards; guidelines on how to share and use PHI; conditions under which PHI usage and disclosure is possible; the patient's rights over their PHI; and the definition of PHI.

Three elements that are affected by this privacy rule are **health plans**, **health care providers**, and **health care clearinghouses**. Other institutions that are affected by these HIPAA guidelines include business associates who deal in healthcare-related information for the three aforementioned entities.

The usage and disclosure of PHI are only possible if it is permitted under the privacy rule, or the individual has authorized it in writing. The security rule focuses on electronic PHI. The rule outlines the organizations that should follow the security rule, the information that is protected by the rule, and what organizations should put in place to safeguard the information. To ensure data security, the security rule requires that the entities ensure the availability, confidentiality, and integrity of data; staff are trained to ensure the compliance requirements are followed; the electronic PHI is protected from all kinds of threats, and that suitable policies and procedures are adapted that promote security and protect electronic PHI from impermissible disclosure and use.

To ensure the security rule is adhered to, HIPAA requires that all covered entities perform a risk analysis of their businesses. This risk analysis process should involve doing the following:

- Identifying potential risks to PHI

- Creating a risk management plan

- Putting safeguards in place to address physical, technical, and administrative issues

- Conducting HIPAA training for all staff members

- Documenting the entire risk analysis process

- Conducting risk analysis processes annually to identify, mitigate, and protect against new risks

Regarding the third rule, the breach notification rule, the HIPAA regulations direct that any unpermitted disclosures and use of PHI comprise a breach of HIPAA regulations. Upon discovering a breach, the entity in charge of PHI must alert the affected individuals within 60 days. Other parties that should be informed of the breach include the media and the Department of **Health and Human Services** (**HHS**). However, the media should only be informed when deemed necessary. Otherwise, only the affected individuals and the HHS should be informed of the data breach. The CISO executive is tasked with performing this role and relaying the information to both the HHS and the affected people. For the CISO executive and the covered entities to be considered to have followed the HIPAA guidelines, they should follow the protocol of relaying this information, as well as take measures to prevent further data breaches.

In some circumstances, however, breach notifications may be excused under special conditions. These conditions are as follows:

- The organization has a reasonable belief that the person that PHI was disclosed to would not have retained the PHI and does not have the PHI.

- The erroneous disclosure was done unintentionally, was done in good faith, and was within the scope of the authority of the covered entity.

- The disclosure was done unintentionally between two people who are authorized to access PHI.

These three special conditions are considered to be secured breaches, so the breach alert requirement does not apply. However, the business is expected to take measures to ensure that such unintentional breaches are not repeated. A repeat of these mistakes would be considered a violation of the HIPAA guidelines and subject to stiff penalties and fines. These fines are meant to ensure that organizations tasked with handling PHI take all reasonable efforts and measures to ensure the security of PHI and assure patients of their privacy.

This section provided important insight into the HIPAA statute and the various laws that govern personally identifiable information in the healthcare and insurance sectors in the United States. The next section addresses another statute in the United States referred to as the CCPA.

Introducing the CCPA

The **California Consumer Privacy Act** (**CCPA**) is a state statute that came into effect in May 2018 and is similar in many respects to the European Union's GDPR. In some cases, it resembles GDPR, but in some cases, it is poised to have further-reaching repercussions than GDPR and will mainly affect United States companies. The statute affects Californian residents and is a measure by the Californian legislature to protect its citizens against possible data breaches by companies that use their data. Unlike GDPR, the CCPA takes a wider view of what constitutes private data. With this broader view, this means that the companies face more difficulties in implementing the statute compared to GDPR.

What does the CCPA entail?

The CCPA is a law that provides Californian citizens with the right to request any corporation that has their private data to provide them with all the details of the private data they have on them, as well as a list of all third parties that the information has been shared with. Additionally, Californian citizens can sue these companies if they can identify a violation of the CCPA guidelines, regardless of whether the company has experienced a data breach. This strict provision in the CCPA forces companies to be extra vigilant in their operations and ensure that they are CCPA-compliant to avoid time-consuming court cases that may injure their reputation or waste resources.

The CCPA lists the type of companies within the United States that must comply with these laws. Any company with annual returns exceeding $25 million in revenue must abide by the CCPA laws. Companies that collect and store personally identifiable information for more than 50,000 individuals must also comply with the CCPA. Other companies that must comply include companies that collect more than half of their revenues as a result of sales of personal data collected from their users. The law affects companies both in the United States and abroad. It does not matter where the company is located to comply. So long as the information that's collected includes the information of a Californian resident, the company is subject to this law. In this regard, the CCPA and GDPR statutes are similar in application.

Recent amendments to the law have seen a few companies being excluded from the list of companies that are subject to CCPA compliance. The excluded companies include insurance institutions, support organizations, and agents. They have been excluded because they are already subject to similar laws under the **California Insurance Information and Privacy Protection Act**.

The CCPA rights

The CCPA statute provides Californian citizens with rights that guarantee the privacy of their data by companies that obtain such information from them. The CCPA offers Californians new rights, which include the following:

- The right for the person to know all the details that pertain to the information a company gathers from them, including how the information will be used and shared.

- The CCPA offers individuals the right to request that their information be deleted from a company server. This rule has exceptions, though, and people who engage in criminal activities cannot successfully request this right.

- The CCPA offers individuals the right to opt out of any potential sale of their personal information to third parties.

- The right to non-discrimination for any individual who wishes to exercise their CCPA rights.

The CCPA directs businesses to give all their users notices that explain their data practices. Failure to provide users with explanations of such data practices constitutes a violation of the CCPA guidelines and makes the business liable to fines and penalties.

Personal information

The CCPA provides a distinctive definition of what it classifies as **personal information**. Any information that can be used to identify an individual, link to an individual, or relate to an individual is considered personal information. This information includes details such as email addresses, browsing history, geo-location data, fingerprints, social security numbers, names, home addresses, records of products purchased, and inferences from other personal information that can be used to infer identity. Information that is publicly available from federal, local, or state records is not considered *personal information*. Information that can be obtained from public records may include professional licenses and real estate information of property owned.

Failure to comply with the CCPA

Companies in violation of the CCPA have up to 30 days to address these violations and comply with the CCPA requirements once they have been notified by the CCPA regulators of this violation. The consequences of failing to comply with these regulations after the 30 days have elapsed are dire. A fine follows failing to comply. A fine of $7,500 per record of the data in breach of the regulations is imposed. In any data breach, the number of affected records is huge, which means that the number of fines can run into millions of dollars for any company in breach of the regulations. These tough measures and regulations for compliance are meant to deter companies from non-compliance and ensure the security and privacy of user data.

A company can be sued by individuals if there is a violation of the CCPA regulations. If a data breach occurs and personal information is stolen, then an individual can sue the business if the business failed to take reasonable precautions and failed to comply with some of the CCPA guidelines, which could have hampered the data breach or made it more difficult for the breach to succeed. An individual can sue and receive compensation of $750 or any amount suffered as a result of the data breach.

This section provided insight into the CCPA statute, which was created to protect Californian state residents. It mainly affects companies in California but can affect organizations outside California that may seek to collect, store, and use personal data from Californian people. The next section handles the HITECH statute.

Understanding the HITECH Act

The **Health Information Technology for Economic and Clinical Health Act (HITECH Act)** statute was passed in 2009 by the Obama Administration in the United States as part of a recovery plan from the economic recession that had hit the world. The statute aimed to address the shortcomings of the HIPAA Act and improve on some issues regarding delivering healthcare to the people of the United States. The proponents of the statute aimed to improve the use and adoption of technology to deliver healthcare in the United States.

Of particular interest in this chapter is **subtitle D** of the HITECH Act, which focuses on the issue of privacy and the security concerns that result from using technology to disseminate healthcare services. With the increased use of technology, increased privacy and security concerns were an expected outcome. Due to this, the statute intends to address these concerns by offering guidelines that healthcare providers in the United States can follow to ensure the sensitive information is safely transmitted across their healthcare networks and systems.

They tightened the language in HIPAA where the provisions appeared to be general and ambiguous, which helped increase the understanding of the regulations, as well as aiding in their implementation. Also, the HITECH Act developed more provisions that aimed at strengthening the criminal and civil enforcement of the HIPAA rules. This was to ensure that the security and privacy concerns in the healthcare sector, especially regarding transmitting electronic data, would be addressed by the institutions that handled the data. Therefore, the HITECH Act was meant to improve both the implementation of the regulations, as well as ensure their enforcement.

Important HITECH amendments and provisions

The HITECH Act revised some Social Security Act provisions to improve their effectiveness. Some of these revisions established are as follows:

- The revisions established four categories of violations that clearly defined the various violations.

- The four categories of violations also created four tiers of penalty amounts that significantly differ in terms of minimum penalties for each violation committed by healthcare industry institutions.

- The revision established a maximum penalty of $1.5 million for the total violations of a particular provision. This meant that regardless of the number of violations per provision, the maximum penalty charge for a single provision would be $1.5 million.

- The revision of the Social Security Act also introduced some form of relief for companies that had violated the provisions but had reasonable justification for such violations. For instance, the revision eliminated the blanket imposition of fines on companies just for violations and sought to ensure that the institution must have been aware of the violations or should have reasonably been aware of the provisions. If it was determined that the institution was not aware and could not have reasonably been aware of the violations, then the fines could either be non-existent or would fall under the lowest tier of fines.

- The amendment of the security act also sought to relieve institutions that corrected violations within 30 days. These institutions would be saved from fines if the violations were proven to have occurred not out of neglect and that the institutions had taken measures and corrected the violations within 30 days.

These amendments, along with new provisions, sought to tighten regulations and improve security and privacy safeguards within the healthcare sector. In many ways, they also helped clarify some ambiguity that was existent in the HIPAA regulations while also recognizing the changing digital space.

Goals of the HITECH Act

The HITECH Act was created mainly to help promote the adoption of information technology in the healthcare industry. This was done in a manner that protected the privacy of citizens and ensured the security of the data that was transmitted within the healthcare sector. Therefore, the goals of HITECH were as follows:

- The HITECH Act anticipated increased use of electronic records after the adoption of more information technology in the healthcare industry. It sought to ensure that these electronic records were safeguarded by all the institutions that handled them. Without proper safeguards, the government understood that increased adoption of information technology, coupled with increased transmissions of healthcare records, increased privacy risks and that the benefits of adopting information technology would be counteracted by the potential loss of privacy.

- HIPAA was the main statute that sought to address the information and data exchange challenges in the healthcare sector. However, with changes in the information technology world, the HIPAA statute was proving harder to implement and needed few modifications. Therefore, the HITECH Act was meant to tighten a few provisions, make amendments to already identified problematic areas, and clarify some HIPAA provisions that were considered ambiguous. These changes would help the institutions in implementing the provisions and adhering to the regulations, which would ultimately improve the security and privacy of the citizenry using the healthcare system.

- The HITECH Act also introduced tougher penalties for institutions that were caught violating these regulations. This helped ensure that all the institutions that handled electronic records in the healthcare industry followed stringent measures. Tougher penalties were meant to deter carelessness among these institutions.

This section provided insight into the HITECH statute. These laws and regulations, including the HIPAA laws, are meant to offer data protection in the healthcare and insurance sectors in the United States. The next section addresses the EFTA.

Getting to know the EFTA

The **Electronic Fund Transfer Act** (**EFTA**) is a statute that offers protection to consumers when transferring funds electronically. The law protects consumers that use credit cards, debit cards, and **Automated Teller Machines** (**ATMs**). The law also protects these consumers from transaction errors, as well as handling liabilities that may result from the loss or theft of a debit or credit card. Electronic fund transfers are transactions that rely on computers, phones, or magnetic strips to authorize financial institutions to transfer funds. Electronic transfers are done at point-of-sale terminals, automated teller machines, with checking and savings accounts, or using pre-authorized withdrawals and automated clearinghouses. The EFTA law protects all electronic transfers, regardless of where the transaction takes place.

The EFTA provides guidelines that banking and other financial institutions should follow when handling errors or fraud cases. Under the law, consumers can challenge any error that occurs in the financial systems and avoid penalties or incur minimal penalties as a result. For instance, if a person loses their credit card and the thief proceeds to use that card to make payments, the customer is required to report this to the financial institutions within a specified period. This report is used to limit the damage the thief can cause as a result of having the card in their possession. However, if a customer fails to report the loss of their card, then the law does not protect them as the law is also meant to ensure fairness and considers the position of the financial institutions. The law is fair in that it protects the financial institutions from possible misuse of the statute by the users of electronic transfers.

The EFTA has several guidelines that banks and other financial institutions need to follow. One such law is provisioning certain information to customers. The law requires that banks inform their customers of all the steps they can follow to reduce the liability on their transactions in case their cards or passwords are compromised. This information helps the customers take precautions to reduce liability on their part. The customers are made aware that they should report any loss or misplacement of their cards to reduce the risks associated with the loss of the card. The report ensures that the customer's liability is reduced and that the bank can protect its customers better. For instance, upon reporting the loss of a card, the bank locks the card, and no further transactions are possible through it.

The customer needs to report to the bank within 60 days to avoid missing out on protection from liability. If a report is made between 3 days and 60 days, the maximum liability a customer can incur is $500. However, upon elapsing these 60 days without reporting that they've lost their card, then a customer loses any protection under the law for the liability that occurs as a result of the card being used. The customer will even be liable to overdraft charges if the card is used to overdraw money from the financial institution. Therefore, the customer will lose all the money on the card, as well as possible overdraft money, and they will incur charges that result from the card being used in that period. It is in the best interests of a customer to report the loss of a card to enjoy the protection EFTA offers to consumers using electronic fund transfer services.

History of the EFTA

By the 1970s, the United States had seen unprecedented growth in the use of ATMs across the country. With this increased use of ATMs and electronic money transfers, the need for more protection arose. Congress passed the EFTA law in 1978 to ensure the growing number of electronic transfers were protected from possible fraudulent activities. This act was also in response to the overall growth of electronic banking. The **Federal Reserve Bureau** (**FRB**) was in charge of its implementation as a regulation to protect consumers from fraudulent activities. These regulations address both the consumers and the financial institutions. Both parties of an electronic transfer were addressed by the regulation as it outlined the rights and responsibilities of both the consumer and the financial institution handling the electronic transaction.

The FRB was the body tasked with implementing these regulations from the time of their passing in 1978 until 2011, when the authority was transferred to the **Consumer Financial Protection Bureau** (**CFPB**). This process followed new laws that were created during the enactment of the Dodd-Frank Wall Street Reform and Consumer Protection Act.

The EFTA requirements for service providers

The EFTA requires any financial entity that deals in electronic fund transfers to disclose the following details to its consumers:

- A summary of all the liabilities that a customer is likely to incur in the case of unauthorized transfers and transactions.

- A description of how to report an error, how to request more information, and the amount of time a consumer has within which they can make a report.

- Details of the financial institution's liability to a consumer if they fail to stop certain fraudulent transactions from happening.

- Details of all the consumer rights to receive periodic statements of all the transactions that affect their account, including all point of sales receipts that affect the consumer's bank balances.

- An outline of the conditions that must be met before the financial institution can share a consumer's account details and activities with a third party. These incidents mostly occur when fraudulent activities are investigated by the financial entity or an authorized government agency is investigating the financial entity or the consumer.

- Details on what a consumer can do with their account, the kinds of transfers they can make, the amount they can take with each transfer, as well as the total amounts they can send to/receive from their accounts. These details should include all the fees that were incurred for these transactions, as well as their limitations.

- Details of the contact information of the person(s) that should be contacted in case of unauthorized transactions on the account, along with all the details of the procedures to follow to make formal reports on the case and make claims on the amount of money that was affected.

These details are furnished to the consumer so that they have control over their funds and the decisions they can make regarding them. It also enables them to understand the risks involved and increase their knowledge regarding the available options in case of unauthorized transactions affecting their funds.

This section has addressed the EFTA statute in the United States. These laws govern electronic money and funds transfers and seek to protect consumers using these services in the United States. The next section will address the COPPA statute.

Introducing COPPA

The **Children's Online Privacy Protection Act** (**COPPA**) has its roots in the 1990s period in the United States, when there was unprecedented growth of e-commerce businesses, the internet, and its usage. With the increased use of the internet and data collection activities on the rise, this led to calls to address the issue of privacy, especially regarding children under the age of 13. Until that point, very few websites had privacy policies regarding collecting data that involved children under the age of 13. The *Center of Media Education* petitioned the **Federal Trade Commission** (**FTC**) to look into this matter, especially regarding deceptive actions by companies that focused on children's data. The report by the FTC indeed found reason to create legislative action that sought to protect children under the age of 13.

This decision led to the COPPA laws being drafted, whereby websites were required to seek parental and guardian permission when collecting user data involving children under the age of 13. Collecting and using data involving kids under the age of 13 was limited. The COPPA also sought to increase industrial-wide regulations on matters that touched on privacy and ensure compliance with the regulations that governed the collecting and using data on the internet. As of 2016, the FTC has since approved several programs that seek to create provisions and regulate the collection and use of data online to safeguard children from potential abuse. Some of these organizations include ESRB, Aristotle Inc., PRIVO, CARU, and TRUSTe, among others. These organizations' primary purpose is to create a safe internet environment for children under the age of 13.

COPPA violations

The FTC provides a court penalty of up to $43,000 for each COPPA violation in any civil litigation. Failing to comply with COPPA regulations is a costly affair for websites and the FTC has since brought many civil actions against companies that fail to comply with the regulations. Google and TikTok are two high-profile companies that have faced the wrath of the TFC regarding COPPA violations.

In 2004, UMG Recordings was given a fine totaling over $400,000 for COPPA violations that involved promoting games to children under the age of 13. In 2006, the Xanga website faced similar action that led to penalties of over $1,000,000 for gross COPPA violations, which included allowing children under the ages of 13 to register on their website without getting consent from their parents.

Inappropriate contact with minors is not allowed as per the COPPA regulations. Dating applications have since faced the wrath of COPPA regulations for not taking measures to ensure that minors do not access the websites or register for their services. In the most recent major violations, YouTube was fined in 2019 for tracking the viewing history of children aged 13 and under to perform targeted advertising. YouTube has since required their channel operators to mark videos and channels as *child-oriented*, which excludes these marked pieces from tracking without the consent of the parents. Violations against COPPA regulations are costly affairs and can lead to huge financial penalties that can damage both the reputation of a company and threaten its financial resources.

COPPA compliance

The COPPA regulations affect all companies in the United States, as well as companies outside the United States that collect data from United States residents. Parental notice is one of the basic requirements for companies to comply with COPPA regulations. Secondly, parental consent is required for companies that seek to collect and use data concerning children under the age of 13. Companies are required to post privacy policies that are clear and detailed regarding the data they collect and the uses of the collected data. These companies should take reasonable efforts to notify and receive consent before collecting data regarding children aged 13 and under. Parental consent should be verifiable before companies can proceed with collecting and using such data.

Websites are prohibited from forcing a child to provide more information than is necessary before they can use their services. If websites make changes to their privacy policies, they should alert the children's parents and receive consent afresh before continuing to gather information or using the information they've already gathered. It does not matter that the parents had consented to the data being used previously. A fresh notification and consent must be sought to ensure compliance with COPPA regulations.

Retention of the collected data should only be done for the period where the original intentions for the data collection have been stated. Holding data past the period that was originally stated puts a company in violation of the law. Websites should provide reasonable means through which parents can review the information that's been gathered about their children so that they can decide whether they want to refuse further use or permit it. The companies that are running online websites and services should engage in reasonable efforts to ensure they can guarantee the confidentiality, integrity, and security of the information they collect.

This section provided insight into the COPPA statute in the United States. The law seeks to protect children from people that may seek to benefit from collecting, storing, and using their information. The next section will address the Sarbanes-Oxley Act.

Learning about Sarbanes-Oxley

The **Sarbanes-Oxley Act** is a federal statute that establishes laws that protect auditing and financial activities in public companies and holds corporate officers, accountants, and auditors accountable for accounting and other auditing activities in a company. The law seeks to protect employees, shareholders, and the public from dubious accounting activities and accounting errors that may be intentional or otherwise. These sets of laws are enforced by the **Securities and Exchange Commission** (**SEC**) in the United States. These regulations target the following areas:

- Regulation of accounting activities.

- Increasing penalties and other forms of punishments for people in violation of the regulations.

- Offering additional protection that was non-existent in previous laws, such as the **Securities and Exchange Act** of *1934*.

- Ensuring corporate responsibility. Without regulations, shareholders, employees, and the public would remain at the mercy of corporate executives, who are more than likely to seek ways to serve their selfish interests at the expense of the masses.

This section has offered an introduction to the Sarbanes-Oxley Act. The next section will offer insight into the history of the act.

History of the Sarbanes-Oxley Act

By the turn of the 21st century, the cases of corporate crime had been on the rise, with more and more cases being reported. The level of public confidence had hit all-time lows, with people becoming increasingly skeptical of investments in publicly traded companies. The reduced investor confidence was a blow to the economy and SEC had to find a solution to get people's confidence in publicly traded companies back. At the start of the 21st century, high-profile cases such as that of *Enron Corp.* shocked many Americans since it was one of the most successful companies in the United States. In addition, other companies, such as WorldCom, were also hit with high-profile scandals that led to the need for new laws that would protect the citizenry from such acts. The act was sponsored by lawmakers Sen. Paul Sarbanes and Michael Oxley, a US house representative from Ohio. Upon congressional approval, the act was signed into law in 2002 by the then-president George W. Bush.

Key provisions of the Sarbanes-Oxley Act

The Sarbanes-Oxley Act is a set of laws that are categorized into various sections and titles. Of particular interest, however, are *sections 302* and *404*. Section 302 pertains to the responsibilities that befall corporate people in companies, especially toward financial information and reporting. The **chief executive officer** (**CEO**) and the **chief financial officer** (**CFO**) are the two corporate officers that are tasked with ensuring that the financial reports in a company are accurate and that they represent the true financial situation of the company. These two individuals are also tasked with ensuring that the internal controls are working. At the end of the year, a report is required that details the various internal auditing controls, and any material changes to the controls should be included in the report.

Section 404 handles the assessment procedures of the internal controls that are set to safeguard the financial information and assets in the company. Accounting procedures and standards regulate the normal accounting processes in any company. In addition to the normal accounting procedures, this section demands further action, whereby the corporate executives are required to certify and confirm the accuracy of the statements, as well as the controls that have been put in place to ensure information is safeguarded.

The act has an additional provision known as the **Whistleblower Protection Act**, which protects any employee or contractor working with the company from any form of reactionary measures that may befall them for testifying or reporting a company's fraudulent activities. Employees are protected from dismissal and/or discrimination.

This section addressed the Sarbanes-Oxley Act in the United States. This act offers protection to consumers through the regulation of financial and auditing activities of public companies in the United States. The next section will offer insights into the FISMA statute.

Understanding FISMA

FISMA is an acronym that stands for **Federal Information Security Management Act**. It is a law that was passed in the United States in 2002 that sought to regulate federal agencies and ensure that they took up measures that protected sensitive data in their possession. The **National Institute of Standards and Technology** (**NIST**) is tasked with maintaining and updating the laws and documents that ensure FISMA compliance. NIST ensures that federal agencies comply with the minimum standards that are required for information security plans as the necessary procedures that ensure this is possible. The organization tells the various federal agencies the types of systems they can use, as well as approves the vendors the federal agencies can work with. The list of approved vendors is carefully vetted by NIST to ensure that they have secure products and that they help the federal agencies protect their sensitive data. Also, NIST assesses risks and standardizes the risk assessment processes that various organizations, especially federal agencies, can use in their risk analysis processes and efforts to secure their systems.

Reasons for creating FISMA

The amount of electronic information and the sensitivity of the information being held by federal agencies is huge. The increasing cases of successful data breaches mean that federal agencies are at risk of data breaches and are often the targets of sensitive data. Due to this, FISMA was created to ensure that federal agencies developed, documented, and implemented information security plans that could protect and support their operations. FISMA is one of the many laws that was created in a larger set of laws, called the **E-Government Act**, to protect all aspects of online information systems. In 2014, FISMA was amended to enable it to handle new challenges that come from these new technological systems and advancement.

FISMA compliance

When the FISMA laws were created in 2002, the laws only targeted federal agencies that handled federal information on behalf of the federal government. However, these laws have since evolved and now the laws also apply to all state agencies that handle federal programs and, therefore, federal data. Examples of federal programs that lead to state agencies needing to comply with FISMA include *Medicare*, *Medicaid*, and *Unemployment Insurance*, among others. Even private companies that do business with state corporations and federal agencies and handle federal data by association also need to be FISMA compliant.

To be FISMA compliant, an organization needs to have various information security controls that are approved and recommended by NIST. Some of the requirements for FISMA compliance are as follows:

- **Risk categorization**: Agencies must categorize their security and risk requirements and document the same.

- **Information system inventory**: Agencies must maintain an inventory record of all their systems and how they integrate.

- **System security plan**: Agencies must have a documented security plan on standby for handling security issues. The security plan must be updated regularly to address new security problems.

- **Risk assessments**: Agencies must perform scheduled risk assessments whenever there is a change to a system. For instance, when it comes to updating software that is part of the system, the agency must run a three-tier assessment of the system to ensure that threats are identified and that measures to handle these threats have been put in place.

- **Security controls**: Agencies must implement the list of 20 security controls that are listed with the NIST 800-53 documents.

- **Certification and accreditation**: Agencies must hold annual security reviews before they can be certified and accredited. These yearly security reviews are meant to ensure that the agencies are capable of implementing, maintaining, and monitoring their systems and hence that they are FISMA-compliant.

This section has defined the FISMA statute and how to be FISMA complaint. Next, we will list the penalties for non-compliant agencies.

FISMA non-compliance penalties

Agencies that are required to be FISMA complaint face tough repercussions for failing to comply with FISMA requirements. The main penalty is the loss of federal funding from the federal government. For federal agencies, loss of federal funding means that the agency cannot operate and will need to address its issues before it can continue. However, for a contractor that relies on federal funds, this loss of funding could mean the end of the company.

Apart from the loss of funds, the agencies and companies that need FISMA compliance can suffer in other non-monetary ways. They can suffer a loss of reputation after successful data breaches, which could greatly impact their operations or spell permanent doom for their businesses. The companies could also miss out on opportunities to bid for federal projects in the future. If the companies solely or mainly rely on the federal projects for survival, missing out on the opportunities to bid for the projects spells the end of the business.

This section provided insight into the penalties of the FISMA statute in the United States. It regulates federal agencies and how their federal data is handled. The next section will address the PIPEDA statute.

Finding out about PIPEDA

PIPEDA is an acronym that stands for the **Personal Information Protection and Electronic Documents Act**. These are Canadian federal privacy laws that are meant to regulate the private sector organizations operating in Canada or that deal with Canadian citizens.

PIPEDA targets any business that collects personally identifiable information from Canadian citizens. Examples of such information include names, age, medical history, comments, opinions, ethnicity, and marital status. The PIPEDA laws are based on 10 fair information principles that require that businesses obtain the consent of the users before they can engage in data collection and l use. The laws also require that all companies that engage in this data collection exercise be transparent as to the reasons for and purpose of the data collection. Under the PIPEDA laws, Canadians have the right to demand access to their information and challenge the accuracy of this data.

The PIPEDA laws also hold organizations responsible for any misuse of the data that's collected, using the data in ways that violate the PIPEDA requirements, and for the loss and theft of information while under the care of an organization. Organizations are required to take reasonable steps to protect the data once they have engaged in data collection exercises. Therefore, if there is data loss or theft and an organization is found to have not engaged in sound security processes that are required to safeguard the data under their care, then they can be held liable under these laws, which have stiff penalties. In the event of a data breach, affected organizations are required to report the breach to the privacy commissioner of Canada, as well as all the individuals that have been affected by the breach. Failure to do this will subject the organization to a fine of up to 100,000 CAD.

The next section covers IT compliance and addresses the role that a CISO executive plays within the regulations and compliance initiatives.

Understanding IT compliance and the CISO's role

IT compliance is tasked to CISO executives in a company. They need to ensure that their company is compliant with all the necessary laws, including those listed in this chapter, that govern companies in their jurisdiction. For instance, the PIPEDA laws are Canadian laws that affect all organizations that target Canadian people's information, regardless of where the companies are located. This means that if you sell products to people in Canada or Canadian people can come to your online business and need to provide the business with their personal information, then the PIPEDA laws will apply to the business as well. GDPR works similarly. It is meant to protect EU citizens, regardless of where the business seeking their information is located.

As a CISO executive, it is important to understand the demographics of the business and understand all the laws that apply and that could affect the business, as well as ensure that the business complies with all of them. However, most of these laws are based on the same principles, and being compliant with one set of laws often automatically helps a business comply with another set of laws. To ensure compliance with the various laws, the CISO executive must have a deep understanding of all the aspects of the business to ensure that they are following the laws and that they avoid penalties that could affect the business.

Summary

This chapter addressed the issue of compliance and provided information about some of the major statutes across the globe that seek to protect data that's handled by companies that engage in collecting, storing, and using data from consumers. This chapter provided insight into statutes such as GDPR, HIPAA, the HITECH Act, COPPA, the EFTA, PIPEDA, Sarbanes-Oxley, the CCPA, and FISMA. All these laws require companies and agencies to put mechanisms in place that ensure the safety of the data they collect, store, and use. They also ensure that the companies only use data for the purposes that were initially stated, and outline penalties for companies that fail to comply. The CISO's role is to ensure that their organizations are compliant with the regulations that govern their operations.

The next chapter will address the role of CISOs in *human resource management*.

Further reading

The following are some resources that you can use to gain more knowledge of the topics covered in this chapter:

- *IT Security versus IT Compliance*: `https://www.bmc.com/blogs/it-security-vs-it-compliance-whats-the-difference/`

- *Commodity*: `https://www.investopedia.com/terms/c/cftc.asp`

- *Federal Information Security Modernization*: `https://www.cisa.gov/federal-information-security-modernization-act`

- *Sarbanes Oxley Act*: `https://searchcio.techtarget.com/definition/Sarbanes-Oxley-Act`

- *Children's Online Privacy Protection Act*: `https://epic.org/privacy/kids/`

- *Complying with Coppa Frequently Asked Questions*: `https://www.ftc.gov/tips-advice/business-center/guidance/complying-coppa-frequently-asked-questions-0`

- *Regulatory Reform Proceedings*: `https://www.ftc.gov/enforcement/rules/rulemaking-regulatory-reform-proceedings/childrens-online-privacy-protection-rule`

- *Electronic Fund Transfer Act*: `https://corporatefinanceinstitute.com/resources/knowledge/finance/electronic-fund-transfer-act-efta/`

- *Electronic Fund Transfer Act 2*: `https://www.investopedia.com/terms/e/electronic-funds-transfer-act.asp`

- *HITEC Act*: `https://www.hipaajournal.com/what-is-the-hitech-act/`

- *California Consumer Privacy Act*: `https://www.csoonline.com/article/3292578/california-consumer-privacy-act-what-you-need-to-know-to-be-compliant.html`

- *CCPA*: `https://oag.ca.gov/privacy/ccpa`

- *HIPPA – Main Components*: `https://dancetherapystudios.com/what-are-the-five-main-components-of-hipaa/`

- *HIPPA – GDPR and PCI DSS*: `https://cloud.netapp.com/blog/data-compliance-regulations-hipaa-gdpr-and-pci-dss`

- *Data Compliance Standards*: `https://www.insightsforprofessionals.com/it/leadership/data-compliance-standards`

- *Data Compliance Essentials*: `https://blog.netwrix.com/2019/08/06/data-security-compliance-essentials-only/`

- *Compliance News*: `https://www.erdalozkaya.com/category/iso-20000-2700x/`

4
Role of HR in Security

The **chief information security officer** (**CISO**) role is one of the most important management positions in recent times, and organizations are increasingly taking a more serious approach to the hiring of such an executive. A CISO plays an integral role in the **human resources** (**HR**) department. The main reason for their integral role is the fact that internal security is an essential part of organizational security and, more often than not, security breaches result from the exploitation of an internal security weakness.

Social engineering a staff member, obtaining a password from a staff member, or getting a staff member to click on an email containing an intrusive program meant to help a hacker gain access into a system are some of the main methods that attackers use. Therefore, the HR department plays a critical role in ensuring the security of an organization. Hiring practices must ensure that the right personnel is acquired for the position, and hiring processes must also ensure that the hired people have the requisite basic skills to comprehend security policies and help implement some of the security policies meant to keep an organization safe.

A staff member arguably poses a security threat to the system in a similar way to an external worker. Carelessness on the part of staff could help a potential attack to succeed. However, good hiring practices, along with training of staff members, goes a long way in helping CISOs protect their organizations from data breaches.

This chapter addresses the role of CISOs in **HR management** (**HRM**) and intends to show how the HR department is critical to the security of an organization and how CISOs use HRM to improve organizational security. The chapter will address the HRM function through the following topics:

- Understanding security posture

- Exploring human error and its impact on organizations

- Hiring procedures

Understanding security posture

Security posture is a term that refers to an organization's readiness to react to cybersecurity threats. Organizations face several kinds of threats that can lead to data breaches. Attack vectors have increased with the rapid development of technology. Any combination of these vectors can cause security threats to an organization. This has led to increased complexities for CISOs. These challenges may come in the form of **incident response** (**IR**). Security controls, vulnerability testing and management, detection of attacks, recovery processes, compliance, and reporting are some CISO activities that determine the status of a company's security posture. A good security posture increases the chances of an organization succeeding in mitigating security threats that it faces. On the other hand, a bad security posture means that *attack surfaces* are highly vulnerable to attacks, and chances of data breaches are high. The work of a CISO is to ensure their organization has a good security posture.

Security posture features

To determine the level of security posture for an organization, the following measurements need to be completed:

- Measurement of an organization's ability to detect and subsequently contain attacks

- Measurement of an organization's ability to react and to recover following a security event

- Measurement of an organization's level of security program automation

- Measurement of the visibility that the security team has into all attack surfaces and asset inventory

- Measurement of all the controls that an organization has in place to safeguard an organization from any cyber-attacks

Now that we have listed various security posture features, the next section will provide insights into various **information technology** (**IT**) assets in an organization that are critical to the security situation.

IT assets inventory

The aim of a security posture is to ensure that all **IT assets** are kept secure from possible threats, either from *internal* or *external* threats. However, it is common knowledge that any security team is incapable of protecting assets they are unaware of. Therefore, CISOs and their teams need to keep an accurate inventory of all the assets that an organization has. Assets in a modern organization include all mobile devices, third-party assets, infrastructure, applications, cloud, or on-premises assets.

It is not enough just to keep an inventory of all the IT assets an organization has—the security team needs to perform a critical analysis of all assets to determine the nature of their criticality in terms of security. This analysis should yield a breach risk level or figure. The breach risk level should then be quantified in terms of **United States dollars** (**USD**) (or any local currency). Quantifying the breach risk serves to calculate the business impact on an organization in case a breach affecting that particular asset occurs.

Security controls

Security controls encompass all the processes in place to detect, prevent, and recover from cyber-attacks. Security controls can generally be categorized into two groups of controls: categorization by *type* or *function*. Under **type categorization**, security controls include *physical*, *administrative*, and *technical* controls. Under **function categorization**, security controls include *preventive*, *detective*, and *corrective* forms of security. The security team needs to have a list of all the controls that their organization has implemented. This list also needs to have a description of the efficiency of each control in helping reduce cyber risks to the organization.

Attack vectors

An **attack vector** is a term that refers to methods that attackers use to infiltrate or breach an organization's systems. Examples of attack vectors include **man-in-the-middle** (**MitM**) attacks, **phishing**, **compromised credentials**, **ransomware**, and **malware**. Attack vectors can be categorized into types of vectors—those that infiltrate by targeting weaknesses of the security assets, and those that target human users gaining security clearance to access the network.

This chapter will focus more on the second category of attack vectors as they impact decision-making processes as well as hiring practices in the HR department.

Attack surface

An **attack surface** refers to all the means through which an attacker can gain access to a system using any breach method. It is a description that includes a combination of the asset inventory and the attack vector.

Automating the security posture

Automating security posture management is a critical aspect that ensures an organization's defenses are ahead of those of potential attackers. Many attacks are automated, and attackers use tools that continuously probe the systems for vulnerabilities. With vulnerabilities being identified all the time, it is not enough to have controls for responding and recovering to attacks. The impact of newly identified vulnerabilities cannot be quantified beforehand and, therefore, successful exploitation of such vulnerabilities can be fatal to the continuity of any organization.

Ways of improving an organization's security posture

In order to improve the security posture of an organization, these three processes must be executed:

1. Analysis of the current security posture.
2. Identification of possible gaps. This is done through assessment of the current security posture.
3. Taking measures to ensure that identified gaps are addressed.

After listing ways to improve the security posture, we will address how to assess an organization's security posture in the next section.

Assessing an organization's security posture

The *assessment* of an organization's security posture is the first step toward addressing cybersecurity risks and attaining the required levels of compliance. Without an understanding of the current processes, it is not possible to tell exactly which vulnerabilities affect a business, how these vulnerabilities can be exploited, the risk involved in case these vulnerabilities are exploited, and the business impact of these risks. Without this knowledge, a business will be running blind in an increasingly *dangerous IT landscape*. In assessing the security posture, the following list of questions needs to be asked. A CISO and their team should be able to answer the questions posed:

1. How safe is our organization?

2. Does our organization have the right cybersecurity strategy to defend the company's IT assets?

3. How good are the security controls we have in place?

4. Are we in a position where we can accurately measure our cybersecurity resilience and breach risks for all our assets?

5. What is our level of vulnerability to possible attacks and potential data breaches?

6. Do we have a vulnerability management program, and how effective is the program?

7. Can we effectively evaluate the various business risks as well as benchmark the various risk owners in the business?

8. Do we have an adequate process through which our reporting of the security posture is made to the board of directors, including a discussion around the security posture?

On answering all these questions, the organization should be in a position to fully understand the current situation of the security posture and, based on the understanding, make adequate plans to address concerns as well as future needs.

Important steps in security posture assessment

Effective security posture assessment is completed in three key steps, and we will look at this in the next few sections.

Determining an IT asset inventory

Organizational assets include all the gadgets that have access to the business' network and data. In inventory-taking processes, the security team needs all the details of all these assets. These details should comprise up-to-date information about the assets as well as a deep understanding of the assets, which includes all risks associated with the asset. Needed details at this stage include the following:

- Categorization of all assets based on location, type of asset, the role of the asset in the organization, and whether it connects to the internet or not.

- Determining the criticality of each asset.

- In-depth information details of all software and hardware details for the asset such as users, ports associated with the asset, and services linked to the asset.

- Asset licenses. Details of all licenses and ensuring that the assets are running up-to-date license software and adhering to the business's security policies.

- Ensuring that actions are triggered to automatically alert security personnel when an asset deviates from organizational security policy procedures.

- Decisions on which assets to decommission and stop using when they are no longer up to date or no longer usable.

Tracking and keeping a detailed record of assets is a basic process that is integral to maintaining security standards and is a requirement for most internal regulations and standards such as the **Health Insurance Portability and Accountability Act** (**HIPAA**) and **Payment Card Industry** (**PCI**) standards. With an accurate list of organizational assets, the security team can create effective plans that cover all assets.

Mapping all attack surfaces

An **attack surface** is any point in an organization's network where an attacker can gain access to the network. Essentially, these are data points where attackers can potentially access and compromise an organizational asset.

Understanding cyber risk

The last step to security posture assessment includes an understanding of the business risk of attack surfaces. **Cyber risk** is the potential loss that can result from a successful cyber-attack. To accurately determine the cyber risk, the following factors need to be considered:

- The criticality of the asset

- The threat level
- The severity of the vulnerability of that particular asset
- Risk-negating effects as a result of certain security controls

Understanding the security posture and subsequently addressing the identified issues ensures that an organization remains in control of the security aspects and greatly minimizes the business risk while simultaneously increasing the chances of business success. A CISO plays a critical role in an organization with their carefully recruited team of security experts. Users pose as much a security threat to an organization's system as infrastructural weaknesses. Therefore, for CISOs to ensure good security postures, they need to ensure that the HR department hires the right personnel and fires or penalizes people in breach of the various security protocols meant to protect an organization's security posture.

This section has addressed the important role of a CISO in guaranteeing a good security posture that ensures the minimization of business risk. The next section will address the second key HRM function of human error and the impact this has on organizations.

Exploring human error and its impact on organizations

Employees pose a big threat to the security of an organization. While many organizations have invested heavily in setting up perimeter walls to keep intruders out, it is the *insiders* that remain a major problem as far as the security of an organization is concerned. Insiders that pose a threat to an organization range from former employees, current employees, business partners, interns, customers, to contractors. Arguably, they pose a greater threat because of their knowledge of the systems and because of the trust the organization may have in these employees. More often than not, it is insiders that either cause an attack themselves or through whom an attack is possible. Laxity on the part of organizations in terms of security policies involving employees is well documented. In 2001, for instance, the **Federal Bureau of Investigation** (**FBI**) revealed that a Russian spy had worked within their ranks for 20 years and had helped the *Russian intelligence services* to infiltrate the US's systems for years without the knowledge of the FBI administration. The news was a major lesson not just for the FBI but also for other organizations that hold sensitive information that may be a target for malicious attacks. Therefore, for the security team to be effective at keeping an organization safe, the focus should not only be on internet-based attacks; insiders, especially employees, should also be monitored.

Preventing insider security threats

Insider threats are a major threat to an organization. Firewalls and other forms of authentication can only help keep outsiders out. However, there are several means of dealing with this threat. Some examples of effective ways of preventing insider threats include the following:

- **See something, say something**: Encouraging employees to report fishy behavior they have witnessed among their colleagues because all employees are a vital component of a company's security posture. Employees should also be encouraged to conduct a self-audit of their activities to determine whether they are a risk to the company or whether their actions help increase the risk aspect.

- **Educating employees**: This will help prevent an accidental breach of security. However, it will not help prevent an intentional data breach.

- **User access hygiene**: This means that all user accounts should be evaluated. All dormant and orphaned accounts should be deleted from the system—for instance, temporary accounts may be created for purposes of a given project that may provide users with access to sensitive data. After completion of such a project, these user accounts are no longer necessary and should be eliminated from the system.

- **Strong authentication**: Weak authentication procedures just help attackers infiltrate the system. The system should require employees to use strong passwords as well as **multi-factor authentication** (**MFA**) to safeguard their user accounts.

- **Third-party access**: Control third parties such as vendors, contractors, and consultants whenever they are accessing the company's facilities. Their movements should be monitored, and they should be provided with an escort while visiting a company's facilities.

- **Sentiment analysis**: This refers to the use of behavioral analysis techniques to handle potential threats. For instance, erratic employee behavior should be considered a potential risk to the company and, therefore, remote logins and other security credentials should be limited or monitored.

- **Compromised accounts**: An organization should invest in the detection of compromised accounts. Compromise may result from actions such as malware downloads. Such accounts should then be restricted from accessing the system, and this will probably help prevent a major incident.

- **Data exfiltration**: Monitoring data and access to data within a company's servers should help prevent successful attacks from insiders. For instance, file movement from servers to a file-sharing site is an irregular process and such actions should raise an alert, with automated action taken to prevent these actions from completing.

- **Privileged access abuse**: Stopping privileged access abuse will help stop insider threats. Tools that monitor privileged access users and control changes to sensitive information will help reveal efforts to abuse privileges and hence reveal possible attacks.

- **Monitoring user behavior**: The monitoring of employees is the first and most obvious means of protecting the system from possibly threatening a company's informational assets.

This topic has addressed various components of the HR factor in organizations and how it affects the security situation. The next section will provide insights into hiring procedures and how integral these are to security policies imposed to improve the security posture of an organization.

Hiring procedures

Recent research finds that more than half of all data breaches occur due to **human error**. It is therefore critical for CISOs to establish a system that reduces human error and its impact on their organization's security posture. Responsibilities begin with setting the right criteria and mechanisms to hire employees with knowledge and awareness of security risks facing their daily work routine. These include, among others, the following:

- Verification checks for job candidates

- Security education and training program

- Policies for **identity and access management (IAM)**

Hiring procedures are an essential function of the HR department. Hiring procedures ensure that an organization not only gets the most competent job applicants out there but also that employees fit the mission and vision of an organization. Some of the factors that an organization seeks in job candidates are school qualifications and relevant experience. However, to find certain types of employees that fit an organization's vision, virtues such as integrity, honesty, intelligence, determination, and loyalty may be considered during hiring.

With the increased use of technology and its increasing importance for security, a CISO must influence all aspects of an organization. The HR department is no different. A CISO needs to help ensure that the HR department gets the right people into the business that can help safeguard the system. Ideally, staff should have some IT knowledge to appreciate the importance of IT security and the application of various security policies. It is harder for non-IT candidates to understand the impact of their actions and reasons for the implementation of certain security policies that may seem overly cumbersome.

Some of the reasons for the involvement of CISOs in hiring practices will be covered in the next sections.

Performing verification checks for job candidates

It is absolutely critical for an organization to get employees that can pose as little a threat to the security of business information assets as possible. Verification checks are important as they ensure that those hired are people without questionable character and that their intentions are clean. Ideally, people whose backgrounds are unclear should be avoided. People whose backgrounds show a history of dedication to work and family should be positively reviewed, and they have an increased likelihood of employment.

In case it is not possible to perform a thorough verification of job candidates, then an external bureau that specializes in background checks can be used. The aim is to ensure that a company employs people of unquestionable character. Such people can help enhance the security posture of a company by adhering to security policies.

Security education and training

Security education and training is a function that requires both CISO and HR department input. Employees may be hired to work within various departments but need security training, as all the sectors of a business can prove to be an attack surface. Security operations apply to all sections of a business and, therefore, all employees need to be educated on the security policies and the reasoning behind the policies. Employees who understand the reasons behind the security policies are more likely to adhere to these policies. However, a lack of education will lead to more accidental security incidents by employees who are either resistant to the security policies or those who see those policies as bothersome company regulations.

Whenever CISOs implement new security features or installation of new systems, employees need to be educated on the new systems and their role in ensuring the system is safe from malicious attackers. Therefore, the CISO, along with the HR department, will work toward preparing education and training sessions for employees to teach them of their requirements in the new system and their obligations. An update in employee security obligations needs staff to be educated. Due to frequent system upgrades, educational and training programs should be run as often as possible.

CISOs should work in unison with the HR department during hiring periods to ensure that new employees are enrolled for training immediately before they can start using the system. Interns should also have a training program to ensure that everyone who works with the business system is aware of the security needs and their role in ensuring that security requirements are met.

Security risk awareness

CISOs have an important role in improving the security posture, and this is only possible with improved security awareness among employees. Employees pose a security threat to an organization and security controls are often put in place to ensure a company is protected from insider actions. However, security controls are not foolproof, and increasing the security awareness of employees is the best way of reducing business risk. As mentioned before, the use of training and educational activities is the main way of increasing the security awareness of employees. The hiring of employees that are technology-savvy is another way of ensuring higher security awareness among a company's employees. Clearly laying out consequences for breach of security controls is another great way of improving security risk awareness. If employees know of the consequences of security breaches and they feel this will result in termination, suspension, warnings, and fines, then they will engage in due-diligence activities.

Hiring practices should adhere to security protocols. The CISO should work with the HR department in creating job requirements and hiring procedures that ensure security awareness is an important factor that should be tested among potential job applicants. A job applicant with a high level of security awareness should be considered. The importance of security awareness has necessitated increased vigilance and hiring practices that ensure hired employees are aware of security threats and that they actively participate in ensuring they are not part of the problem.

Organizational culture

The **organizational culture** is an important aspect of security for an organization. Usually, employees have a certain culture that influences most of their actions and, more often than not, management has an important role in creating this organizational culture. Users may know the right thing to do but fail to do it—for instance, users may know that they need their security cards to get into some parts of the building but may use their colleagues' after misplacing their cards. More often than not, such habits create a culture of insecurity in the long run as they open up loopholes that can be exploited by malicious individuals.

CISOs need to stamp out such a dangerous organizational culture and encourage the strict implementation of security controls and policies. This can be done through warnings, unscheduled audits, camera monitoring, and terminations. Having an organizational culture that is rooted in security measures is an effective way of improving the security posture of an organization. Regular education and clearly pinned security protocols to remind workers of the protocols should enhance awareness and create a culture rooted in a good security posture. Another effective means of maintaining security awareness is job rotation to ensure that an employee does not retain one workstation indefinitely for them to grow complacent and engage in sub-optimal security measures.

This section has provided insights into the employee role and how they can contribute toward increasing the threat risk to security. The next section will handle policies created by security leaders to address both internal and external security threats.

Policies for IAM

Policies are a crucial aspect of the security posture of an organization. Policies are internal regulations that are created in accordance with the unique needs of an organization's business activities. In this section, we will address policies that are crucial to ensuring denial of access to information assets within an organization without proper authorization.

Implementing security policies

Security policies are the main solution to limiting the kind of damage possible from an insider threat. They reduce the carelessness of employees and reduce the chances of attackers taking advantage of complacency from employees to access the system. Security policies should include clearly laid-out procedures that employees should follow for the security of an organization. In addition, the consequences of breaching any of these policies should be clearly outlined. Employees should understand that their actions can put the business at risk, and so they should follow security guidelines as instructed to ensure that the business protects its assets from malicious attacks. Consequences could be in the form of legal liability, fines, suspensions, and termination of contracts based on the extent of the breach or the likelihood of damage from their actions.

Security policies should outline the limitations of all employees, the kind of data they can access, and the consequences of accessing such data. Mishandling data and accessing data an employee should not be handling is a red flag that should put such an employee in line for serious consequences. Spelling out the consequences also helps to eliminate the chance of unfair penalties being applied to employees if they are in the wrong. The HR department handles employee issues, and these guidelines should be part and parcel of the employment contract that an employee signs when accepting employment. Also, whenever there is a change of security policies as a measure to improve security or in response to the installation of new security systems or guidelines, the employees should be informed and required to read and agree to the changes in their contractual obligations.

Physical security

Physical measures to improve security are a simple yet effective way of keeping insiders in line and a system safe from mishandling from employees. Every employee has their station of work within an organization. Sensitive locations such as servers that house sensitive information should be kept in the furthest room in the building to make it harder for people to access it, and this applies to both customers and employees. Only authorized personnel should be able to access the room. Physical restrictions from accessing the servers should help keep the servers secure and safeguard against tampering.

Some of the available technologies to implement physical safeguards include the following:

- **Two-factor authentication (2FA)**: Using key cards to access certain rooms is a common physical security measure to keep unauthorized people out of certain areas. However, with trust among employees, one of them can borrow a card or use another's card to access certain areas of the building they are not mandated to access. The use of 2FA helps increase a layer of security that will make it harder for people to access certain restricted areas of the system.

- **Biometric authentication**: Fingerprint and face scanners are common biometric authentication systems that help enhance physical security. This option is possible for large and profitable organizations given the expensive nature of installing such systems. Organizations that can afford this kind of system are more reliable compared to simple key card use that can easily be exploited internally.

- **Lock and key**: The simplest form of security that does not require advanced technology, yet it remains an effective layer of security in modern times. Thieves and kleptomaniacs among employee staff can steal sensitive information or unsecured pieces/hard copies of sensitive data. Therefore, employees should have lockable drawers in their workstations to safeguard the sensitive data they are responsible for.

CISOs have an important role to play in the HR department toward ensuring personnel security among staff members in an organization. Personnel security is a priority engagement and is made possible through the implementation of various procedures that guide various business functions with contractors, vendors, and consultants. These procedures also include hiring practices.

General safety procedures

To ensure a safe business environment, an organization should engage in activities such as the following:

1. **Physical security incident responses**: An organization needs to have procedures and policies that outline activities that the company's personnel should engage in in the event of personnel safety concerns. One way of ensuring employees are safe is to conduct employee training.

2. **Training and drilling**: Employees should be aware of the possibility of physical security threats to their organization that may target the organization's information assets and they should receive training and practice on how to respond to such cases. Training and drills should be done to practice for such things as storms, fires, pandemics, active shooters, and so on.

3. **Succession planning**: A company should have plans in place that detail the succession procedure regarding the person that should take over the management of the company in case a person(s) in management is fired or is incapacitated. Such procedures ensure the safety of information assets, as only select staff will be accorded access to these assets.

4. **Traveling**: It is expected that organizational leaders may have to travel from time to time to other regions of the country or world. Safety procedures may include the use of third-party security services or escorts. In such cases, the procedures should outline how these services should be contracted to ensure the security of the organization and eliminate the possibility of leakage of such information. Additionally, several senior staff can travel on separate airlines or different mediums of transport to reduce the risk of an organization losing multiple members of the management staff in case of an accident.

5. **Operational security**: This form of security is often referred to as **OPSEC**. OPSEC requires that personnel should learn to keep sensitive information to themselves and learn what to give away in case they are conversing with other people wherever they are. OPSEC works on the assumption that attackers can glean sensitive information that can enable them to successfully attack an organization by piecing together several strands of sensitive information. Practicing good OPSEC means that personnel should limit the information they share regarding their work with other people, and this includes their fellow workers.

Employment procedures

The management of the life cycle of employment processes is part and parcel of personnel security. Some of the procedures that should be managed to ensure personnel security include the following:

1. **Employment screening procedures**: Before hiring employees, an organization needs to have in place employment procedures that they follow when employing staff members. These procedures ensure that hired staff members are suitable for the roles they will play in the organization. These procedures will include drug screening, background checks, credit checks, and security clearance requirements.

2. **Employment policies and agreements**: To ensure personnel safety as well as safety of an organization from threats emanating from employees, before hiring them an organization needs to ensure that they sign the following documents: **non-disclosure agreements** (**NDAs**), ethics agreements, code of conduct policies and conflict of interest policies. These documents ensure that employees follow the expected behavior, and it helps protect the information assets within an organization.

3. **Employment termination procedures**: These are safety procedures followed when an employee is fired or has their contract terminated. These procedures encompass such actions as completing an exit interview, reviewing the NDA, revoking company **identifier** (**ID**) badges, returning company keys and any other company assets, disabling user accounts, changing passwords, and escorting the individual off the premises.

Vendors, contractors, and consultants – procedures

Physical security procedures do not just deal with matters pertaining to employees—they should also have provisions for third parties that visit an organization's facilities. These third parties include such people as vendors, contractors, and consultants. Some of the procedures that should guide their visits to organizational facilities include the following:

1. Escorting visitors while they are within the premises of the organization.
2. Verifying their identities and ensuring that there are proper access-control mechanisms in place.
3. Verifying visitors' licenses and other forms of identifications they may have.
4. Asking visitors to complete a sign-in sheet as well as sign out when they leave the facilities.
5. Issuing visitors with a name badge and requiring them to always carry these badges while within the premises.
6. Ensure that appropriate agreements with these visitors are in place.
7. Ensuring they sign NDAs.
8. Ensuring that these visitors are screened properly before engaging them on a contractual basis.

While this section has provided a list of procedures that should be used to handle vendors, consultants, and contractors when they visit an organization, the next section will address the issue of hiring practices and how to ensure they contribute toward tightening the security situation.

Tight hiring practices

A background check on new staff members is an effective means of keeping internal systems safe. An attacker can pose as an employee to gain access to a system from within—therefore, investing time and resources into performing background checks is an important security measure that helps a business safeguard its systems. Background checks can be expensive, and an organization may not have the resources to perform them effectively. In this case, it is advisable to outsource these services to professional security firms that can conduct effective background checks to reveal more information than the HR department can access. Background checks can be performed not only on employees but on business partners and vendors as well. Before engaging a vendor or outsourcing work that may require granting access to your systems, an organization needs to perform background checks to assure them of the integrity of business partners or vendors.

Using strong authentication mechanisms

Passwords can be cracked. With increased hardware and software capabilities being readily available to people, it has become easier for this to happen; therefore, it is no longer prudent to use simple passwords. Employees should be educated on the need to use strong passwords for their computer systems. In addition, they should be discouraged from using the same password they use on personal devices and online accounts to safeguard company assets. Attackers focusing on an employee will hack easier accounts to determine a password used elsewhere and try the same password, as many employees prefer easy passwords they have used over the years. These habits should be discouraged as they put a business at enormous risk. MFA is one of the solutions that can be used to enhance password security.

Securing internet access

Companies can help secure their computers from access to certain sites and hence keep their employees in check. Group policies enable management to set configuration details on company computers that limit an employee from the kind of sites they can access while working with company systems. An organization can limit internet-based services to the company website and a handful of other sites that are considered necessary for an employee's work. This will limit employees from accessing all kinds of sites while using company devices that could provide an avenue for potential hackers targeting the company employees. Accessing company files should be restricted among employees and should be allowed only on a need-to-know basis.

Investigating anomalous activities

Log data is an important source of data that can be used to perform investigations into network activity. For internal users, the internal **local area network** (**LAN**) should be a good source of log data that can be used to investigate any anomalous activities among company staff. Based on recent investigations of insider data breaches, it has been shown that insiders often do not attempt to cover their tracks as they do not seem to expect to be caught. While external hackers go to great lengths to cover their tracks, insiders do not do the same. However, it is important to note that logging of data among non-domain controllers such as **New Technology** (**NT**)/**Windows 2000** (**Win2K**) servers is often disabled by default, and this proves difficult during investigations due to insufficient log data on internal LANs. However, enabling this system enables the internal logs to keep data of internal staff operations, which can then be analyzed in case of investigations or in an attempt to detect anomalous activities.

Refocusing perimeter strategies and tools

In most company security strategies, the focus is on internet-based attacks and keeping malicious attackers away. Perimeter tools to keep external attackers away are vigilant and often do a thorough job. However, the same cannot be said of internal systems. By refocusing the perimeter wall strategies toward internal mechanisms, a lot can be achieved, and internal threats averted. Internal patching is one such strategy that is used on the external perimeter wall to safeguard email and web servers on the internet domain; however, it is rarely done on internal systems. Applying such strategies to internal systems will dramatically increase the safety of these systems and reduce the risk of internal damage.

In addition, vulnerability assessment for internal systems—a strategy that is commonly used to safeguard external-facing services—can be used on internal systems as well. The assessments can be done by scanning all critical servers that are used by employees to determine any weakness that can be exploited by internal staff and by taking the necessary steps to safeguard the systems from exploitation of vulnerabilities.

Monitoring misuse of assets

In addition to having security policies that employees need to follow to ensure a good security posture, monitoring of employees is often a requirement that radically improves the security posture. The use of video cameras and keystroke logging are examples of additional monitoring mechanisms that can be used in this case. However, some of these measures can be illegal—for instance, they can be an invasion of privacy, and the company can be sued and suffer reputational as well as financial damage if found in breach of privacy laws. Therefore, any monitoring should be done within the confines of the law. Web content filters can be used to monitor and restrict employees' access to websites such as competitor websites, pornographic content, and hacker tools sites where an employee can access tools to use for hacking. To be safe, organizations should inform their employees of all the mechanisms they use to monitor them so that the employees can agree to such monitoring or restrictive actions within their job environment that can lead to the exposure of information they would wish to keep private.

Summary

In this chapter, the essential role of CISOs in HRM has been discussed in great detail. The potential threat from insiders has been highlighted, explaining the need for CISOs to be involved in HRM. The chapter has shown that insider threats are just as risky as external threats and need to be handled with the seriousness with which external threats are handled. The chapter has reiterated a need for a good security posture that is ready to respond to cybersecurity threats.

In the next chapter, we will handle the documentation function of CISO and its importance in a company's security posture and implementation.

Further reading

Here are some resources that can be used to gain more knowledge on the topics covered in this chapter:

- Security posture: `https://www.balbix.com/insights/what-is-cyber-security-posture/`

- Human error in security breaches: `https://blog.usecure.io/the-role-of-human-error-in-successful-cyber-security-breaches`

- Preventing insider security threats: `https://searchsecurity.techtarget.com/feature/Ten-ways-to-prevent-insider-security-threats`

- Human error and cybersecurity: `https://thehackernews.com/2021/02/why-human-error-is-1-cyber-security.html`

- *How to Prevent Human Error: Top 4 Employee Cybersecurity Mistakes*: `https://www.ekransystem.com/en/blog/how-prevent-human-error-top-5-employee-cyber-security-mistakes`

- Human error threats: `https://nevadaitsolutions.com/prevent-human-error-threats/`

- Data breaches: `https://securitybrief.eu/story/more-than-half-of-personal-data-breaches-caused-by-human-error`

- Job listing: `https://www.bmc.com/blogs/it-job-listing/`

- IAM: `https://www.bmc.com/blogs/identity-access-management/`

- *The history of data breaches*: `https://www.erdalozkaya.com/the-history-of-data-breaches/`

5
How Documentation Contributes to Security

Documentation is an information systems security exercise that entails recording security processes, procedures, and policies to allow security leaders to enforce security measures. It also ensures the easy maintenance of security systems in an organization. This chapter will look at the role documentation has in security and the sectors that need to be documented. Documentation helps keep all the security processes in check and aids in evaluating the current security situation to determine whether updates are required.

The documentation aspects of security management encompass several issues. These issues, listed as follows, will also act the various subtopics for this chapter:

- Why information system documentation for security is important
- Understanding compliance with documentation
- Describing some examples of cybersecurity documents
- Tips for better security

Why information system documentation for security is important

Data breaches have been on the increase in the recent past and the potential for such security incidents has grown. This has necessitated companies to raise their efforts to mitigate the risks of these security incidents occurring. Data breaches affect a wide variety of organizations, including financial organizations, public-sector entities, and healthcare organizations, among others. Attackers aim to infiltrate these organizations' systems and access their information.

Information is the most valuable resource in organizations, which is why it's the main target for attackers. Information is often secured in elaborate information systems where it is stored in such a way that it can be safely stored and accessed conveniently when the need to do so arises. **CISOs** create measures that ensure the protection of these information systems and ultimately the information stored therein. Information is an important asset, and the security of **information systems** aims to protect this asset from theft or destruction. Proper *information system security* ensures that the stored data retains its integrity, confidentiality, and availability.

The section addressed the importance of information system documentation. In the next section, we will define what information system documentation entails.

What is information security documentation?

Information security documentation refers to all the processes involved in recording all the procedures that encompass the development, operation, and maintenance of organizational projects. All information technology systems pass through the development phase and every stage of development, from the *feasibility studies* phase to the *implementation phases that need documentation*. The documentation of all these stages lets you easily use and maintain the systems and lets you assess the system, which is a basic requirement for security functions.

A **project document** contains all the processes that are involved in developing a project and specifies how all the different components of the project function and integrate. A project document enables users to understand the system, assess the weaknesses of the system, and, subsequently, upgrade the system. **System documentation**, in this case, acts as a component that enables communication, monitoring, and control of the information system. A good system document enables users who were not involved in developing the system to easily understand it. It also enables developers to repair and maintain the system, regardless of whether they were involved in the development processes or not. Therefore, a system document is integral to the proper and safe use of a system and is integral to enabling security leaders, such as a CISO, to effect security measures to protect information assets.

System development documents are not just information system documents, though. Other information security documents include cybersecurity policies, guidelines, standards, and procedures that help users use an information system in an organization securely. This set of documents enables an information system to ensure the availability, confidentiality, and integrity of all their client and customer data by enforcing various security practices and controls. These documents are critical in enabling security leaders to proactively protect the data that's stored and processed within the organizational systems. These documents are also critical to maintaining compliance with various regulatory frameworks, as well as customer requirements. They are also instrumental while you're assessing the security protocols.

Some examples of documentation processes are as follows:

- Identifying and documenting threats
- Documenting organization's information security program
- Documenting security policies
- Reviewing documentation regarding security policies and procedures and updating those records
- Documenting all the information technology assets that belong to the organization
- Documenting the risk assessment procedures
- Documenting the risk assessment results
- Designing documentation procedures that ensure convenient access and production of information documents, such as reports and employee feedback

Now that we have defined what information system documentation entails, let's address why we should use such documentation processes.

Why document?

Organizational and financial data are key attributes of modern systems that revolve around data and information technology. As the use of IT in organizations and internet connectivity is increasing to enable many business functions, so is the necessity for having secured information systems grow. Continually being able to develop information systems, either by upgrading to beat the competition or to resolve vulnerabilities within the system, is now a basic need for all organizations.

Innovation and being able to **develop** systems are, therefore, continuous processes that rely on documentation. Such documentation enables better planning as well as decision-making during these phases. This ultimately leads to better end products and effective information systems. *Accuracy* and *reliability* are greatly improved when every process can be documented, which enables you to review and assess the projects during the latter stages of development. These system documents help project managers remain on track during development and enable them to achieve their goals as they can allocate resources and report to management. The CISO, as a security leader, is an integral member in the development processes and systems documents to enable the security leaders to meet the set project goals.

This section has highlighted the various reasons for documenting and how it is crucial to ensure that all the security activities are recorded for future reviews. The next section addresses how to **document**.

How to document

Incomplete or otherwise missing documentation is supremely consequential to the future of an organization. It is critical to document every process thoroughly and correctly. Documentation is important during project management, when developing information systems, as well as for the operation of the system. Appreciating the importance of the document during the development process is an important aspect. Resource allocation, as well as allocating responsibilities to the documentation process, helps ensure that the project's development is successful in the end. Some of the areas that should be considered during the documentation process are as follows:

- The feasibility studies, the project plan, the project report, and the project's evaluation
- The analysis of the project phase, the drafts, and the final cost-benefit analysis so that the costs of the project's development can be analyzed
- A manual of how the project will be used

The information system documentation should be complete enough to enable the employee *users* to answer all the customer queries regarding its use and assessment. It should also be able to guide any security team employee in their understanding of the system and all its functionalities.

The documentation should include various policy statements that define the position of the organization regarding the security standards that are required, as well as the guidelines to be followed, to achieve this level of security.

International Organization for Standardization (**ISO**) standards define the guidelines for information system documentation. According to ISO, the documentation should do the following:

- Assess the user's needs

- Develop a comprehensive strategy for informational development

- Provide staffing and help form information-development teams

- Manage all translation processes

- Review and test the information that's required by users

- Publish and deliver the required information from users

- Evaluate the organization's maturity

- Evaluate the customer's satisfaction and the information's quality

Documentation helps new users learn the system easily, lets them quickly access information from *authorized users* when required and helps reduce the cost of maintenance and support. With good documentation, security leaders can review the system and find innovative ways of addressing possible vulnerabilities and improving the quality of the system.

At this point, you know how to document information system security. The next section handles *approving* the security documentation, its maintenance, as well as how to communicate it to others.

Approving the security documentation

Security documentation must be approved to help it effectively enforce security strategies in an organization. Without approval, the employees in an organization will find it difficult to follow the policies, procedures, and processes that are outlined in these security documents. The security documents are approved by the security leaders in an organization. For organization-wide security policies, the documents are approved by the CISO. Lower-level security officers can authorize system-specific documentation.

Maintaining the security documentation

The threats that face an organization keep evolving. This means that the effective security policies, procedures, and processes at this time may render themselves ineffective. Especially due to rapid changes in technology, effective security controls need to be reviewed constantly.

Such a review should be done *annually*. These annual reviews are meant to ensure that the security documents are up to date, that they address the current trends in the threat environment, and that they contain the most recent security protocols that are effective in ensuring the security of information assets. Without constant reviews of the security controls to ensure that the controls in these documents are up to date, more resources will be required to address the vulnerabilities. So, such reviews must be done to update the current security policies, processes, and procedures in the security documents.

Communicating the security documentation

Communication is a vital element in security documentation as it helps ensure its effectiveness. Communication is required to inform all the **stakeholders** of the requirements of the security documents and the policies therein to follow for the security of the organization.

The security documents are approved by the CISO for the *organization-wide security* documents, as well as for *system-specific security*, which should be published and communicated to all stakeholders. Employees need to be aware of the changes that have been made to the policies before they can follow these guidelines. Without communication, it is impossible to enforce policies in an organization. The reasons for such changes, as well as the introduction of new policies, need to be explained to the stakeholders as well. All the stakeholders play a key role in the security strategy and its implementation, so they should understand the reasoning behind the security requirements for ease of implementation.

With that, you have learned about how to *approve*, *maintain*, and *communicate* security documentation. In the next section, we'll address the compliance requirements of documentation processes.

Understanding compliance with documentation

CISOs, with their role of documenting security operations within an organization, need to *comply* with some guidelines to ensure that the system security documentation is effective. One such standard is **ISO 27001**.

ISO 27001

This international standard addresses the need for system documentation and provides several controls that need to be instituted in an organization to ensure that the documentation processes are effective. When correctly instituted, these controls ensure two things, as follows:

- That the auditors are satisfied with the controls that have been put in place to safeguard the information assets in the organization.

- That the informational assets are correctly maintained and secured and that the risk of attackers successfully breaching and gaining access to these assets is minimal.

The ISO 27001 is a specification that "*provides a model for establishing, implementing, operating, monitoring, reviewing, maintaining, and improving information security management systems.*" This security specification is risk-based and takes a top-down approach in terms of its requirements for information system security. The six-part planning process that's detailed in the standard specification is as follows:

1. Define a security policy.
2. Define the scope of the **Information Security Management System** (**ISMS**).
3. Conduct a risk assessment.
4. Manage the identified risks.
5. Select control objectives and the controls that need to be implemented.
6. Prepare a statement of applicability.

The specification also details the process of documenting the entire process, managing the responsibilities of the security leaders and stakeholders, internal audits, continual improvement, as well corrective actions. In addition, the specification demands that all the departments of an organization work in unison.

This section has addressed the topic of compliance regarding documentation regulations and provided an example of the ISO 27000 standard. Documentation is a regulatory requirement that helps ensure that security measures can be reviewed on demand. The next section will provide examples of cybersecurity documents.

Describing some examples of cybersecurity documents

With data breaches becoming more common, the need to take measures to mitigate the risks of internet attacks is huge. However, with some documentation, an organization can be more prepared for possible attacks and offer guidance during security incidents. Some of the must-have security documents include the following:

- **Information security policy (ISP)**
- **Incident management plan (IMP)**
- **Disaster recovery (DR)** and **business continuity plans (BCPs)**

We will explore each of these in detail in the following sections.

Information security policy (ISP)

This is a document that outlines how an organization's security program works, the roles of all the members of an organization concerning security, a list of all actions that need to be performed by the workforce members, as well as the procedure for performing these actions. This document acts as an operating manual. It includes a list of all the daily security activities that keep the security program running alongside the wider organizational-wide security picture. An organization must have a clear and well-understood document that is based on an organization's business processes. This allows the organization to cover all possible infiltration surfaces. This also ensures that an organization is ready for security incidents.

The recommended best practices for creating an effective information security policy are as follows:

- Integrate the document into the business's mission objectives; security aspects are core to an organization and should never be viewed as an afterthought.

- Ensure that the document is understood by staff at all levels of the organization. This ensures that they can follow the policies that are being developed.

- The document should apply to all the members of an organization and should not only apply to the IT staff.

- The document should naturally fit into the business processes and not hinder any business process. Instead, it should be an enabler of business operations.

Next, let's look at the *incident management plan*.

Incident management plan (IMP)

An organization should be ready for security incidents, especially adverse security incidents. The **incident management plan** (**IMP**) is a written document that details a plan that is created and purposely exercised in readiness for adverse security incidents. The purpose of drawing an IMP is to have written procedures that define all the actions that can be taken in the event of an attack, as well as the actions that cannot be performed. It defines all the resources that are needed at this time and how these resources can be used to help address the impact of the attack or subdue the attackers. These processes should be developed in advance and enacted well before such an attack is possible. The aim is to prepare an organization and to ensure they are ready to face possible attacks. An effective IMP should be able to guide an organization, from identifying an attack to recovering from an attack.

Just like the **information security policy** (**ISP**) document, the IMP should be integrated with the business operations and should be a natural part of an organization. All the members of an organization should be included in creating and providing the program to increase the chances of success during implementation. Including all the employees in the security drills ensures that they are aware of their roles during security events, which will drastically reduce the chances of successful attacks or reduce the negative business impact that may result from the security incident.

Risk management

Risk comes from the Italian verb *risico*, which meant the hazards of sailing through rocky coasts. Logically, organizations want to reduce risks and most people have some risk aversion. Most managers prefer to have a relatively safe benefit to a major unpredictable benefit (it is better to earn $100 than have one chance out of ten earning $1,000), even if the mathematic expectation is the same. Organizations prefer to have a stable and supported expansion regarding the volatility of their activities.

However, risks represent benefits for organizations. The principle consists of an expected risk bonus or additional benefits at the time of participation for risky activities. For example, an organization that implants BETA software is exposed to greater risks (bugs, inconsistency with other applications, untrained employees, and so on) but expects effectiveness benefits that are superior to the incurred costs.

Organizations are exposed to several risks. Normally, financial risks are distinguished from non-financial risks. The following diagram shows all the risk categories:

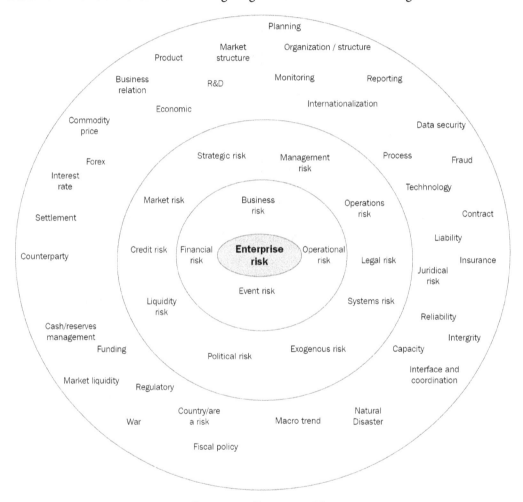

Figure 5.1 – Enterprise risks

In information security, it is necessary to take not only the technology risks into consideration but also all the types of risks that can have an impact on how informational assets will be protected. In summary, risk management focuses on one thing – that is, keeping data safe. With that in mind, risk management involves the following:

- **Identification**: All the assets, vulnerabilities, controls, and known vulnerabilities/threats should be identified.

- **Assessment**: All the information that's been gathered in the identification phase will help define the risk based on the following:

  Risk = (threat x vulnerability (exploit likelihood x exploit impact) x asset value) – security controls

- **Treatment**: Once the risks have been assessed, they need to be treated:

  - **Remediation**: This is a control that fixes the risks, such as finding a vulnerability and applying a patch for it.

  - **Mitigation**: This means minimizing the risks or their impact but not fixing them in full. As an example, if a patch is breaking the system because of a bug, a workaround can be implemented by setting up a firewall rule to cut the connection to the internet.

  - **Transference**: This is done by transferring risk to another entity so that you can recover if ever it happens. This is similar to buying insurance so that you can cover any losses.

  - **Risk Acceptance**: This is when you accept a low risk if there is no sensitive data present. Fixing it would cost more than it would cost if the risk occurs.

  - **Risk Avoidance**: This involves removing all risk exposure, such as when servers are near death and no patches are available. You may have all the data stored and transferred to another one.

Disaster recovery (DR) and the business continuity plan (BCP)

A **disaster recovery** (**DR**) plan is a written document that outlines all the steps an organization should take in the aftermath of an adverse security incident to have a successful recovery. For instance, after a natural disaster destroys an *information technology* infrastructure, a DR plan should outline the actions that should be followed after the disaster, as well as what the organization should do. The document should also outline the people that are responsible during this period and their respective duties. On the other hand, the **business continuity plan** (**BCP**) handles the bigger picture in the aftermath of an adverse security event. The BCP is concerned with the continuity of the business and will outline all the processes that should be undertaken during the recovery phase, as well as their priority, to ensure continued business operations – for instance, prioritizing vital operations before other operations can be brought back up.

While you're documenting the DR and BCP documents, the following should be kept in mind:

- As business situations change, it is important to update the documents for them to remain relevant.

- Do not just rely on desktop simulations – it is critical to conduct real-life enactments of possible examples to ensure that the processes that are outlined in the documents work.

- Untested processes in these documents are less likely to work in real-life situations, hence the need to test these activities regularly to determine their effectiveness and relevance.

As a CISO, it's your job to manage the security's functionality, as well as its compliance, and the CISO's primary task is reviewing the risks and inheriting the current security landscape based on risk management. Let's take a look:

- **Critical Systems and Data**: The CISO needs to determine all the information assets, networks, and systems that are critical for the business.

- **External Threat Management**: As the security landscape gets more sophisticated, the CISO's team needs to keep everything up to date, including the systems, software, and security protocols.

- **Internal Threat Management**: To minimize insider attacks, role-based authorization should be enforced, along with multi-factor authentication, for all external-facing systems, as well as employee logins. The CISO needs to establish internal controls over system and network access.

- **Vendor Risk Management**: The CISO should keep a close eye on the vendor's data, if any. Such storage requires encryption, as well as their security controls to be monitored and managed with role-based access.

- **Continuous Monitoring**: To identify system and network vulnerabilities, the CISO should implement automated monitoring for internal and external controls to enable better controls.

- **Business Continuity and Incident Response**: The CISO needs to establish and enact appropriate cybersecurity strategies to minimize possible breaches. Later in this chapter, we will cover how CISOs can build cyber strategies.

As we mentioned, earlier, the CISO needs to be in full control of any security implications relating to sensitive data for their organization based on a risk management approach.

The CISOs needs to tackle various issues and do the following:

- **Communicate and Collaborate**: Collaborate with stakeholders as soon as possible. It's the CISO's role to explain the risks to business executives so that they understand the business risks early on in the process. This will ensure that the CISOs have full management support and will be in control of security concepts that cannot be pushed aside to meet the deadlines of other stakeholders.

- **Create a Cyberculture or Change the Current Culture If Needed**: Security teams cannot be seen as roadblocks that slow things down. The CISOs need to ensure that while IT enables the business to run, the security team works with them to verify if the necessary security has been added.

- **Change the Perception**: As we mentioned previously in this chapter, the CISO's role is to establish a security and cyber risk management strategy and communicate that with the rest of the organization. This change in perception should include providing a governance policy on security, regular training that gets updated often, and being open to new developments in the threat landscape and adopting new technologies where possible.

- **Build a Common Language**: The CISOs need to ensure that the business and technology teams are fully aligned and are the bridges to ensure those teams will communicate. The security strategy can be aligned with standards such as ISO or frameworks such as NIST. The business goals and strategies should be based on this common language, and a shared mindset on both the technical and business sides should be set.

This section provided examples of important cybersecurity documents that organizations must keep to ensure they have good security. In the next section, we will provide tips that will help ensure you have better security in your organization.

Tips for better security

The following tips will help ensure you have better security through your security documentation:

- **Write down your security processes**: Practicing drills frequently can prove a challenge and can be resource-consuming. It can even be impractical. Therefore, many workforce members may be confused in the case of a security response because they have not been given the experience to reenact these drills during real-life situations. So, in this case, writing down incident response plans can prove very effective. These rules and processes can be used as a manual and help you avoid confusion. Also, creating written playbooks to simulate different kinds of security incidents can serve the same purpose. Conducting a swift and orderly response to an attack or other security incidents can fast-track the recovery process and lessen the possible negative impact on the business.

- **Consistently format your documents**: Sound document policies should be used across the organization. These rules should ensure that all the security incident cases, including security-related matters, are documented consistently. The consistency in the document communicates a message of confidence to employees, who will be more confident that, in the case of an attack, the required information will be available. The policies should outline what should be documented and how it should be documented. It should not be left to employees to decide what to record and what to ignore.

- **Keep up-to-date documentation**: It is critical to ensure that all the documents regarding the information systems in an organization are updated consistently and that they have the most current information. For instance, if there is a technical system repair and this repair is not documented correctly, then the subsequent changes to the system may have negative unintended consequences since the changes will be made based on outdated information. In this case, a bad situation may get worse.

- **Document your resolutions**: In the case of a security incident, all the resolutions that were used to solve the problem should be written down. Documenting these resolutions will provide subsequent cases with a playbook to follow to resolve similar security incidents.

- **Secure your documentation platform**: An organization needs to have a central repository for safekeeping all its security documents. This will allow for easy access to this information in case it is required. The central repository should have all the necessary security protocols in place, such as encryption for data authentication mechanisms, to keep unauthorized personnel away from the information. The sensitivity of these documents can lead to the destruction of a business, so they should be kept under tight security protocols. Only reputable vendors of such systems should be used.

These five tips are important for security leaders to ensure they benefit from documenting security plans and operations. These tips can be implemented by all kinds of organizations, regardless of their size and security needs.

Building a cyber strategy plan

A cyber strategy is a documented approach toward various aspects of cyberspace. It is mostly developed to address the cybersecurity needs of an entity by addressing how data, networks, technical systems, and people will be protected. An effective cyber strategy is normally on par with the cybersecurity risk exposure of an entity. It covers all the possible attack landscapes that can be targeted by malicious parties. Cybersecurity has been taking center stage in most cyber strategies. This is because cyber threats are continually becoming more advanced as better exploitation tools and techniques are becoming available to threat actors. Due to these threats, organizations are advised to develop cyber strategies that ensure the protection of their cyber infrastructure from different risks and threats.

> **Note**
>
> This section on *Building a cyber strategy plan* and its subsections have been taken from my previous book that was published with Packt, *Cybersecurity – Attack and Defense Strategies - Second Edition.* You can find this book at `https://www.packtpub.com/product/cybersecurity-attack-and-defense-strategies-second-edition/9781838827793`.

Why do we need to build a cyber strategy?

Organizations are constantly dealing with threats emanating from hardened professionals in terms of cyber-attacks. While hardening systems and installing more security tools would have worked just fine a few years ago, today, organizations need a tactful cyber strategy to guide their cyber defense approaches.

The following are some of the reasons why cyber strategies are essential:

- **A move from assumptions**: Some of the cybersecurity defense mechanisms that are used in organizations today are based on assumptions from the IT department or cybersecurity consultants. However, there is always a chance that assumptions could be misleading and perhaps tailored only toward a certain goal, such as compliance. Cyber strategies, on the other hand, are informed plans of action that cover different cyber threats and risks. They are also developed with a common end goal in sight.

- **Better organization**: Cyber strategies bring centralized control and decision-making to matters regarding cybersecurity since they are built in collaboration with different stakeholders. This ensures that different departments in an organization can set and work toward achieving a common set of security goals. For instance, line managers could discourage junior employees from sharing login credentials to prevent phishing. Such small contributions from different departments, as informed by the cyber strategy, help improve the overall security posture of an organization.

- **Details on security tactics**: Cyber strategies lay out high-level tactics to ensure the security of the organization. These tactics touch on incidence response, disaster recovery and business continuity plans, and behavioral responses to attacks to help calm stakeholders. These can help inform stakeholders about the preparedness of an organization when it comes to dealing with cyber-attacks.

- **Long-term commitment to security**: A cyber strategy ensures that the organization will commit considerable efforts and resources toward securing the organization. Such commitment is a good sign to stakeholders that the organization will remain secure during attacks.

- **Simplifying cybersecurity to stakeholders**: A cyber strategy helps break down the complexities of cybersecurity. It informs all the stakeholders about the cyberspace risks and threats before explaining how these are mitigated through a set of small, achievable goals.

The following diagram summarizes the cybersecurity strategy:

Why do you need a Cybersecurity strategy?

Without strategy
- You will end up with complexity
- You will not optimize your investment
- You can not prioritize the needs

What is a "Cybersecurity Strategy"?

A **Cybersecurity Security Strategy** is a plan for managing
organizational security risk according to a defined risk tolerance
for the organization to meet the business/organizational
objectives and goals
- Your goal should be securing as needed

Figure 5.2 – Cybersecurity strategy

Cybersecurity strategies might take two approaches toward security – defense or offense. From the defense perspective, the cyber strategy focuses on informing stakeholders about the defense strategies that an organization has put in place to protect itself from identified threats. On the other hand, with the offense perspective, cyber strategies might be focused on proving the effectiveness of existing security capabilities to find flaws and fix them. Therefore, the strategies might extensively cover the different methods that will be used to test the organization's preparedness for attacks. Lastly, some strategies might be a mix of the two perspectives, so they will cover testing and strengthening the existing defense mechanisms. The next section will discuss some of the commonly used cyber-attack and defense strategies.

How to build a cyber strategy

In this section, you will learn how to build effective cyber defense strategies. These steps should not always be taken in the order they've been provided here; they have been provided to give you an idea of how to create one. This means that you can customize it as you wish.

Understanding the business

The more you know about your business, the better you can secure it. It's really important to know the *goals* of your organization, the *objectives*, the *people* you work with, the *industry*, the current *trends*, your *business risks*, the *risk appetite and tolerance* of the risks, as well as your *most valuable* assets. Everything we do must be a reflection of the business requirements, which are approved by senior leadership, as has been manded in ISO 27001.

As Sun Tzu said in the 6th Century BC, "*If you know your enemies and know yourself, you will not be imperiled in a hundred battles; if you do not know your enemies but do know yourself, you will win one and lose one; if you do not know your enemies nor yourself, you will be imperiled in every single battle.*"

Sun Tzu also said, "*A strategy without tactics is the slowest route to victory. Tactics without a strategy are the noise before defeat.*"

Understanding threats and risks

It's not very easy to define risk since, in literature, the word *risk* is used in many different ways. According to ISO 31000, risk is the *effect of uncertainty on objectives* and such an effect is a positive or negative deviation from what is expected.

The word *risk* combines three elements: it starts with a potential event and then combines its probability with its potential severity. Many risk management courses define risk as *Risk (potential loss) = Threat x Vulnerability x Asset*:

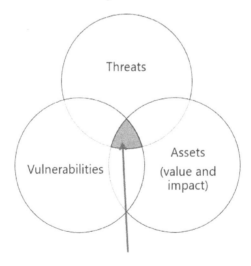

Figure 5.3 – Risk definition

It's really important to understand that not all risks are worth mitigating. If the mitigation is going to be more costly than a single occurrence or if it's not a major risk, then the risk can be accepted.

Document

As in everything else, documentation is really important and it's a key aspect of every strategy. When it comes to treatment settings or helping ensure business continuity, documentation plays a critical role. Documenting the cyber strategy will ensure efficiency, consistency, and peace of mind for anyone who is involved. Documentation helps establish standardization between processes and ensures that everyone in your organization is working the same way toward the same outcome.

The following diagram shows what good cyber strategy documentation should look like:

Figure 5.4 – Elements of a good strategy

A good strategy document should list what the strategy is and why it's needed. It has to be clear and easy to understand. It should highlight any urgencies with some mitigations options, which should also highlight the benefits of the given choices and how it's going to address the business issues.

Having such cyber strategy documents can help you easily align with the business strategy, as well as with the business drivers and goals. Once this has been aligned, you can build the technical aspects and the cyber transformation plan to become more cyber safe.

It is important to appreciate the mindset of a hacker to implement an effective cyber strategy. In the next section, we are going to discuss cyber-attack strategies.

Best cyber-attack strategies

One of the best ways to secure an organization is to think like a hacker and try to breach the organization using the same tools and techniques that an adversary would use. The following are the best cyber-attack strategies that organizations should consider.

External testing strategies

These strategies involve attempting to breach the organization externally – that is, from outside its network. In this case, cyber-attacks will be directed at publicly accessible resources for testing purposes. For instance, the firewall could be targeted via a DDoS attack to make it impossible for legitimate traffic to flow into the organization's network. Email servers are also targeted to try and jam email communication in the organization. Web servers are also targeted to try and find incorrectly placed files, such as sensitive information stored in publicly accessible folders. Other common targets include domain name servers and intrusion detection systems, which are usually exposed to the public. Other than technical systems, external testing strategies include attacks directed at staff or users. Such attacks can be carried out through social media platforms, emails, and phone calls. The most commonly used attack method is social engineering, whereby targets are persuaded to share sensitive details or send some money to pay for non-existent services.

Internal testing strategies

This includes attack tests that are performed within an organization to mimic other insider threats that may try to compromise the organization. These include disgruntled employees and visitors with malicious intentions. Internal security breach tests always assume that the adversary has standard access privileges and is knowledgeable of where sensitive information is kept, can evade detection, and even disable some security tools. Internal testing aims to harden the systems that are exposed to normal users to ensure that they cannot be easily breached. Some of the techniques that are used in external testing can still be used in internal testing, but their efficiency often increases within the network since they are exposed to more targets.

Blind testing strategy

This is a testing strategy that aims to catch the organization by surprise. It is conducted without prior warning to the IT department so that when it happens, they will treat it as a real hack rather than a test. Blind testing is done by attacking security tools, trying to breach networks, and targeting users to obtain credentials or sensitive information from them. Blind testing is often expensive since the testing team does not get any form of support from the IT department to avoid any alerts about the planned attacks. However, it often leads to the discovery of many unknown vulnerabilities.

Targeted testing strategy

This type of testing isolates only one target and carries out multiple attacks on it to discover the ones that can succeed. It is highly effective when you're testing new systems or specific cybersecurity aspects, such as incidence response to attacks targeting critical systems. However, due to its narrow scope, targeted testing does not give full details about the vulnerability of the organization.

Best cyber defense strategies

The bottom line of cybersecurity often comes down to the defense systems that an organization has in place. There are two defense strategies that organizations commonly use – defense in depth and defense in breadth.

Defense in depth

Defense in depth, also referred to as layered securing, involves employing stratified defense mechanisms to make it hard for attackers to breach organizations. Since multiple layers of security are employed, the failure of one level of security to thwart an attack only exposes attackers to another security layer. Due to this redundancy, it becomes complex and expensive for threat actors to try and breach systems. The defense in depth strategy appeals to organizations that believe that no single layer of security is immune to attacks. Therefore, a series of defense systems is always deployed to protect systems, networks, and data. For instance, an organization that wishes to protect its file server might deploy an intrusion detection system and a firewall on its network. It may also install an endpoint antivirus program on the server and further encrypt its contents. Lastly, it may disable remote access and employ two-factor authentication for any login attempts. Any threat actors trying to gain access to the sensitive files in the server will have to successfully breach all these layers of security. The chances of success are very low as each layer of security has a complexity of its own. The most common components in defense in depth approaches are as follows:

- **Network Security**: Since networks are the most exposed attack surfaces, the first line of defense is usually aimed at protecting them. The IT department might install a firewall to block malicious traffic and also prevent internal users from sending malicious traffic or visiting malicious networks. In addition, intrusion detection systems are deployed on the network to help detect suspicious activities. Due to the widespread use of DDoS attacks against firewalls, it is recommended that organizations purchase firewalls that can withstand such attacks for a continuous period.

- **An Endpoint Antivirus System**: Antivirus systems are essential in protecting computing devices from getting infected with malware. Modern antivirus systems come with additional functionalities such as inbuilt firewalls, which can be used to secure a host in a network.

- **Encryption**: Encryption is often the most trusted line of defense since it is based on mathematical complexities. Organizations choose to encrypt sensitive data to ensure that only authorized personnel can access it. When such data is stolen, it is not a big blow to the organization since most encryption algorithms are not easy to break.

- **Access Control**: Access control is used as a way to limit the people that can access a resource in a network through authentication. Organizations often combine physical and logical access controls to make it hard for potential hackers to breach them. Physical controls involve using locks and security guards to physically deter people from accessing sensitive areas such as server rooms. Logical controls, on the other hand, entail the use of authentication before a user can access any system. Traditionally, only username and password combinations were used but due to increased breaches, two-factor authentication is recommended.

The following diagram illustrates defense in depth:

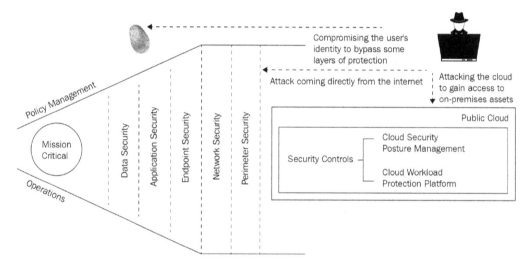

Figure 5.5 – Defense in depth

Layered security is the most widely used cyber defense strategy. However, it is increasingly becoming too expensive and quite ineffective. Hackers are still able to bypass several layers of security using attack techniques such as phishing, where the end user is directly targeted. In addition, multiple layers of security are expensive to install and maintain, which is quite challenging for SMEs. This is why there is an increase in the number of organizations when it comes to the defense in breadth approach.

Defense in breadth

This is a newly adopted defense strategy that combines the traditional security approaches with new security mechanisms. It aims to offer security at every layer of the OSI model. Therefore, when hackers evade the conventional security controls, they are still thwarted by other mitigation strategies higher up in the OSI model. The last layer of security is usually the application layer. **Web Application Firewalls** (**WAFs**) are increasing in popularity since they are highly effective against attacks targeted at specific applications. Once an attack has been launched, the WAF can thwart it and a rule can be created to prevent future similar attacks until a patch has been applied.

In addition to this, security-aware developers are using **Open Web Application Security Project** (**OWASP**) methodologies when developing applications. These methodologies insist applications being developed that meet a standard level of security and address a list of common vulnerabilities. Future developments will ensure that applications are shipped while they're almost fully secure. This means that they will be individually capable of thwarting or withstanding attacks without relying on other defense systems.

Another concept that's used in defense in breadth is security automaton. This is where systems are being developed with the ability to detect attacks and automatically defend themselves. These capabilities are achieved using machine learning, where systems are taught their desired states and normal environment setups. When there are anomalies either in their state or environment, the applications can scan for threats and mitigate them. This technology is already being fitted into security applications to improve their efficiency. There are AI-based firewalls and host-based antivirus programs that can handle security incidents without the need for human input. However, defense in breadth is still a new strategy and many organizations are apprehensive about using it.

Summary

This chapter addressed the role that CISOs and other security leaders play in an organization in terms of documenting security processes. This documentation process ensures that all the processes are recorded for future review, to provide guidance on the use of a system, and to enforce policies and procedures across the organization. Some of the main documents that have been identified in this chapter include incident response plans, disaster recovery plans, business continuity plans, and information security plans.

Documenting processes include project development phases, which help us understand the development aspects of a system for future evaluation and improvement. Processes, procedures, and policies are also documented to help enforce security requirements in an organization. Every aspect of documentation should be consistent with the business objectives and should fit within the business objectives; they should not hinder business operations.

The next chapter will look into planning for security incidents and will focus on two security plans and documents, that is, *disaster recovery* and *business continuity* plans.

Further reading

The following are resources that you can use to gain more knowledge on the topics that were covered in this chapter:

- Better security tips: `https://www.msspalert.com/cybersecurity-guests/documenation-tips/`

- Cybersecurity documentation: `https://www.tripwire.com/state-of-security/security-data-protection/cybersecurity-documentation-the-best-defense-is-a-good-offense/`

- Cybersecurity documentation – The Best Defense is a Good Offense: `https://www.tripwire.com/state-of-security/security-data-protection/cybersecurity-documentation-the-best-defense-is-a-good-offense/`

- Importance of documentation: `https://www.msspalert.com/cybersecurity-guests/documenation-tips/`

- Importance of information system documentation: `https://lifars.com/2020/07/importance-of-information-systems-documentation-for-security-what-how-and-why-to-document/`

- Documentation standards: `https://it.umn.edu/resources-it-staff-partners/information-security-standards/documentation-standards-information`

- Guidelines for security documentation: `https://www.cyber.gov.au/acsc/view-all-content/advice/guidelines-security-documentation`

- Cybersecurity documents: `https://www.tylercybersecurity.com/blog/3-must-have-cybersecurity-documents`

- Documenting an information security policy: `https://www.itgovernance.eu/blog/en/how-to-document-your-information-security-policy-2`

- Mandatory documentation: `https://www.erdalozkaya.com/checklist-of-iso-27001-mandatory-documentation/`

6
Disaster Recovery and Business Continuity

In the wake of increasing data breaches, ransomware attacks, and—based on recent happenings—global pandemics, the need for businesses to prepare for these eventualities has never been greater. Businesses are losing hundreds to millions of **United States dollars** (**USD**) every other day from successful attacks on their organizations. Since the cost of these attacks is huge, businesses need a plan in readiness for these events. Two plans, in this case, can prove helpful to a business when handling a security incident: a **disaster recovery** (**DR**) plan and a **business continuity** (**BC**) plan. While these two plans are similar and to some degree share the same objectives, a DR plan is a subset of a BC plan and is more concerned with getting the business back up and running immediately following a disruption. On the other hand, a BC plan does more than this. In addition to ensuring the business is up and running within the shortest time possible, it also seeks to address the impact of the incident from both the business's and the public's point of view. It addresses issues such as reputation risk, media coverage, and publicity issues, among others.

The aim of having a DR or BC plan is to ensure that the business can absorb shocks resulting from attacks, with the most minimal of impacts. These kinds of plans are required to simulate real-time attack vectors and to ensure that an organization is ready for such an attack when it does happen. The sophistication of attackers and the increasing success of attacks on organizations globally means that keeping attackers away is increasingly becoming a futile task. Instead, having an additional plan to rescue a business from a possible demise in case attackers are successful in getting into the systems ensures that customers, suppliers, employees, and other interested stakeholders are protected from the negative impact of attacks. The plans are guidelines of all activities to be conducted at the time of the security incidents, the procedures to follow during this period, and the people to carry out all the required duties at that time. These plans help reduce confusion during these critical periods and ensure that a business survives despite an attack. The competitive nature of businesses has seen more demand for businesses not to afford to go offline for long periods. Doing so can see competitors capitalizing on an organization's misery, which could lead to a loss of business or even a total collapse of a business enterprise.

This chapter will cover cyber attacks, data breaches, and how you can build a cyber response and DR plan based on risk management. We will look at the following topics:

- Integrating cybersecurity with a **data protection plan** (**DPP**)
- **Business impact analysis** (**BIA**)
- **DR as a service** (**DRaaS**)
- Understanding the relationship between cybersecurity and BC
- Learning about supply chain continuity
- Introducing the key components of a BC plan

The first topic addresses how to integrate cybersecurity and data protection, so let's dive right into it.

Integrating cybersecurity with a DPP

Chief information security officers (CISOs) have a challenging role in keeping intruders out of systems. Since this task is becoming increasingly difficult, the backup plan that is gaining popularity by the day is to have a long-term plan that is geared toward protecting the business following any attacks. Having a **DPP** in place is one way to keep data safe from attackers in case they get into the system. In current times, most businesses have taken to cloud technology to reduce operational costs and also to protect data from physical damage by having and running servers at the business premises. This has led to an increase in the popularity of such technologies as **hyper-scale clouds**, **edge services**, and **software-as-a-service (SaaS)** applications. These technologies encourage businesses to use applications from the cloud and other virtual environments that are maintained by third parties.

This has made data protection more challenging. While a business has total control over its business environment, it has limited control over these third-party **service providers (SPs)**. These new challenges have called upon CISOs to develop new means of keeping data safe, which forms part of a long-term plan to address security incidents when they do occur. Encryption of data, use of **virtual private networks (VPNs)**, and beefing up security at the endpoints for remote workers are just some of the innovative measures that CISOs have had to implement to keep their organizations' data safe.

After this insight into how to integrate cybersecurity with a DPP, the next section handles the BIA processes for DR and BC planning.

BIA

Conducting a BIA is an essential component of a BC plan. An impact analysis seeks to conduct a risk assessment of all possible attack vectors and the financial and other business-related costs in case these security incidents are successful. This engagement is also a regulatory requirement and serves other purposes, such as legal, employee safety, and financial fallouts. Recent studies have shown that a majority of companies (more than 70%) are making DR as well as BC plans without up-to-date BIA information.

This means that these plans are more likely to fail in case of a security incident. The cybersecurity landscape keeps evolving, and new attack vectors keep coming up all the time. In addition, the technologics in use at companies keep changing with the times as well. For instance, companies that use third-party services such as cloud services and edge technologies are reliant on software that keeps being updated all the time. This software keeps being updated to ensure that clients keep receiving the best services from these companies and also to enable them to scale their services and process more data, as well as store more data. All these changes impact businesses in many ways, and a BIA needs to be reviewed regularly to ensure that it is based on the most current information.

Prioritization of information assets is a huge factor in impact analysis processes. It is too costly for businesses to protect all assets equally using the most effective of solutions. In most cases, it is not necessary to do so, and a business can also cut down on costs by prioritizing and safeguarding the most critical assets. A BIA reveals the criticality of every information asset in the company. Loss of some information in a company cannot hinder business operations and will have minimal impact on a business. However, loss of some information can bring a business to a standstill or lead to issues such as legal problems from stakeholders. Also, some information assets are rarely required and run minimal and less sensitive operations in a business—for instance, a server can run some operations once and at the end of the month. Other servers are needed to run core business operations daily. Therefore, safeguarding the servers that run core business operations consistently is the natural priority in this case.

The section has addressed BIA for DR and BC purposes and how it impacts the prioritizing of security processes. We will now look at the classification of data to determine data that needs priority protection and why this data has the biggest impact on a business.

Classification of data

Not all data in a business needs protection. Data that is essential to business operations is that which is more critical and worth protecting. However, to determine data that needs protecting and separating it from data that does not need protecting, it is essential to engage in the **location**, **identification**, and **classification** of data. Classifying data enables a business to prioritize sensitive data over data that is less sensitive. This enables the business to make cost savings. In any case, most businesses are in operation to make a profit. Making cost savings on some business operations enables a business to meet one of its most fundamental objectives. Some classes of sensitive data that need to be prioritized include **regulatory required data**, **customer data**, **credit card data**, **intellectual property**, **patient data**, and **private communication**, among others. In this day and age when the amount of data can be overwhelming even for small businesses, there are automation tools that can help a business in data identification as well as classification.

We've now had an insight into data classification as a determinant in data protection decisions. Next, we will look at handling DRaaS solutions for organizations.

DRaaS

DRaaS is an option that is increasingly being offered by third parties to firms, especially small- and medium-sized firms as a means of getting the best DR tools and services but at less costly means. This has enabled many businesses that opt for this to achieve higher levels of **information technology** (**IT**) resilience and meet regulatory needs while achieving cost savings. Using this option also offers businesses an advantage due to the agility and flexibility they obtain from using the option. While the DRaaS service is a relatively new technological service, it has rapidly been growing, and the vendors offering this service are expanding its scope and functionalities.

In the following section, we will address how to develop an effective **communication plan** for use during DR periods.

Developing a communication plan

DR and BC rely on getting servers back up and running and businesses getting back to their normal operations in the shortest time possible. However, without a communication plan in place, getting the servers back up and running may not save a business. Having a communication plan ensures that everyone knows their role during a security incident. This includes the means of communication during a security incident, and who executes this. The communication plan handles issues both *internally* and *externally*. For internal use, it ensures that all employees know their duties during a crisis and how they are expected to behave and communicate during this period. It also offers employees a way to communicate or report potential security incidents. Reporting potential security incidents to the right person enables them to take immediate action on the issue—for instance, reporting a possible incident to a colleague not involved in matters with security may delay getting to the person who can effectively address it.

An **external communication plan** is even more important in this day and age. The era of social media and fast communication means that the manner of handling external communication must be solid to protect a business from negative and potentially harmful impacts following a security incident. There needs to be a plan on how to communicate with the legal team in case of possible legal repercussions and a procedure for contacting legal authorities to report an incident. External communication also includes how to inform customers and other stakeholders whose data is potentially compromised because of a security incident. An external **public relations** (**PR**) team is required in this case. How a PR team handles the release of information to the public, updating the public of solutions to the incident, as well as assuring them of avoiding a repeat of the same, is core to the BC objectives. The business's reputation is at stake this time and having a solid communication plan could make all the difference between keeping the business going and the collapse of the business.

Now that we have covered communication strategies during DR, let's look at how to handle the automation of data recovery plans.

Automated testing processes

Normally, a DR plan needs to be tested to ensure it is effective. A *table-top* exercise is the typical means of testing such processes, and this involves the coming together of key players (usually managers) to play out simulated DR scenarios. Recent research, conducted by *Osterman Research,* has, however, revealed that most businesses do not consider these table-top exercises as an effective means of testing. These perceptions mean that many businesses avoid conducting these tests or rarely conduct them. The downside of this is that businesses miss out on effectively preparing for evolving and newer threats in the cybersecurity landscape. As a solution to these perceptions and to help improve the success of DR exercises, **automated** tools have been developed to help companies conduct these exercises with limited resources while maintaining the required levels of security. These tools are capable of conducting backup and recovery processes continually to ensure that the processes established continue to work amid the changing business environment.

In case of identified issues, the business can then address the problem, which ensures that it has a DR plan capable of protecting the business. Also, the automated market has seen more modern automated tool solutions that create sandbox environments that do not impact the production environment and ensure that the testing process is done without hindering production processes, while efficiently testing out all possible scenarios.

Now that we have information about the automation of data recovery plans, we will move on to addressing **immutable data backups**, data reuse, highlighting the importance of **continuous updates** on DR plans, and long-term security planning.

Immutable data backups

Immutable data backups refer to copies of data that are not subject to possible changes from the production environment. A company should maintain three copies of data—one copy at the production environment and another at the recovery site, with the third copy being the immutable copy. *Air gapping* is a term that is used to refer to recovery environments that are not connected to the production environment. The immutable copy should be air gapped. The reason for the increasing usage of immutable copies of backups is the recent trend of attackers targeting recovery environments, especially cloud server environments.

Data reuse

Data recovery processes aim to ensure that a business can recover from a disruption caused by attackers; therefore, data backups are used only to restore operations. However, recent trends are suggesting that businesses could further benefit because of these recovery efforts. Recovery efforts are redundant and costly to any business. It is a necessary expense to a business to ensure its business survival in case of a security incident. The in-store data can be used to further the business prospects of a business entity. Businesses can now consider using an intelligent strategy that can encompass **regulatory requirements**, **DR procedures**, and **data analytics**. This solution can see a business advance its digital transformation efforts as a result of the DR efforts that, until now, seemingly only serve the purpose of recovery processes.

Continuous updates

Continuous changes in the business environment due to robust modern environments also hugely impact DR processes and, ultimately, the BC prospects of a business. For instance, a global pandemic such as the Covid-19 outbreak saw a huge number of companies opting to move their business operations to **remote working**. This change in the business environment was huge. It meant that companies now had workers using private networks from the comfort of their homes while accessing the company servers. The home and private networks were not subject to company safeguards, and hence, the changes affected the security of the businesses. This called for businesses to conduct frequent and regular updates of their recovery plans to reflect changes in the business environment, an increase in risks, and potential changes in recovery operations. Other changes in the business environment include the expansion of a business, which can add extra infrastructure and increased risks that also impact recoverability operations. DR and BC plans should therefore continually be updated.

Long-term planning

Traditionally, DR and BC planning have been reactive in nature. These two plans aim to have procedures ready in case of an attack and to activate these procedures whenever there is a security incident. However, this has not stopped disasters from recovering. In fact, the number of disasters and data breaches keeps increasing by the day. The results of these data breaches are also becoming more devastating. This has called for a change in mentality among security leaders. There is an increasing need for DR and BC plans to be more proactive as opposed to reactive. As reactive strategies, they are increasingly becoming less useful. A proactive approach will require planning to get ahead of threats—for instance, when there is an increasing trend in a given attack vector, a business can choose to update its systems to address such a vulnerability instead of waiting for such an attack to take place. Long-term planning for DR and BC operations provides security leaders in an organization with an opportunity to find creative ways to keep the business out of potential danger.

The previous few sections provided information on immutable data backups and data reuse and highlighted the importance of long-term planning and continuous updates, as these enable a business to resume operations after a security incident.

In the next section of this chapter, we will seek to provide insights into the relationship between cybersecurity and BC.

Understanding the relationship between cybersecurity and BC

Cybersecurity and **BC** go hand in hand. BC is often associated with natural disasters. For long periods, businesses have planned for BC by making long-term plans in case of disasters such as hurricanes, storms, floods, earthquakes, and so on. The most common form of planning for those businesses to engage in is an investment in a backup generator in case of power blackouts. Needless to say, a power blackout in a digital environment means a complete cessation of business. However, increased cybersecurity threats have seen cyber threats rise in consideration, and these now stand alongside natural disasters and have a similar potential impact on a business. The higher likelihood of a cybersecurity incident occurring as compared to a natural disaster means that cybersecurity planning in a company must be included in BC planning.

Cybersecurity and BC share common goals—for instance, they both have the goal of ensuring reliable business operations and stable networks. When a business plans for BC, it plans to ensure that disruption to networks and infrastructure is promptly averted, and stability and reliability are returned. Cybersecurity also has similar goals. All plans to address the security of information assets are geared toward ensuring that the networks remain stable and reliable to enable business operations to continue with minimal-to-no disruptions. In many organizations, it is common to find separate departments for cybersecurity headed by the CISO and the BC departments. More often than not, efforts by the BC team lead to resources that prove valuable to the cybersecurity team. In this regard, BC and cybersecurity are similar.

In some cases, the cybersecurity team may work separately from the BC team. The cybersecurity team focuses on specific threats that are most likely to affect the company, and in its singular focus, fails to capture the bigger picture of BC. However, many of its efforts overlap either in function or objectivity; therefore, it is only prudent that these two teams work in unison to achieve their objectives. In so doing, they may also cut down on costs due to the elimination of redundancies. Also, the company will benefit from increased security from a more comprehensive long-term BC plan that addresses all aspects of the company's operations.

BC and cybersecurity objectives also show similarity in areas such as the following:

- **Threat evaluation**
- **Risk assessment**
- **Mitigation planning**
- **Service prioritization**

In terms of threat evaluation, both evaluate all possible threats and find a means to mitigate those threats in the event the company must face them. Regarding risk assessment, BC will assess the risk factor from each of the identified threats and then determine how these risks will impact the company. After assessing the risk, BC and cybersecurity will make plans on how to mitigate the threats. Also, both BC and cybersecurity teams will use the risk assessment and business impact of each threat to prioritize the risks and mitigation efforts.

Now that we have covered the relationship between cybersecurity and BC planning, let's explore how to plan for common attacks such as **ransomware** and **denial-of-service (DoS) attacks**.

Planning for ransomware and DoS attacks

Ransomware is a popular means of attack in which attackers infiltrate a system, get hold of the data on the servers, and then encrypt the data using a key only they have access to. Once they have achieved this, the attackers then contact the affected company and blackmail the company into offering them a ransom in exchange for keys to decrypt the data. Without a proper backup plan, an organization will not have other copies of the encrypted data and will be forced to part with the ransom to regain access to their data. Ransomware attacks have been on the rise in the recent past and trends suggest that these kinds of attacks will not stop soon. However, with effective data recovery and a BC plan, a business can address the threat of ransomware attacks. All a company needs is a **backup data source**. In case of such an attack, the company can quickly cleanse its servers and then reload the backup and resume operations without needing to pay any ransom.

DoS attacks are also similarly used by attackers. In this case, the attackers will target a company's network transmissions and spam the network until it fails to address required functions, hence denying legitimate functions and transmissions that require service. Attackers use this as a means of extortion to demand a ransom from firms to leave them alone. A company without a backup plan will have to part with a ransom to stop disruptions to its services. However, with a proper DR and BC plan, a business will have an alternative means of getting its servers and functions back up online, hence enabling it to avoid the DoS extortion.

The next section emphasizes the importance of using **quality backups**, because the use of poor quality backups may fail a business intending to recover from ransomware and DoS attacks.

Using quality backups

The data recovery process is an exercise filled with redundancies. These redundancies include both the data aspects and the infrastructure. A company must invest in *duplicates*. However, it's a common habit of companies to focus on the production copies and data and invest heavily in protecting data in use in the production environment, while similar efforts do not apply to duplicate copies at recovery centers. Therefore, attackers may find it easier to break into recovery centers and get hold of the data compared to breaking into the production environment.

In some cases, the backup files are powered down and sit idling on the shelves, waiting for security incidents in order to be used. In other cases, there are hot sites that are always live and ready for use immediately in case of a security incident. These sites rarely get the security attention and preparation the production environment copies get. These sites are more prone to infiltration as well as physical penetration from malicious individuals.

Unencrypted files, poor maintenance, and insecurity of backups are general themes in the case of most organizations' backup positions. Security leaders that prepare security in the production environment and develop security policies for use at live sites need to duplicate their efforts at recovery sites to ensure the security of data. Otherwise, attackers will only need to determine the location of the backup sites and target the recovery center instead, where their chances of success are much higher.

This section has shown the importance of investing in quality backups. The next section highlights why organizations need user training and education.

User training and education

User training and education is an important component that helps ensure the efficiency of any DR and BC plan—for instance, during a security incident, all users involved have to know their role in the DR plan. They need to be aware of the means of communication during this period and the kind of information they can communicate to outsiders. Therefore, user training is necessary for the success of the plans. User education is important for security operations because this helps raise the level of awareness in a business. It is more likely for an employee to notice something amiss with the system and then inform or report to relevant authorities instead of relying on experts to notice the problem. Without a group of educated users, the chances of successful attacks are higher. Therefore, for a business to maximize the chances of the BC plan succeeding, they need to invest some resources in user education to raise their level of awareness as well as help them understand their roles during security incidents so that they can be part of the solution and not part of the problem.

You should now have an understanding of the various aspects of cybersecurity, such as user training and education, and how user knowledge helps reduce security threats posed by internal users, hence increasing the chances of success of a BC plan. Next, we will walk through an insight into **supply chain continuity**.

Learning about supply chain continuity

Supply chain continuity is a subset of BC and is an often-overlooked side of BC. While businesses will look at the internal aspects of their business when assessing levels of risk and creating ways to safeguard their business in case of security incidents, they fail to look at the entire supply chain to determine the risks that emanate from the supply chain and plan for continuity of the supply chain in the case of security incidents. A business needs to invest in resources for the monitoring and evaluation of the entire supply chain for cybersecurity threats that may result from it. After assessing the entire supply chain and determining the cybersecurity threats that the supply chain causes the business, the next step is to prioritize these threats and decide on risks that are tolerable based on a BIA. The lowest risk threats can be tolerated with minimal security resources, while the bigger threats have to be addressed in the supply chain continuity planning process. Investments toward supply chain partners may be necessary to ensure BC.

After providing an insight into supply chain continuity, we are going to describe other key components, besides the supply chain continuity we have just covered, that are crucial to BC planning.

Introducing the key components of a BC plan

A BC plan is integral during the aftermath of a security incident due to the guidance it offers regarding the handling of various issues that are crucial to the recovery of business operations. In this section, we will look at various business components that are essential to BC planning.

The following are key components in any BC plan:

- **Strategy**: These are all the strategic objectives that a business uses to complete its day-to-day business operations.
- **Organization**: These are objects that encompass employee responsibilities, skills, organizational structure, communications within the organization, and so on.
- **Applications and data**: Applications and the data being processed by these applications to enable business functions.
- **People**: Users of the business system.
- **Processes**: IT processes and other critical business processes for the smooth running of the business.
- **Technology**: Network, technology architecture, and things such as secure backups.
- **Facilities**: Objects that seek alternatives in case of the destruction of production copies.

Next, we will look at how security leaders can identify BC risks.

How to identify BC risks

The CISO and their team need to be able to identify business risks associated with the company's business operations. To identify risks, the CISO needs to thoroughly understand the **IT infrastructure** at the company on which the business operations are reliant. The key points that need to be considered to help in the identification process include the following:

- Critical systems that maintain daily business operations

- Critical data and information needed for business operations

- Critical parts of the network that are necessary for normal business operations

- Critical software needed for normal business operations

- Natural disasters that are capable of impacting critical systems, networks, and software

- Cyber risks that can impact critical systems, networks, and software

- Critical third-party services that are necessary for core business operations

- Controls that have been put in place to safeguard critical systems, networks, and software from cyber risks

- Off-site data centers, and other backup data recovery services used by the business

- Encryption of data in transit, especially affecting remote work

- The availability of endpoint encryption options in case of security incidents affecting business operations

- Defined processes that are used during emergencies to implement required administrative authorizations

The section has provided insights into how security teams can identify BC risks that affect an organization. The next section lists and describes types of DR with the various business risks, helping to determine the various classifications.

Types of DR

These fall into categories such as the following:

- **Network DR**: This type of recovery planning involves the assessment of a company's network and the determination of threats to the company emanating from the network. Problems that may affect a company's network may be caused by intentional or unintentional human activities, disruptions due to natural hazards such as floods, or due to network provider inherent issues.

- **Virtualization DR**: With the virtualization of server technologies, the recovery options allow more flexibility in that companies do not need to have the same physical servers in the production environment as those at the secondary recovery site. With flexibility, companies can save on the cost of having to invest in lots of server hardware, which is a costly affair given that it needs upgrading and maintenance for effectiveness as well.

- **Cloud-based DR**: Cloud-based recovery involves the recovery of remote machines that operate on a cloud-based platform. These cloud-based recovery options are available in form of **infrastructure as a service** (**IaaS**) and ensure data backup of sensitive system data on off-site cloud servers away from the production environment.

- **Data center DR**: This kind of recovery involves organizational plans on means to resume operations in case of an unexpected event that results in the destruction of data, software, and infrastructure. It is a contingency measure meant to address unforeseen events in case they do happen.

The section has listed and described types of DR. The next section addresses key differences between DR and BC plans.

Key differences between DR and BC plans

While DR and BC share lots of similarities and are often handled together, they do have contrasting differences. These include the following:

- A DR plan aims to restore operations as they were before the security incident. The priority, in this case, is the restoration of only critical applications and critical data for use in availing core business operations.

- On the other hand, a BC plan is more of a long-term strategy that defines business operations during and after a security event. While DR is concerned with getting the systems back up, a BC plan considers the timing of the downtime, power outages, and other disaster impacts, and how these affect the business going forward.

- The differences between the two plans are magnified during the implementation stages. However, there are several overlaps between the two plans, especially during the recovery phase.

The section has explained the key differences between DR and BC plans. The next section addresses the role **artificial intelligence** (**AI**) can play in DR and BC planning.

Using AI for DR and BC processes

Natural disasters have been much more unpredictable, and traditional planning for such disasters did not require much thought. However, with the digital landscape, security disasters have become more certain, highlighting the need for effective DR planning. AI strategies are increasingly being required to help enhance the efficiency of the available DR options. With AI, the following strategies can be implemented:

- **Predicting potential outcomes**: During the assessment of threats, the use of AI technologies can greatly advance the threat assessment processes. The use of **deep neural networks** (**DNNs**) is better and more robust than manual assessments and will enable the development of more powerful recovery plans.

- **Better protection**: AI will enhance both a risk assessment and BIA, which will ultimately help security strategists draft better plans for DR operations.

- **Automating the DR process**: AI can be used to control various parts of a DR plan, as well as automating the process. The automation will not only help prevent some security incidents but will also help in adapting to new data and updating the available processes.

- **Enhancing incident response (IR) actions**: AI can quickly analyze a security incident and determine the reasons behind attacks. AI can also be programmed in such a way that it can initiate auto-recovery processes, hence reducing downtime and drastically improving BC chances.

- **AI learning from each security incident**: AI is based on **machine learning** (**ML**) principles and will learn from each security incident that affects an organization. With better learning capacity and analysis potential compared to humans, AI can greatly improve the security aspects of an organization and can help it respond better in upcoming security incidents and improve on reporting downtime issues.

The section has shown how AI can be used in DR and BC planning efforts. The next section provides insights into new and **emerging technologies** that are enhancing DR and BC efforts.

Emerging technologies in the DR and BC landscape

With an increasing need for businesses to protect themselves against impending threats, the need for better DR and BC has become more critical. Fortunately, emerging technologies are being developed to address this need. Some of these technologies are listed here:

- **Virtualization technologies**: These help to make restoration easier during recovery time.

- **Backing up data and recovery for mobile users**: This helps broaden the DR landscape.

- **Disc-based backup solutions**: With massive amounts of data being stored in huge data centers, it has necessitated the need for disc-based data backup solutions.

- **Cloud-based solutions**: These solutions have been created for cloud platforms that are increasingly being used by more companies. They have enabled companies to access automated data recovery options and save on costs, with a DRaaS option being available on these cloud platforms.

The next section will now provide tips on how to build an effective DR plan.

Tips on building a strong and effective DR plan

Organizations invest a lot in security systems, yet most of these security systems end up being based on the increasing number of successful security breaches being reported. The failure of these security defenses often leaves firms in worse situations in the periods following security incidents. Therefore, organizations need to plan ahead to be able to better protect their informational assets from cyber attacks. The following three tips are crucial to building a strong and effective plan:

- Be wary of insider threats and stay safe from them as they have as much potential to cause destruction as outsider threats do.

- It is critical to involve employees at various levels of mitigation planning.

- Always document, implement, and update plans regularly as business processes change.

The next section highlights the importance of a certified and skilled **cybersecurity workforce** to an organization and why this is critical to effective BC planning.

Importance of a certified and skilled cybersecurity workforce

A CISO and their team need to be certified and skilled enough to handle all cybersecurity challenges that are certain to come their way. The team has a critical role to play in identifying, protecting, detecting, and responding to vulnerabilities in an organization's system. The team has a responsibility to create security policies and defense mechanisms to protect an organization as well as develop a disaster management plan. The major duties of this team include the following:

- Mitigating company vulnerabilities and threats

- Protecting company data

- Protecting networks and systems

- Performing weekly offsite backups

- Monitoring both internal and external threats

- Regularly updating organizational security procedures and policies

- Improving awareness and training of staff to be able to handle DR and emergencies during security incidents

The listed duties are the core responsibilities of a cybersecurity team in an organization. These roles, however, have been evolving as the CISO role keeps adapting to changes in the cybersecurity space as well as rapid developments in the IT world.

Summary

This chapter has addressed a major CISO role of enacting systems to help an organization during and in the aftermath of a security incident. In the current times of increasing security incidents, it is important for an organization to be prepared for security events and lay down procedures to tackle security incidents if and when they do occur. These plans are laid out in two documents referred to as **DR** and **BC** plans. DR planning focuses on getting systems and servers back up and running after a security incident. BC planning, on the other hand, focuses on the business impact of a security incident and strategizes on ensuring the security incident has minimal impact on the business and that the business can fully resume operations in the aftermath of the incident.

In the next chapter, we will tackle the concept of **stakeholder onboarding** where various organizational stakeholders and their cybersecurity roles will be discussed.

Further reading

Here are some resources that can be used to gain more knowledge of the topics covered in this chapter:

- BC and DR: `https://www.eccouncil.org/business-continuity-and-disaster-recovery/`

- Cyber defense teams in BC: `https://www.cybersecurityeducationguides.org/business-continuity/`

- Importance of BCDR: `https://searchdisasterrecovery.techtarget.com/definition/Business-Continuity-and-Disaster-Recovery-BCDR`

- Integrating cybersecurity with BC: `https://www.resolver.com/blog/integrate-cybersecurity-business-continuity/`

- Basics of DR and BC: `https://www.csoonline.com/article/2118605/business-continuity-and-disaster-recovery-planning-the-basics.html`

- Impact of cybersecurity on BC and DR: `https://www.lmgsecurity.com/how-cybersecurity-impacts-business-continuity-planning-and-disaster-recovery/`

7
Bringing Stakeholders On Board

Stakeholder onboarding refers to the process of **chief information security officers** (**CISOs**) bringing all the relevant stakeholders of an organization on board with their security planning. The reason for CISOs needing to bring stakeholders on board is because of the costly activities of security planning and implementation. Security initiatives, which form the core role of a CISO in an organization, increasingly need more resource allocation to ensure their effectiveness.

The threat landscape is worsening and threats continue to evolve, which has necessitated organizations to increase their budgets toward security initiatives. However, continually requesting more resources is a goal that directly conflicts with the basic business goal of making a profit and maximizing benefits. A major way of maximizing benefits and profits is to reduce costs and make operations less costly. The stakeholders—mainly the investors—and the board of directors that manage these interests have an automatic say in matters that require a huge investment in company resources. Therefore, a CISO is tasked with the role of having to bring stakeholders on board by explaining the strategies in place and why the chosen strategies can work for the company and will not threaten a company's long-term need for survival and continuity.

In this chapter, we will evaluate the CISO task of security onboarding under the following main topics:

- Evaluating business opportunities versus security risks
- Optimal budgeting

Evaluating business opportunities versus security risks

The ever-evolving role of a CISO has seen this executive role get more management responsibilities to a point they can only be seen as part of management. Among these evolving and new roles is the evaluation of **business opportunities** *vis-à-vis* the respective **security risks**. Every business opportunity, however lucrative it may seem, comes with its share of risks. Some business opportunities carry with them far higher risks compared to others. Unfortunately, a majority of high-risk business opportunities are also the most promising in terms of potential rewards to the company. Investing in high-risk business opportunities is a perilous strategy that is highly likely to sink a business. However, balancing risks is a delicate venture that can ensure a business thrives. Risk management, therefore, is a critical management role in which security leaders such as a CISO play an integral role. While other managers may consider other aspects of a business operation in terms of likely resource allocations and the likely profits from the business opportunity, the CISO will evaluate opportunities from a security point of view.

A business identifies many business opportunities they may be interested in investing in. The CISO has to evaluate the security impact of all these opportunities. Essentially, the CISO has to fully understand all the functionalities of these business opportunities and how they will integrate with the current system. If a new opportunity presents similar risks to the current system, integrating the system with the current one should be easier, with few modifications required. However, most business opportunities will present different risks as various factors—including the business location and infrastructure, and the users in the new environment—impact the risk levels presented by a business opportunity. Some factors to consider when evaluating a new business opportunity include the following:

- The system to be used by the new business opportunity. If the new business opportunity will run on the same system that the CISO understands, evaluating the system will be easier, and decision-making processes should be easier to complete.

- The amount of capital investment required before the organization can take on the new business opportunity. If the amount of the capital required is high and the opportunity does not promise high rewards, then it would be prudent not to consider such an opportunity.

- The impact of the new opportunity on current business operations, as undertaking a new business opportunity may cause a ripple effect on these. For instance, hospitality businesses joining delivery apps such as *Uber Eats* or creating a unique business may have a significant impact on the business operations of the company. This may force the business to re-evaluate the current business as well as consider the new factors. A big impact means higher risks. However, if the risks are manageable, then the business can be considered a worthwhile venture.

- The technological aspects of the new business opportunity. The more digitalized a business opportunity is, the higher the risk potential concerning cybersecurity. Therefore, less digitalized environments are easier to evaluate and enable us to determine the risks involved.

The section has introduced the role of a CISO in evaluating new business opportunities to determine the risks they carry and the impact of these risks on a business, which is crucial in decision-making processes. The next section will address the role of the CISO in **risk management** and provide various security functions in executing this role.

The role of a CISO in risk management

A CISO has a core role of reviewing all business aspects, including new business opportunities, to determine the level of risk associated with all business operations. A review will enable the CISO to make informed decisions and strategies on how to combat and mitigate these risks. Some of the functions for the CISO in risk management include the following:

- **Reviewing critical systems and data**: A review of critical systems and data is necessary whenever there is increased use. This helps determine which assets, networks, or systems are critical to continued business operations.

- **Management of external threats**: Whenever there are increased malicious activities such as ease of access to sophisticated tools by hackers, the security team needs to ensure there are automated mechanisms to regularly update software and systems.

- **Continuous monitoring (CM)**: The use of automated software and tools enables better threat and vulnerability identification.

- **Business continuity (BC) and incident response (IR)**: A CISO is tasked with ensuring the enactment of strategies to handle the business in case of a security incident and in the aftermath of a security incident.

- **Internal threat management**: Ensuring authorizations and **multi-factor authentication** (**MFA**) are in use to help secure systems from internal threats.

- **Vendor risk management**: Vendors also introduce risks to a business entity. The security team must monitor and manage security controls handled by vendors and other third parties to ensure the security of organizational data.

This section has listed and described functions of the CISO concerning risk management and why CISOs need to consider all aspects of an organization that present risk to the business, addressing these risks because this is their primary role as security leaders. The next section will look into the optimal budgeting role of a CISO and how financial resources aid a CISO in implementing security initiatives in an organization.

Optimal budgeting

While CISO roles used to be limited in the past, changing security threats and increasing roles in an organization have seen CISOs become ever more involved with the budgeting process. Security planning now involves almost all aspects of a company, given that most parts of organizations have been digitalized and, hence, need security from external and internal threats. This means that any changes to business processes in any part of the company will need a review to be carried out by the security team to ensure they meet the regulations and security standards set for the company.

The idea of **optimal budgeting** is a process of budgeting for security resources while keeping in mind that the budget is limited and that the business needs to make a profit at the end of the day. A cost-benefit analysis of the security initiatives should guide the CISO in making optimal budgeting decisions. A **cost-benefit analysis (CBA)** will require the security team to consider all available options, perform risk assessments of all identified risks, look at the business impact of identified threats, and then determine whether the benefit of the security initiative or strategy will outweigh the cost of implementing it.

After understanding what optimal budgeting means, the next section addresses how **communication** plays an integral role in getting management on board.

Communication

Regular notifications to the board of management are a key CISO activity to bring stakeholders on board. Strategizing on your own and coming up with a plan that will cost the company money at the end of the day may not be well received by the board. However, regular communication and briefing the board of the security situation, threats, and possible solutions prepare the board for such strategies when they eventually may need to be implemented.

The board is not the only stakeholder that needs to be notified of plans and security initiatives. The organization's management is first in line. Departmental managers and the **chief executive officers** (**CEOs**) are part and parcel of the daily management of the company. They understand the business operations better than the board of directors. Any security initiatives affect their duties and responsibilities in the company. Therefore, they have to be included in the security planning and review of proposed security initiatives before they are presented to the final board for resource approval.

Hopefully, you now have an understanding of the role of communication in management onboarding and why it needs to be done in the right way to enhance the chances of getting them on board. The next section will address the concept of **corporate governance** and why this is crucial to the stakeholder onboarding discussion.

Corporate governance

According to the dictionary, *corporate governance* is a term that is used to refer to the many rules, processes, and practices by which a company is controlled or directed. The basis of corporate governance is the balancing of interests by the many company stakeholders such as customers, shareholders, government, community, and **senior management executives** (**SMEs**). Recent needs have seen information security increasingly become a major corporate governance issue. Information security involves issues such as risk management, reporting controls, testing and training, and executive accountability. All these mentioned issues are the responsibilities of management in corporations, therefore it is no longer possible to separate the management of a company from the security aspects of the company. The security team must therefore involve firm management in all matters pertaining to security strategizing.

Corporate governance by its very definition revolves around policies and controls by which a company operates. In this respect, security controls are part and parcel of corporate governance. Therefore, the security team needs to work with the company management in instituting controls for the company that do not hinder business processes but that capture the firm's unique culture as well as enhance business operations. People, processes, and technology are the three key components of corporate governance. All these components are essential to cybersecurity. People are the users of the system and could pose internal threats to the informational system. A process represents business procedures that could potentially be exploited by malicious individuals to access the system. The technology component is a system that could have inherent flaws or that could be exploited during a security incident. Corporate governance and information security cannot be considered separately in the modern business environment.

After understanding the concept of corporate governance and how intertwined it is with information security, the next section will list and describe the various duties of top management concerning security initiatives.

Duties of top management in an organization

The top management of any firm has core duties to play to ensure the success and continuity of an organization from a security perspective. They are outlined here:

1. **Creating a safe business community for all stakeholders**. The top management in any company has the responsibility of ensuring that the business environment is safe from exploitation by would-be attackers. The environment should be safe for customers and other parties such as business associates that deal with the company and that may share sensitive information with the firm.

2. **Abiding by regulations and laws that govern business practices**. Due to the potential for exploitation even from top management, governments in various countries and internationally have created laws and regulations that govern business operations. The top management in the company is responsible for ensuring that these laws are implemented and that the company operates in full compliance with the law.

3. **Ensuring internal controls are developed and implemented well within the company**. This will ultimately translate to a secure business environment and security of information assets within the company. Internal controls must be structured in such a way that they secure all consumer information. A failure to implement this will see a company facing severe penalties for neglecting to make their business environment secure.

As can be seen from the three aforementioned top management duties, it is imperative for top management to be in the loop of all security strategies that the security team is brainstorming and what it wants to implement. The CISO thus has to ensure that all the security policies and controls they intend to formulate are approved by top management and the board before they can be implemented. At the end of the day, the security of the business environment is the responsibility of a firm's top management. Even though the CISO may perform the actual work, the success and failure of controls will be attributed to top management.

The section has listed and described the various roles of top management concerning security initiatives, and hence the need to get them on board with security-initiative strategizing. The next section addresses the role of a CISO in terms of reporting security initiatives to the board of directors.

Reporting to the board of directors

Reporting to the board of management is a CISO responsibility. CISOs and their security team have to report security initiatives, as some of these initiatives are regulatory responsibilities that are tasked to corporate governance. Some regulations emphasize that corporate governance is a compliance issue that all firms need to ensure a safe business environment. During **information technology** (**IT**) discussions, the board must be included due to the risk management aspect of security initiatives. The board is responsible for creating management strategies to combat business risks and the business impact that could arise from such risks. Their inclusion in security discussions ensures that these discussions have the backing of management and that management offers the necessary oversight and advice needed to protect the company data and the company. Any breach of company data puts a company at risk of failing to continue operations or could be a blow to the company's reputation, which may prove impossible to recover from. The importance of security initiatives thus needs the full knowledge and involvement of the corporate board.

The section has provided insights into the role of the security team concerning reporting all security initiatives to the board of directors to enable the board to carry out some of their corporate governance responsibilities. In the next section, we will look at how to get **employees** on board.

Getting employees on board

Employees are a key part of a company and have a direct influence on the success as well as the failures of a company. In terms of threats, employees are a potential threat to a company's informational assets, just as external threats are to these assets. In many cases, it is easier to protect a company from external threats than it is to protect a company from internal threats. Therefore, it is essential for the CISO and the security team to get company employees on board in their security initiatives and arrangements. Security initiatives have to be incorporated into the company values and culture. For this to happen, employees have to fully embrace these initiatives. Employees' training sessions are a key factor in getting them on board. If employees do not understand the security initiatives, then they are less likely to follow them. Training and security conferences are important avenues for management—and the security team, in particular—to explain the security features in place and the importance of embracing these initiatives for the benefit of the company.

Rewarding employees is a major way to get them on board. Security policies may include such things as sign-in schedules and sign-out forms at the entrance and exit of the business premises. These forms are important security protocols for a company to ensure that they keep a record of all employees that come in and out of the business premises. Rewarding employees that are good at following security protocols can help employees to appreciate some of these initiatives and to make these controls part of the organizational culture.

Management must lead by example. The various departmental managers and supervisors have an important role to play in helping lower-level users and employees in an organization to adopt new security initiatives. These managerial figures must follow these security protocols, and the rest of the employees can follow their examples. Therefore, the security team needs to engage the managers and supervisors first and get them on board before the security controls are rolled out for the rest of the users to adopt.

The security initiatives need to be reasonable and not hinder smooth business operations. If security controls make work difficult for users, then they are less likely to embrace the protocols and may use shortcuts whenever they have a chance to do so. Having a culture where the employees are resentful toward security initiatives is risky to a company. Therefore, when brainstorming new security initiatives and controls, the CISO and their team need to think about the impact these controls will have on the users and their work. The security controls should not make the working environment overly stressful but should promote the business. Security initiatives, such as the use of security cameras, should be implemented sparingly and only in needed areas such as common rooms, the reception area, entrances, and exits. Some rooms, especially private rooms and changing rooms, should not have security cameras installed. Such measures may be interpreted as disrespectful and an invasion of privacy by employees. Security initiatives must be considerate of all factors and should ensure they cause as little friction among employees as possible.

After getting to understand various ways we can use to get employees on board in the section, the next section seeks to show how to get **customers** on board as well.

Getting customers on board

Customers are an essential part of a business enterprise. Without customers, a business is doomed to fail. A business is built to impress customers to get them to come back for more goods and services from the company, therefore customers have to be totally on board with the security operations in a company for them to engage with the company. If customers feel that their data is not safe within your organization, then they are likely to take their business elsewhere. They need to feel safe. There are several actions that a firm can undertake to ensure that customers get on board with their security initiatives, and some of them are outlined here:

- **Customers must see security controls in action**: Customers will be more convinced of the security of their data and information in the hands of an organization if they see some good security practices being implemented. For instance, in a bank, customers will see bank tellers and other staff members only accessing staff areas using security cards. Such a measure can be seen by customers and will enhance their confidence in the security initiatives implemented by the organization.

- **Customers should experience some of the security controls**: Malicious individuals often pose as customers to access premises of their target companies either for surveillance purposes or to gain access to some information assets in the business premises. Therefore, some security initiatives and controls should be applicable for customers as well. An example of a security control is a request for full identification from a customer before they can access their data from the system or make any transaction. When customers experience such controls, they gain confidence in the system and are confident that their data is safe in the hands of the organization.

- **Use of physical limitations and security cameras**: The use of cameras at reception and waiting areas and other customer-accessible areas will help keep customers in check. Customers can see the cameras, and the presence of these cameras will help increase their confidence in the company's operations. Customers will know that any malicious person posing as a customer will also be subject to such surveillance and will then have more faith in the security operations and initiatives by the company to safeguard their information.

- **Some policies need to be communicated in print and displayed for customers to see**: It is common for organizations to print security rules and display them on notice boards or walls of waiting rooms and reception areas. Customers can then read and follow these while they are waiting to be served. Such a display of security policies aids in reiterating security initiatives and gaining the confidence of customers.

After getting to understand the importance of getting customers on board and how to get them on board in this section, the next section addresses why and how to get **shareholders** on board.

Getting shareholders on board

Shareholders are an important aspect of a company. Their investments allow companies to expand and to grow, as well as handle financial challenges that may face them. A company needs to get shareholders on board with all the security initiatives in place. The board of directors will normally take care of the interests of the shareholders. The shareholders meet at **annual general meetings** (**AGMs**) and choose representatives on the board to manage their interests. Therefore, a firm needs to get the board of directors to share similar sentiments regarding security and to approve of these security initiatives.

Some methods an organization can use to get shareholders on board include the following:

- Hiring a qualified and competent security team including a CISO executive. Hiring such a team inspires confidence that the firm is doing the right things to secure data and address business risks arising from data security issues.

- Developing and then subsequently implementing security initiatives such as physical controls that limit access to sensitive company sections such as servers. Such controls will raise confidence in security operations.

- Using qualified and reputable security contractors and vendors for security projects, systems, and products. A firm using questionable vendors to procure products will not inspire much confidence in the security situation within the organization. On the other hand, using reputable consultants and market-leading security products is a sign of a firm taking security initiatives seriously.

This section has addressed the importance of getting shareholders on board and provided tips on how to get them on board. In the next section, we will look at the benefits of getting the community on board and tips on how to get them on board.

Getting the community on board

The community plays an integral part in the success of a business and, therefore, they also play a role in the security aspects of a firm. A firm's physical location could be targeted by malicious individuals who may want to cause havoc and cause issues such as fires, burglary of IT products, and so on.

Getting the community on board in the security aspects of a firm will help raise security levels of the physical location and keep malicious individuals away. Some ways to get the community on board include the following:

- Investing in the community as corporate social responsibility and providing the community with vital social services, such as scholarships and donating toward health and sporting activities, will get the community behind the firm. The community, in turn, will help safeguard the company's assets by reporting any suspicious activities that may happen around the firm's premises.

- Employing people from the community. When a firm employs people from the community, the people in the community become invested in the success of the business, as the employees and their families form part of the company. Therefore, a community that is more invested in the success of the company is more likely to report suspicious activities as well as help safeguard business premises from external threats.

We have now provided insights into the role of the community and why a CISO needs to get them on board because they pose a potential security risk to an organization, but they can also be included in a plan that will help improve the security situation of an organization.

Summary

This chapter has addressed the important role of the security team and getting stakeholders on board with security initiatives. We have looked at issues such as optimal budgeting strategies and why it is important for a CISO to make budgeting considerations in their security planning to ensure that they prioritize risks and balance the cost of implementing security operations against the business benefits. Some of the stakeholders that need onboarding include the board of management, shareholders, employees, customers, and the community. When the security team gets all the stakeholders on board, then then the implementation of security initiatives becomes easier, and this also translates to access to resources to implement them as well.

The next chapter will look at other CISO tasks, such as contributions to technical projects, evaluating employee behavior, financial reporting, and partnering with internal and external providers to ensure the effectiveness of their security strategies.

Further reading

Here are some resources that can be used to gain more knowledge about the topics covered in this chapter:

- Linking information security and corporate governance: `https://www.computerworld.com/article/2564800/the-link-between-information-security-and-corporate-governance.html`

- *Security planning on a budget for CISOs:* `https://www.intelligentciso.com/2021/07/22/security-planning-on-a-budget-for-cisos/#`

- *Principles of Corporate Governance:* `https://corpgov.law.harvard.edu/2016/09/08/principles-of-corporate-governance/`

- Understanding corporate governance: `https://www.investopedia.com/terms/c/corporategovernance.asp`

- The roles of CISOs: `https://hyperproof.io/resource/chief-information-security-officers/`

- The CISO's role in risk management: `https://ctovision.com/the-cisos-role-in-risk-management/`

8
Other CISO Tasks

The **Chief Information Security Officer (CISO)** has a critical role to play in an organization as far as safeguarding an organization's informational assets is concerned. In the previous chapters, we saw their increasing involvement in the long-term strategic planning activities for an organization, given that all long-term planning and investments affect the security aspects of a company and will need the CISO's input. In this chapter, we will look at the other important roles they play in an organization by covering the following topics:

- Contributing to technical projects
- Partnering with internal and external providers
- Evaluating employee behavior
- Financial reporting
- Addressing cybersecurity as a business problem

The first section will address how and why CISOs contribute to technical projects. Let's dive right into it.

Contributing to technical projects

Technical projects include projects that have been undertaken by a company to develop infrastructure and other informational assets that are crucial for managing data in an organization. Such technical projects may include such projects as developing an information management system and upgrading the system to a more modern system that encompasses newer technologies and better safety features. Other technical projects may include expansion plans for the current system to enable it to scale with ease. This will allow it to incorporate the expected growth in the company or engage in increased business operations.

A business cannot use the same system indefinitely. The growth of technology, as well as the ever-evolving security threat landscape, demands that companies keep updating their systems to incorporate the latest recommended security features. Upgrading the current system may be a regulations requirement or company policy. Either way, a company is poised to benefit from engaging in such plans as it will keep attackers away, as well as ensure that it reduces possible security incidents and the potential damages associated with such security incidents.

The role of the CISO in such technical projects is clear. Their responsibility for keeping the company safe from attacks ensures that they evaluate all the attack surfaces and take the necessary precautions to ensure that the system's vulnerabilities are not exploited by attackers. One of the ways of ensuring attack surfaces are safeguarded is to plan and develop technical projects. System security aspects can be addressed during the development stages of the system. Instead of waiting until the system is rolled out and needing to take additional measures to safeguard the system, which will prove to be a costly venture, it is more impactful to address the security issues during the development phases. By the time a system is rolled out, it is less vulnerable to attacks and, therefore, less risky to a company.

This section has provided insights into how and why CISOs contribute to technical projects, enabling us to understand how that enhances the security posture of an organization. The next section will look into various partnerships that are necessary for CISOs, both internally and externally, and how they help the CISO be a better security leader.

Partnering with internal and external providers

Partnering with both *internal* and *external* providers is an essential task for CISOs in an organization. The work of the CISO touches on all the aspects of a company. In the modern business landscape, where many business operations have been automated and digitalized, any of these automated points can present a vulnerability to the business, hence impacting the security posture of an organization. It requires CISOs and their security teams to understand all the aspects of the business properly to ensure that they can perform effective evaluation and vulnerability testing. Therefore, the security team will need to partner up with other departments within the company to ensure that the CISO not only understands all the aspects of the business but that they can also get the input of the various partners regarding possible security policies and their implementation in the businesses.

Now, let's go through the various business processes that are impacted by partnerships.

Security policies implementation

As we've mentioned in the previous chapters, one of the key functions of the CISO is to create **security policies** in a company, which help safeguard business processes by managing employee behavior, as well as control the production environment from possible security risks. Security policies are essential procedures for safeguarding businesses from cyber threats. However, these procedures affect business operations and could hinder the smooth operations of a business entity. While CISOs may have the best understanding of the security aspects of the company and how a cyber threat could be mitigated, the developed security policies could affect the business negatively by slowing down business operations, making employee working conditions more difficult, and reducing profit margins in the long run.

To avoid these scenarios, it is prudent for the CISO and their team to work with other departmental heads and the supervisors of various sections within the business. The security team will need to brainstorm the security policies with the departmental heads to determine their efficacy and their impact on business functions. The departmental heads and supervisors can suggest changes to the security or even suggest the policies themselves. The aim of including other leaders within an organization in the security discussions has more than one advantage to the business. First, implementing these security policies will require the various departmental heads to implement their departments and sections. These leaders will also be responsible for reviewing the efficiency of these security policies as they will get reviews from the workers.

Second, including other departmental managers in the security discussion encourages them to provide input because of the feeling of inclusivity that such a gesture will have on them. Developing policies on your own and then needing these managers to implement them in their departments will not be the necessary goodwill for better efficiency. The managers, in most cases, have to lead by example. Therefore, a manager who has provided input on a security policy will ensure it is implemented as expected and can show junior workers how to work with the security policies by leading from the front.

Security planning needs resources

Security planning is an expensive process. Buying tools to help with security incidences and safeguarding the business by automating some of the security requirements need capital-intensive budgeting. Due to the ever-increasing threat landscape, the budgeting for security situations in any given company keeps increasing every year. Top management aims to keep expenses low and increase profit margins. These two needs are conflicting. However, both are necessary, so there is a need to compromise. The best way forward for the security team is to create partnerships with the finance departments and the budgeting committee to get the support it needs. Security situations have to be prioritized and without budgeting for these issues, the company may never fully benefit from the required security needs and will operate at higher risks as a result of cyber threats that have not been mitigated properly. A CISO needs to create rapport with the finance and budgeting heads in an organization for this purpose. This will ensure that their security plans are taken care of, which will ultimately improve the security posture of the organization.

Role in recruitment

Internal partnerships between the CISO's security team and the recruitment department are essential to business operations. This is because employees pose a great internal cyber threat to a business that is just as potent as an external threat. In many cases, this internal threat is even greater, owing to the ability to easily get into the system compared to an outsider, who needs specialized skills and equipment to achieve the same thing. Therefore, **recruitment** has proven to be an important role that can directly impact the security aspects in a company, hence the need to have the CISO partner up with the human resources department managers. This partnership aims to ensure that the recruited team does not pose a threat to the company. This can be achieved by carrying out background checks on all the employees joining the company. These background checks will ensure that the company employs people that can help meet the company's visions by maintaining integrity and professionalism while working with the company.

Secondly, partnering with the human resources department heads will help with the training sessions for employees within the organization. This training may be required for security reasons. It will mainly require the top managers, the departmental heads, and other lower-level managers who are subject to higher security clearances and hence may be the targets of attacks by external criminals. This training can even equip the managers with certifications that can be included as part of their resumes. The trainees can then be better equipped to understand the various security implications of their normal business routines and suggest better security policies when the need arises.

Partnering with security tool providers and consultants

As a CISO, you must partner with the **security tool** vendors and security consultants for the benefit of the organization. Partnering with security team providers enables the organization to get customer care support regarding their systems whenever they need to do. It also aids in urgent situations where the organization has issues with the tools and other systems that are used to evaluate the company systems for vulnerabilities. The security posture depends on many security tools, so getting the right vendors to procure these tools from is an important detail in this process. The vendors know how best to use their tools. Partnering with such vendors will enable the security team to get first-hand expertise on how to get the best out of these tools. Understanding the tools at your disposal and how a business can fully benefit from them is a crucial issue that will help in the overall security implementation and help you mitigate cybersecurity risks.

Security consultants are other crucial partners for the security team in an organization. From time to time, a CISO will need to consult on security matters that affect the organization with consultants. Security consultants are expected to have a better understanding of all the security laws affecting the business operations of a company. For instance, when dealing with customers from various regions of the world, some laws, such as data laws, which govern companies globally, may come into play. For instance, the **General Data Protection Regulation** (**GDPR**) statute seeks to protect *European Union* citizens and hence impacts all companies globally that may want to collect EU residents' data. Therefore, when expanding business operations that may potentially lead to dealing with customers outside the location of operation, security consultants may come in handy in advising on what laws may affect such plans, how these laws will affect business operations, and how to work with these laws.

Security consultants and security tools vendors are important information resources that can hugely benefit the CISO and its security team. They specialize in security threats and have a better understanding of the threat landscape compared to a CISO, who focuses on the security situation of their organization. Having such partners will alert the security team of new security threats and possible ways to mitigate such risks. The security systems and tools vendors need to get ahead of trends and get solutions for the evolving threats, hence the need for them to research the market and improve their tools to remain relevant. On the other hand, the security consultants must have up-to-date information to give the best counsel to their clients. Partnering with these two groups of people is poised to give the CISO and their security team huge advantages in their war against potential cyber attackers. The consultants can also inform the CISO of any security conferences, which will allow the CISO to benefit from new information and refresh their knowledge. This also helps them keep themselves abreast of everything that's happening in the cybersecurity industry.

The section has provided insights into the issue of CISO partnerships, both internally and externally, and how they impact security initiatives within an organization. The next section will address the CISO role, which involves evaluating employee behavior and looking at how this is related to cybersecurity.

Evaluating employee behavior

Employees present a huge challenge to the security aspects of a company. They pose potential insider threats to a company. Research has shown that many of the biggest data breaches were instigated by insiders who had access to the system and who could willingly participate in such situations to benefit from it financially, or even as a way to get back at the company. All the aspects of an employee are important in determining their behavior and ultimately deciding on the level of threat they pose to an organization. A scrupulous employee is more likely to help attackers breach an organization's system compared to a professional employee.

The following factors affect employee behavior and could be used as evaluation factors.

Employee motivation

Taking care of your employees is an essential factor in ensuring employees do what is expected of them and directly participate in initiatives that promote business continuity. How you treat an employee determines their likelihood to take care of company assets. Employees with high morale are highly likely to take good care of the firm's informational assets. Therefore, the aim of the company should be to ensure that the employees are properly motivated. To determine whether employees are properly motivated, the security team can conduct anonymous surveys on workers within an organization, where they seek to get the level of satisfaction among employees and where they can also raise issues they have with the company. Employees who feel they are overworked and are not paid enough are dangerous to a company. If a survey reveals that the consensus among employees is that they are bitter about the company, then the level of insider threat potential will be high.

The remuneration and rewarding systems

How a company rewards its employees has a direct impact on employee behavior. Remuneration and other rewarding schemes are important issues that help improve employee morale and motivation. As stated in the previous section, employees with high morale will take better care of the company's informational assets compared to underpaid employees. A bonus system for employees who work hard and other systems that tend to properly appreciate workers goes a long way toward improving employee loyalty and hence better protectors of company assets. As a security leader, determining the various aspects of employees, including their remuneration, will help evaluate their potential to pose cyber threats toward the company.

Employee skill level

Employee skill level is another important metric when evaluating employee behavior. If a firm has highly qualified workers working in an environment that does not utilize their skills effectively, then they are likely to be frustrated with the company. Ideally, a company should recruit employees to work in departments that can effectively utilize their qualifications. In this regard, employees with technical skills are the most dangerous and should be limited in terms of what they can access within a company.

User and entity behavior analytics (UEBA)

User and entity behavior analytics (**UEBA**) is a concept that helps improve the security posture of a company. It helps with detecting users and entities that are compromising the entire system. The process of UEBA works by learning user behavior to determine what and what should not be considered normal human behavior within the system. After learning the behavior of users, a pattern is developed, which is then used to evaluate normal behavior. Any deviations from this pattern are a cause for concern and alert the system of possible fraudulent behavior. For instance, if a user who normally accesses accounting files tries to access data from the information department, the system will be alerted of this anomalous behavior. Similarly, a user who usually downloads small amounts of data suddenly downloading huge amounts of data is a cause for concern.

The UEBA system uses advanced processes aided by machine learning, statistical analysis, and computing algorithms. The system analyzes all the data that goes through the system, all the packets that are received and sent through a network, and helps determine deviations from normal patterns. As opposed to normal systems, where monitoring is done on devices or particular systems, this concept tracks all users of the system and their daily interactions within it. The UEBA system is efficient in terms of insider threat management as it focuses on employee behavior to determine employees who have gone rogue or whose accounts have been compromised.

UEBA is a very effective system in improving IT security in a system as it enhances protection against insider threats. In the current environment, it is almost impossible to keep hackers out of the system. They are used to find weaknesses in the system that they can exploit. UEBA is effective as a last line of defense because it detects malicious users or anomalies within the system, even after hackers have bypassed the normal defenses. Hackers can't mimic normal user behavior while within the system because they will be targeting files they are not supposed to be targeting or will attempt huge downloads from the servers. Such a system should be able to identify such rogue behavior and alert the security team for them to take the necessary action against such attackers.

Advantages of using UEBA

UEBA has several advantages that can benefit an organization and improve the security posture. These benefits include the following:

- **Improves the ability to detect insider threats**: Insider threats are a big security risk to a company and more often than not, it is difficult to accurately control this risk. However, with UEBA, the security team can analyze user behavior and determine when an attack is in progress and stop it before it worsens. It helps protect a company from issues such as sabotage, data breaches, privilege abuse, and policy violations.

- **Pinpointing compromised accounts**: One of the main ways that attackers breach a system is to use an account within the system to conduct their malicious actions. They will target and crack some passwords and then use those compromised accounts to access the systems. The more privileged the account is to the system, the more damage they are likely to do within the system. UEBA helps detect compromised accounts that can then be investigated and suspended to disallow further damage to the system.

- **Detecting brute-force attacks**: Brute-force attacks are common attack vectors used by hackers. The system enables you to detect brute-force attack attempts and then block access.

- **Detecting changes in user accounts and privilege assignment**: Some attacks will require the use of super-users within the system to cause the intended damage. Using an ordinary account cannot benefit the hacker. In this case, they will need to create super-users who have more access to the system and can do more within the system as well. UEBA detects changes to user accounts, as well as accounts that have been granted unnecessary privileges, and flags them.

- **UEBA helps detect breaches in protected data**: It does this by monitoring access to protected and sensitive data. Therefore, whenever a user accesses this kind of data, the system determines whether they have legitimate reasons for accessing the data. If there are no legitimate reasons, then the user is blocked from accessing the data.

The section has addressed the concept of evaluating user behavior and why CISOs need to do that to help enhance their organization's security posture. The next section will provide insights into the financial aspects of cybersecurity and the role the CISO has in reporting any financial implications.

Financial reporting

Cybersecurity has a direct impact on the financial situation of a company and hence the **financial reporting** role of the CISO. Every security initiative from the CISO has to be evaluated for the financial impact it has on the company's business operations. Both the direct and indirect consequences should be evaluated and quantified in terms of the impact they have on the business. The direct impact initiatives include purchasing security tools and systems, as well as paying for security consultancy. These initiatives are easy to quantify and easy to control. The budgeting process for these initiatives can be done alongside the other budgets for other departments in the company. With proper planning, the security team can make plans for gradually improving the security situation based on a prioritized set of security risks and possible business impacts.

The indirect financial costs are much more difficult to determine and control. These result from initiatives such as security policies that impact business operations, making them either smoother or more difficult. Some initiatives make employees' working conditions more difficult, which is likely to reduce employee morale within the company. This will ultimately translate into losses for the company in terms of reduced profits. Such indirect costs on the company are difficult to quantify. However, partnering with various departmental managers and getting their inputs about effective security policies will help in developing initiatives that do not necessarily make life more difficult for the employees. Therefore, internal partnering, as discussed earlier in this chapter, is essential in ensuring prudent financial decisions are made regarding security initiatives.

With that, we have addressed the issue of financial reporting, looked at the financial implications of various security initiatives, and looked at the role that CISOs have in terms of reporting these implications. Next, we will provide information on how CISOs perceive *cybersecurity as a business problem* as opposed to an isolated issue.

Addressing cybersecurity as a business problem

Cybersecurity is a *business problem* and should be addressed as such. Looking at cybersecurity as an isolated problem and tackling the issue in isolation from other business operations will prove ineffective to organizations and lead to resource waste. Cybersecurity is concerned with keeping a company safe from cyber threats. Cyber threats, in the modern landscape, originate from all kinds of sectors. Both insiders, in form of employees, and outsiders, in the form of hackers, are potential threats to an organization. Both these threats aim to access the system and sabotage it or steal customer data for ransom or to be sold on the black market. It may also be a result of the vengeful actions of a disgruntled employee. Whatever the reasons for the attacks, cybersecurity affects the entire business and has a direct impact on business continuity.

Looking at cybersecurity as a business problem is an effective way of handling the issue, given the potential impact cybersecurity incidents have on a company. The security initiatives will require the cooperation of other departmental heads and their input, as well as ensuring they are effective. The main issue lies in the business impact of security incidents. For each security threat, the CISO needs to evaluate the potential business impact on the business, and then use these evaluations to prioritize the implementations of these issues. Looking at cybersecurity as a business problem helps CISOs and their security teams create initiatives that address all the different aspects of the company. It also allows CISOs to play bigger roles in the strategic and financial planning of a business, including playing a critical role in making investment decisions.

Summary

The chapter has addressed various additional roles that CISOs play in organizations that help enhance the security posture of an organization. These additional CISO tasks include contributing to technical projects; partnering with internal and external providers; evaluating employee behavior; financial reporting; and addressing cybersecurity as a business problem.

In their role of contributing toward technical projects, CISOs are involved in designing technical projects and architecting the various security layers to ensure that the final product is secure, with minimal vulnerabilities that can be exploited by attackers.

These CISOs partner with various departments to ensure effective policymaking and the smooth implementation of security procedures. External partners help the CISOs improve their cyber knowledge, which they can then apply to their organization. Evaluating employee behavior helps identify their potential threat to the organization and take measures to mitigate these risks.

CISOs are instrumental in helping report the financial impact of various security initiatives and ensuring that the financial impact of the risks and the initiatives conform with business goals.

Lastly, CISOs address all the aspects of cybersecurity as a business problem, which ensures effective initiatives and planning are done.

The next chapter will address how to get hired as a CISO and what is expected of you, as a CISO, within the first 90 days.

Further reading

The following are resources that you can use to gain more knowledge about this chapter:

- *Understanding CISO roles*: https://www.bmc.com/blogs/ciso-chief-information-security-officer/

- *Cybersecurity for Small Businesses*: https://www.fcc.gov/general/cybersecurity-small-business

- *Information security behaviors*: https://hrmars.com/papers_submitted/5972/Information_Security_Behaviors_among_Employees.pdf

- *User and entity behavior analytics*: https://digitalguardian.com/blog/what-user-and-entity-behavior-analytics-definition-ueba-benefits-how-it-works-and-more

- *Behavioral aspects of cybersecurity*: https://cybersecurity.springeropen.com/articles/10.1186/s42400-020-00050-w

9
Congratulations! You Are Hired

In the previous chapters, we discussed the various roles that the **Chief Information Security Officer (CISO)** plays in an organization. Some of these roles are traditional information security roles – roles that have been evolving over time. While in the past, the security team was largely considered just part of the information technology team, the CISO and their team have increasingly gained influence regarding the management aspects of their respective organizations. They now have a bigger role to play in the company and are involved in both short-term and long-term strategic decision-making processes.

In this chapter, we will discuss the practical aspects of the duties of the CISO, assuming that you have now been hired as a CISO in a medium-sized institution to take charge of security matters. This chapter will show the practical application of what we have learned regarding the duties of the CISO in an organization. We will cover the following main topics:

- How to get hired as a CISO
- Your first 90 days as a CISO

We will begin by looking at the hiring process and what you need to get hired.

How to get hired as a CISO

Cyber security is among the most important concerns in any organization. The ability to secure digital assets in an organization determines the success of a business, with more cases of data breaches being reported every other day. This increase in the prevalence of security incidents has led to CISO professionals being among the most sought-after experts globally. This career is among the best paying careers in the *information technology* sector and being a CISO is considered the pinnacle of an IT career. Therefore, for any aspiring cyber security professional eying a CISO career, there are several issues they need to address before they can be hired. These factors include the following:

- Qualifications
- Experience
- Communication ability
- Leadership skills

This section has provided insights into how to get hired as a CISO executive and listed the various requirements you need to get the job. This list is described in detail in the following sections.

Qualifications for a CISO job

A CISO role involves leading a security team in an organization. Their primary responsibility is safeguarding the digital assets of an organization, which includes both digital infrastructure and the data that's used in an organization. Leading a team of information technology experts will need a CISO to have the qualifications to lead the team. A master's or PhD degree in computer science, computer engineering, or related fields is a basic requirement for such a professional. So, if you are after that CISO job and do not have a master's degree yet in a cyber-security-related course, then you better get those qualifications. However, this is one of several factors that are needed to get you a job as a CISO. For small and medium-sized organizations, lower qualifications, such as a degree, may get you the job with certifications in cyber security, which helps with this process.

Job experience

On average, globally, CISO professionals in top organizations have more than 10 years of experience in the cyber security sector. CISOs require both hard and soft skills and these skills require experience to perfect them. CISOs are leaders in an organization and will often need senior members of the security team to take the leadership positions to lead younger, less experienced members of the security team. Additionally, during security incidents, experience comes in handy in managing several aspects of the company's processes. Stressful circumstances and the ability to rely on previous experience will help you in those scenarios. Therefore, experience plays a major role in the CISO hiring processes in any organization.

Communication ability

Communication is a critical skill for a security leader, just like any other leader in an organization. To effectively lead a team, the CISO needs to be able to communicate their ideas to all team members. In addition, they need to create a good rapport with other managers because the CISO needs to create both internal and external partnerships to aid them in performing well in their duties. A CISO also needs to communicate with the top management regarding various aspects, such as explaining the cyber security risks associated with strategic business acquisitions to enable them to make informed decisions about such issues. The CISO also needs to communicate issues such as resource requests to the top management and get them on board with many security initiatives that need massive resource inputs from top management. Speaking the same language or speaking a common language can help in this case. The world is increasingly embracing diversity and the CISO can lead a team of diverse individuals who speak different languages as their first languages. Being multilingual is an added advantage as far as communication is concerned.

Leadership skills

Leadership skills are an essential requirement for a CISO candidate. Essentially, the CISO role involves leading the security team, which requires a good leader to get the team functioning as required. A security team may have all the technical abilities, but without proper motivation and guidance, they may not perform optimally in an organization. Therefore, leadership and managerial skills are basic requirements for a CISO candidate. So, before being hired as a CISO, ensure that you develop your leadership skills.

The previous four sections have looked at the various requirements you need to get the CISO role. You will need both soft and hard skills as the CISO role encompasses both the technical aspects as well as managerial roles. The next section outlines the steps to follow to become a CISO.

Steps to follow to become a CISO

A CISO role is at the pinnacle of *cyber security* and *information security* careers. Therefore, to get to this pinnacle, you will need to spend several years rising through the ranks in terms of getting an education and gaining the necessary skills. The process of becoming a CISO will typically require passing through the following steps:

- Typically, the process of becoming a CISO will begin with an undergraduate degree in computer science, information technology, or related courses. The process can also begin by getting an associate degree in computer science or information technology. This education will help you obtain both the soft and hard skills required for the CISO career.

- After gaining an undergraduate degree, typically, an individual will begin working in the information technology sector as an entry-level computer person, in networking, or as a system specialist, among other possible careers. At this point, you may work as an analyst as part of the security team, where you will be required to detect, prevent, and investigate cyber threats for an organization.

- At this point in the learning curve, you may also gain experience by researching security systems and measures – especially new security measures – which can be used to address infrastructural weaknesses in the system.

- After gaining experience at this level, you can then move on to the mid-level, where you can take on more responsibilities and more challenging assignments. At this level, you may work as a security engineer, a security consultant, or a security auditor, among other roles. At this level, you are expected to develop both technical skills and interpersonal skills. You may be required to head sub-sections or small projects at this point, hence the need to develop interpersonal skills.

- The next step is to move to the senior level of the cyber security hierarchy. At the top, possible jobs include working as a security architect, an information technology project manager, or as a security director in an organization. These jobs are senior positions in an organization and require you to have organizational, technical, and leadership skills to navigate them. In most cases, you will need to be involved in decision-making, hence the need to have the managerial skills for that.

- A masters' degree comes in handy and plays a critical role at this senior level of management. While it is possible to have a masters-level individual in the lower ranks, to move up the ranks in an organization, a master's degree plays a critical role from moving from the mid-level position to the senior position. A business degree in an associate business course will also help at this point due to the managerial and organizational skills that business-oriented individuals need to handle. However, without a business degree, you can still get senior positions based on years of experience working up the hierarchy and racking up years of managerial experience along the way.

With that, we have outlined the various steps you need to follow to rise through the ranks and ultimately secure a position as a CISO, which is considered the pinnacle of all information technology careers. In the next section, we will look at the top skills you will require to make it as a CISO executive.

The top skills required to succeed as a CISO

The CISO role, as we mentioned previously, requires years of experience as you need to be in a position to handle the responsibilities of the security leader. While going through the ranks, you will need to acquire and polish the following skills before getting the CISO role:

- Knowledge of programming languages. The technical aspects of the CISO role will mostly require you to have an education in programming languages, software systems, computer networks, and cyber security. The study and use of computer software will enable you to understand applications and their limitations, hence giving you the ability to conduct thorough vulnerability testing. This education also enables you to innovate and allows you to grow within cyber security roles.

- Soft skills such as analytical thinking will give you research competency, which can enable you to construct efficient security processes, procedures, and policies. Some other soft skills that are required include effective communication abilities. This is because CISOs are often required to communicate the technical details of their work to colleagues and other individuals, such as shareholders, who may have little or no technical knowledge.

- Great interpersonal skills. These skills are critical to enabling you to work with colleagues and the security team. Communication is helpful in this regard as it smoothens communication with entry- and mid-level employees. In some instances, the CISO has to conduct employee training regarding security aspects, policies, and procedures and need to have great interpersonal skills to relay this information.

- Constructing and implementing incident response plans and procedures. The CISO is required to plan for security incidents and come up with procedures that will be followed to effectively handle a security incident if – and when – it occurs.

- Report writing and security auditing are other important skills that a CISO needs to carry out his/her responsibilities effectively. All security processes need to be documented both for other people who will implement or review the processes and for other employees to follow in case of issues such as security incidents. Report writing and documentation are, therefore, essential skills that CISOs need in their work.

- Familiarity with compliance standards and regulations. A CISO must be familiar with all the industry standards that govern the business operation of their organization. Failure to understand the various industry standards and regulations can lead to major losses and costs. These costs may be in the form of penalties by the government and the regulatory bodies that implement these regulations. Other costs may be incurred as a result of diminished security since these standards are meant to improve the security posture, in addition to safeguarding the interests of users.

- A CISO must be able to understand and then subsequently communicate the business and profit impacts of the various information security operations before implementing them for their organization. This enables the CISO to effectively advise the top management on their investment ventures, as well as on the necessary information security changes in the organization.

Next, we will look at a sample job description, where we will look at many of the job responsibilities of CISO executives in a modern organization.

A CISO job description sample

A sample job description for a CISO will list the following responsibilities:

- Designing and developing an information security system blueprint that aligns and scales with company objectives and enables company growth.

- Leading security testing and assessment processes. These processes include, but are not limited to, penetration testing, secure software development, and vulnerability management.

- Developing and extending security tooling, as well as automation efforts, across an organization.

- Identifying security issues proactively, along with potential threats to an organization, and continually building systems that monitor them and protect an organization from these issues and threats.

- Leading all data and information technology compliance initiatives, including regulatory compliance projects, external audits, and conducting overall security reviews of the systems.

- Communicating all information security plans, goals, and efforts, as well as their impact on the business, to the top management and the board of directors.

- Interfacing with external partners such as consultants, security tool vendors, compliance, and regulatory bodies, as well as legal authorities, during security incidents.

- Provide risk assessment and risk guidance to C-suite officers, as well as the board of directors, on issues such as corporate IT projects or major business acquisitions. Also, evaluate and recommend technical controls and standards.

- Establishing and implementing processes for incident management that effectively monitor, identify, respond, contain any incident, and communicate any suspected or confirmed security incidents.

Now that we've looked at a sample job description for the job of a CISO to understand the job responsibilities for a CISO, you should have a clear understanding of the skills you need to polish before getting hired as a CISO. In the next section, we will look at your first 90 days as a CISO and what you will be expected to do to fulfill this role.

Your first 90 days as a CISO

In this section, we will discuss the practical aspects of the **CISO executive** role. You have spent years gaining experience as a cyber security guru and you have worked your way to the top – rising from being an entry-level computer graduate to the head of security operations in your organization. The first 90 days as a CISO will prove important and may point to the success you will have in the organization.

To get a rough idea of your success within the 90 days as a CISO executive, you need to have conclusive answers to the following questions:

- *Who is my boss and how much influence does my boss have over security initiatives?* The CISO executive role will require you to determine who in the company will be supervising your plans and who will have the final say on the many security plans you will be developing. At some points, you will discuss issues with the C-suite officers, such as the CEO, while at others, you will explain your plans to the board for consideration. However, there are some high-level discussions that you will miss out on as a CISO that will ultimately impact your work. Therefore, it is important to know if the C-suite officer who will be your supervisor and attending these high-level meetings is completely on board with your appointment and will advocate your cause, especially regarding securing resources for your security initiatives.

- *How committed is the organization to information security?* This is another important question that you will have to determine during the first 90 days as a CISO. One way of answering this is by looking at the staff recruitment for the security and information technology functions in the organization. Secondly, you will have to look at the resources being allocated to the security functions before getting the job. This is easier if you are already working in the company and have first-hand information on the security situation. The most important way to determine the commitment level is to determine the kind of empowerment you will have as a CISO, as well as your inclusion in strategic decision-making. This is because a CISO must be empowered enough to influence the organization, especially on matters that directly impact security aspects.

- *What key performance indicators will measure you?* The benchmark that the company will use to determine whether you are succeeding in your role is another important determination you need to make within the first 90 days. The reason for this is the prevalence of attacks. In this day and age, being attacked is a certainty. Therefore, your work as a CISO and your success in your duties is always on the line, and you will be judged on your success during these security incidents. However, you will need to know whether failure in one security incident will mean you are out of a job or not or whether other considerations will be taken to keep you in the job.

- *Where will you be in the next 5 or 10 years*? Your career ambition will help determine the answer to this question. However, the organization's commitment and the kind of empowerment the CISO role will have will help determine some of these decisions. If you have the ambition to move on quickly to a bigger position within the same company or in another, then you need to get ideas implemented quickly after determining the kind of support you will get from management. If you plan to stay in the company for a long time, since you have reached the pinnacle of your career ambitions or feel the company will grow to accommodate your ambitions, then long-term and strategic planning will be necessary from the beginning of your contract at the company.

These questions will adequately prepare you for your responsibilities. Now, let's explore the things you should do within the first 90 days as the CISO in your organization.

List of dos in the first 90 days

The first 90 days in your role as a CISO will act as your honeymoon period at the organization. However, you need to establish the basics as these will determine your legacy in the CISO role. At the end of the day, the CISO role is a security leadership role with a team looking up to you. Within the first 90 days, you need to be able to do the following:

- Define your role in the organization.

- Develop a security strategy for your organization.

- Build professional relationships.

- Secure leadership support.

- Establish trust with the security team.

- Signal your leadership style.

We'll break each to-do down in the following sections.

Define your role in the organization

You will define your role in the organization by meeting with the top management of the company, who will outline the magnitude of the issues you will be facing. However, the job description will guide you as your roles will be documented in your work contract as well. Before meeting the top management officials and the security team that you will be leading, you need to adequately prepare with questions and gather background information about the company from any online sources you can find. Preparing beforehand will help you get the most out of the meetings with the top management, supervisors, and other colleagues you will be working with.

Develop a security strategy for your organization

Before coming up with the security strategy for your organization, you will need to fully understand the functionality of the current system. Determine its advantages and its disadvantages to keep the good aspects and address the weaknesses. Any security strategy will have to capture the organization's culture. Therefore, seek out an executive mentor in the organization that will mentor you on the culture in the organization. This will help you develop a strategy that matches the organization's ideals and principles.

Build professional relationships

You will need to build professional relationships both *internally* and *externally* to be able to execute your functions properly. Within the organization, you will have to build a good rapport with top management, as well as cultivate a good relationship with other managers and supervisors, as you will need to institute policies that will affect their operations. You will also need information and ideas from them in return. Therefore, developing a conducive working relationship will benefit you immensely. With outsiders, you will create partnerships with security consultants, security system tools vendors, and information system vendors, who may have developed the system in use if it was not developed internally.

Secure leadership support

You need the support of the C-suite officers and the board to fully implement some of the security initiatives that you will develop as a CISO. The leadership is in charge of approving resource use in an organization and will need to be convinced of your plans before they can get on board. Therefore, you will need to create a rapport with the leadership to gain their support with the many security initiatives and finance some changes you will need to make in the organization. Since you will need input in some initiatives in an organization, such as recruitment, the leadership will be responsible for empowering you within the organization to execute some of these roles.

Establish trust with the security team

You need to establish trust with the security team that you will be leading. As a security leader, most of the functions, especially the technical functions, will have to be delegated to the security team members. Their proficiency in their work will have a direct impact on your success as a CISO. Therefore, trusting these security team members will be essential to your role as their leader. One way of establishing trust would be to come up with effective strategies that they can believe. The other way would be to talk to them individually and establish a personal relationship with all the team members. Also, let them know that their efforts will be appreciated and that their opinions are welcome and be considered. These strategies will help you establish and promote trust with the security team members.

Signal your leadership style

Signaling your leadership style early on will help you as a CISO within the first 90 days. The security team will be looking up to you for guidance and direction. In addition, they will try to understand how to work with you because people like to work with minimal friction with their colleagues and their bosses. Therefore, it is important to communicate to your security team the kind of CISO they will get and hence the kind of leadership they will experience. If you lead by example, you will direct everything that needs to be done, you will encourage teamwork, and your team's opinions will be stimulated. These are all aspects that help signal your leadership style to the team. The team will know how to relate to you and what to expect whenever they are allocated an assignment.

The first 90 days of getting hired are crucial to establishing the pillars you need to succeed in the role. Establishing these pillars depends on all the factors that are crucial to developing and executing security initiatives. Creating a rapport with people and having a communicated plan is critical to the success of a CISO within the early days of their appointment.

Summary

This chapter focused on the latter stages of the journey of becoming a CISO executive – that is, the part where you get hired as a CISO and the first 90 days as a CISO executive. To get hired as a CISO, we have determined that you will need several things, such as qualifications, communication abilities, experience, and leadership abilities. Qualifications are usually based on a degree in computer science or related fields and several years of experience. Since the CISO position is a senior position in the cyber security ladder, you will often need a master's degree in cyber security issues to get the job. Knowledge of computer systems, security systems, computer networks, and interpersonal skills are some of the key requirements for someone to get the CISO job and to succeed in the CISO role. During the first 90 days, you will need to define your role in the organization, establish trust with your security team, signal your leadership style, build professional relationships, and develop a security strategy for the organization.

The next chapter will look at security leadership and address such issues as building cybersecurity awareness in the organization, building a strategy, telling your story, and presenting your findings to the board and the security team.

Further reading

The following are resources that you can use to gain more knowledge about this chapter:

- *Becoming a CISO*: https://remeshr.medium.com/how-to-become-a-chief-information-security-officer-ciso-f6a4eeb718ff

- *Tips before becoming a CISO*: https://www.linkedin.com/pulse/10-things-think-before-accepting-ciso-job-gary-hayslip-cissp-

- *Hiring a CISO*: https://www.securityroundtable.org/what-to-expect-and-consider-when-hiring-a-ciso/

- *The CISO career*: https://cybersecurityguide.org/careers/chief-information-security-officer/

- *How to become a CISO*: https://www.cyberdegrees.org/jobs/chief-information-security-officer-ciso/

- *First 90 days as a CISO:* https://go.sentinelone.com/rs/327-MNM-087/images/SentinelOne_CISO_eBook_Vol2_How_to_Drive_Success_03.pdf

- *First 100 days as a CISO:* https://www.gartner.com/smarterwithgartner/your-first-100-days-as-a-new-chief-information-security-officer-2/

- *Everything you need to know about CISOs:* https://www.erdalozkaya.com/?s=CISO

10
Security Leadership

In the previous chapter, we had a look at the hiring process of a **chief information security officer** (**CISO**) and the kind of approach you need to take during the first 90 days of working as a CISO executive. In this chapter, we will provide insights into your role as a security leader in an organization and how to lead in the most effective manner. We will achieve this by addressing some of the key roles of a CISO and how to best carry out these roles. While looking at the key security roles and how to execute these, we will address your interactions with various stakeholders, such as the board of directors, as well as other employees in the organization who are not part of the security team.

In this chapter, we will cover the following topics:

- Building cybersecurity awareness
- Building a cybersecurity strategy
- Telling your story
- Presenting to the board
- Leadership and team

Let's dive right in and find out more.

Building cybersecurity awareness

The adoption of the **Internet of Things** (**IoT**) and the increasing use of technology across all facets of life means that more people are now connected through digital infrastructure, and the internet is now playing a bigger role in modern societies than it ever has before. The age of social media is also here. More people and businesses have migrated online and are using the vast potential of the internet to leverage and expand their businesses. For the most part, things are positive. However, cyber attacks have become increasingly rampant and are creating havoc all across the world. The impact of these cyber attacks ranges from no business impact to the total destruction of business operations, so the potential for damage is huge and undeniable. This has led to a need to build cybersecurity awareness in organizations to help increase the security posture of an organization and keep attackers away. Also, increasing cybersecurity awareness leads to more integration of business processes with cybersecurity plans to ensure that they benefit from each other and that neither stands in the way of the other. Cybersecurity is supposed to facilitate business processes, not to hinder them. Building cybersecurity awareness in an organization essentially means getting a non-security team fully on board with various security initiatives and getting them to play a role as required toward enhancing the security situation. The end result is a **human resources** (**HR**) team that aids the cybersecurity cause and not one that presents additional security challenges to an organization.

Some of the actions that help in building and creating security awareness in an organization include the following:

- Developing suitable security policies
- Communicating cybersecurity issues clearly
- Getting a bigger budget for the security team to ensure their security initiatives are fully implemented
- Leading by example
- Having training conferences and seminars for employees

We are going to explore each of these in the next sections.

Developing suitable security policies

Security policies are the basis for implementing security initiatives in an organization. The CISO and the security team offer security leadership by developing security policies that are business-oriented and match the business goals. In addition, the developed security policies should not make the working environment more tedious for employees, as this could then contribute to making them resentful toward these policies and hence reduce the efficiency of the security policies in the long run. As a newly hired CISO executive in the first days of your role, you will need to evaluate the existing security policies to determine their efficiency and areas that may need improvement. After a thorough review, the results may show that the existing system needs a complete overhaul or just an upgrade. A complete overhaul will require drastic changes to the business and working environments. An upgrade will only need additional security initiatives while retaining many of the existing policies.

The ideal case for most employees is to retain the status quo. However, if the security environment is vulnerable and calls for a complete overhaul, the process of developing these new policies will be challenging and will need all the wisdom available to get employees on board and not make working unnecessarily difficult henceforth. The security team will need to get as many employees as possible on board during the development of these policies so that they can get the support they require during policy execution. Therefore, meeting regularly with the various supervisors and lower-level managers that interact with the employees is a prudent idea that will get their input as well as their support during the execution phase.

Communicating cybersecurity issues clearly

Security matters have to be communicated clearly throughout organizations for security initiatives to have the support they need to be effective. Without proper communication, security initiatives may not be implemented as required, and identified vulnerabilities in the system will remain subject to exploitation by potential attackers. Communication ensures that everyone who will be affected by the security initiatives is aware of these initiatives or any changes to them. In some cases where employees may face resistance to some of the security policies, the security team may need to meet with the employees to explain the reasons for the security initiatives and why they are necessary. Getting the opinion of the employees in this phase will help the security team to obtain important feedback that they may use in improving security policies or making any future changes to security initiatives.

Apart from the employees, communication needs to be extended to other stakeholders as well. Some of these stakeholders include top management, the board, and external partners such as security consultants. Any changes to security initiatives and policies should be communicated immediately to any stakeholder who has an interest in the policies or who may be affected by the initiatives. Some of the stakeholders, such as the board of directors, may be responsible for approving some of the security initiatives and will need to be convinced as to their effectiveness before they can get on board in approving resources needed by the security team to implement these initiatives. Security consultants will need to be aware of changes as well, as this may impact how they relate to the business going forward. Since creating positive partnerships is one of the key roles of a security team and helps them execute their roles effectively, communicating with these stakeholders is critical.

Getting a bigger budget

Security initiatives need resources for implementation. After developing security policies that include suggested upgrades to the current system and infrastructure, the security team will need to get approval from top management and the board of directors on some of the expenses. With the ever-increasing budgeting needs for cybersecurity, getting additional funding may prove to be a really difficult assignment. However, it is essential to get the resources needed for the implementation of cybersecurity initiatives and security plans to perform effectively as a CISO. Getting additional funds for the security team is a need that conflicts with the basic goal of many businesses: *to make profits*. Increasing expenses means a reduction in profits. Businesses are always trying to find ways to reduce their expenses, making their business operations more efficient, and this then reduces their expenses and ultimately increases their profit margins. The bigger budgets for security teams go against this basic principle.

One way of addressing this problem is by prioritization of security challenges. The security team will determine all the vulnerabilities that affect the business and then use the possible business impact of these vulnerabilities to prioritize the security risks. The most impactful risk to the business comes first and will get the most funding. The least impactful business risk gets the lowest funding or gets scheduled for another financial period. In the current cybersecurity situation, getting bigger budgets is a necessity that many businesses will need to address as data breaches become more common by the day and the consequences of attacks on businesses become worse by the day.

Leading by example

The best approach by a security team to help increase cybersecurity awareness is to lead the organization in executing developed security initiatives and policies. The security team members need to show other employees the importance of security initiatives by adhering to all of these. For instance, one of the main security initiatives implemented by many businesses globally is the use of security cards to access various parts of the business environment. These security cards ensure that only a person who has a security card can access some sections of the business, with security cards being accorded different privileges based on the business department and level of seniority in the business. However, one common security problem is colleagues sharing cards because one of them has misplaced or lost their security card. While this is expected to happen, it should not be encouraged as it presents a weakness in the system that can be exploited by potential attackers.

In this case, if security team members are also seen to be sharing cards or misplacing these, often flouting organizational policies to access some sections of the business, then the rest of the employees will likely follow their example and flout the rules without understanding the possible consequences of such actions. The CISO is the leader of the security team. While the security team members have a responsibility to show the rest of the employees by way of example, the CISO executive has to show leadership to both the security team and the rest of the organization, especially among managerial staff with whom they interact often.

Having training conferences and seminars for employees

Training employees on security initiatives helps improve security awareness among all employees in an organization. We have seen from previous chapters how the employees in an organization present a challenge to the organization's security as they pose a great security threat to the organization just as much as an *external threat*. In some cases, the *internal threat* could be even more dangerous to an entity given their access to the system and less surveillance compared to the aggressive strategies put out to keep external threats out of the system. Training employees about the security initiatives in place and a need to adhere to all security policies is important in increasing cybersecurity awareness and ultimately leading to a good security posture for the organization.

The security team should organize training sessions and seminars for employees to help educate them on cybersecurity initiatives and any changes the security team implements on the system. For new employees, it is important to have a short security training session before they can get to work using the system so that when they eventually get full access to the system, they should be able to safeguard assets by engaging in safe procedures that adhere to security initiatives and policies from the security team. Some of the training should involve the use of passwords and a need to keep strong and unique passwords, and not to deploy passwords used for social media and other online accounts. The training should also help increase their awareness of various attack strategies and how to be alert in the face of mysterious zero-day attack strategies.

We have now received a detailed explanation of the importance of a CISO's role in building cybersecurity awareness in an organization, showing the impact they have in neutralizing internal threats to an organization from employees. The next section will look at another important CISO role, which is about building a **cybersecurity strategy**.

Building a cybersecurity strategy

Building a cybersecurity strategy is a CISO role that is central to all their security functions. All security initiatives and policies are based on a core cybersecurity strategy that is developed by a CISO and their security team. This cybersecurity strategy acts as a blueprint on which all security actions and efforts are developed and measured and offers direction to the security team in the development of various security policies and initiatives across the organization. All cybersecurity engagements within the organization should align with the cybersecurity strategy in place. The CISO is tasked with coming up with a strategy that will define their work as a CISO in the organization. The strategy has to match the business needs and operations to ensure that it facilitates business operations and does not hinder the progress of the organization. Therefore, a cybersecurity strategy can only be developed after the CISO and their team have developed a thorough understanding of the business and have evaluated all its threats. The threat risk potential will determine the kind of strategy the CISO will use to protect the organization.

Building a cybersecurity strategy is influenced by several factors, one being the resources available to implement the strategy. If an organization has the funds to support huge cybersecurity programs, then the security team will be encouraged to come up with up-to-date strategies that will include the installation of new infrastructure and making major changes to business operations. Other factors that affect the strategy include the kind of business environment involved, the security threat landscape, and the current cybersecurity strategy in place. If the current system is already a modern one, major changes will not be necessary, and the new strategy will be heavily based on the current systems. If there is a need for a change of infrastructure, then the strategy will need to be long-term and incorporate gradual security initiative changes.

You now have an understanding of the importance of a CISO's role in building a cybersecurity strategy in an organization and how this offers a blueprint in developing security initiatives for an organization. In the next section, we will look at how you should handle the role of CISO and the need to take charge of this security role.

Telling your story

As a CISO, you need to be able to *tell your story* and relate the challenges that being a CISO entails. While the challenges of being a CISO may be common across various organizations owing to similarities in the threat landscape for most organizations, there are nevertheless unique challenges that you may face that may not be common among all CISO executives in various organizations globally. Some of these unique challenges may be caused by factors such as the following:

- **First time working as a CISO or leading a security team**. The challenge of doing a particular job for the first time can be onerous for any individual. Therefore, a CISO in such a situation needs to adapt fast and be open to new ideas to enable them to stabilize as soon as possible in their new environment.

- **Need for a complete overhaul of the current system**. If an organization faces serious cybersecurity issues, it needs an overhaul of the current system. This could prove to be a hugely tasking challenge given the need to convince top management about the resources required, the changes to be made, and the impact these will have on other business operations.

- **You need to have total control of the security operations of an organization as a CISO executive**. Your effectiveness in your job will be measured on how secure the organization is, how effective the measures are against possible threats, and how quickly the organization recovers from security incidents. Therefore, a CISO needs to have power and support from top management and the board to carry out all the duties they need to perform well in the organization.

Now that you have an understanding of why you need to take charge of security responsibilities as a CISO executive to ensure effective dissemination of your duties, we will next look at a CISO's role in presenting information to the board of directors.

Presenting to the board

Presenting to the board is one of the core functions of a CISO executive in an organization. A CISO in this day and age is a top management official who needs to interact with top management and be included in the long-term and strategic planning of a business. The reason for this inclusion in planning strategies is that cybersecurity has become a huge determinant in investment decisions and a business investment can be rejected based on the cybersecurity risk it will present to an organization. The threat landscape also keeps evolving, requiring cybersecurity teams to be alert to changes and initiatives that counteract the changing threat landscape and risks to organizations.

The board of directors has the final say on huge capital investments and outlays in an organization. The CISO and the security team need resources to implement their security initiatives, so the CISO will need to convince the board to support these initiatives. In cases where changes are huge, the board may be reluctant to make such approvals. In such cases, the CISO will need to present a convincing case before the board to get the resources they need, not only having to show the board that the initiatives protect the business from potential danger, but also being able to quantify the kind of business impact the security initiatives will have, and the board needs to support them. Any presentation that goes before the board of directors needs to be well researched and thought out, with an actionable plan of possible options.

We have looked at why and how presenting information to the board of directors is critical to the execution of your role as a CISO and getting the required resources. Let's look at the issue of **leadership** and the security team next.

Leadership and team

A CISO leads the security team in an organization. The security team is important, given that a CISO cannot perform all the technical as well as the managerial functions required of them. The main role of a CISO is to come up with a strategy and policies to implement the strategy. After coming up with a plan, the security team comes in handy in implementing the plan. The CISO may lack some technical expertise but provides a managerial function. In the current environment, a CISO plays more of a managerial role than a technical role, thus any technical actions will be delegated to the junior members of their security team. CISOs are then able to concentrate on managerial duties, creating partnerships internally and externally, as well as aiding in the long-term strategic planning and decision making of an organization.

A CISO needs a capable team to execute all technical and security requirements of an organization. The recruitment process is important for the CISO to ensure that they get the right technical team under them to execute all security initiatives in addition to performing vulnerability testing to identify all system weaknesses. The team should have experts in various technical disciplines and they should be in charge of their respective fields in the organization so as to carry out their responsibilities most effectively. The CISO needs to offer capable leadership to the team, as without proper guidance, a team of experts will not be effective at the end of the day. Organizational and communication skills are important for the CISO executive to help them manage their team and provide security leadership for the organization in the best way possible.

Summary

In this chapter, we have tackled the topic of security leadership that a CISO executive is responsible for providing in an organization. A CISO is responsible for all security matters in an organization and is therefore tasked with various responsibilities that will enable them to offer the required security leadership to the organization. Some important CISO roles that enable them to do this have been described in detail in this chapter.

Building cybersecurity awareness helps reduce the potential internal threat that employees pose to an organization's informational assets, which increases their alertness and enables them to adhere to security initiatives and policies. A CISO is tasked with developing a cybersecurity strategy that provides a blueprint for the development and implementation of all security initiatives in an organization. The chapter has shown the need for a CISO to take full control of their security role in an organization, explained why the CISO needs to get the board convinced about the cybersecurity strategy, and highlighted the benefits of providing good security leadership to the organization and security team members.

This chapter marks the end of our book, but it doesn't stop there. *Chapter 11, Conclusion,* will summarize the key takeaways from the book.

Further reading

The following resources can be used to gain more knowledge of the topics covered in this chapter:

- *Building Cybersecurity Awareness: The need for evidence-based framing strategies:* `https://www.sciencedirect.com/science/article/pii/S0740624X17300540`

- *The Roadmap to Cybersecurity Awareness in Your Organization:* `https://www.hoxhunt.com/blog/cybersecurity-awareness-in-your-enterprise/`

- Strategies for building cybersecurity awareness: `https://daneshyari.com/article/preview/5110658.pdf`

11
Conclusion

This book, through the various chapters, has sought to offer insights into the security leadership role of a **chief information security officer** (**CISO**) executive in an organization. It has focused on the main role of tackling cybersecurity issues in an organization, the challenges a CISO has to address, and the many factors that affect the kind of leadership they can offer as security officers in an organization. We have learned, through the previous 10 chapters, that various interactions within an organization and with some parties outside of an organization are crucial to effective security leadership.

In this final chapter, we will review, in brief, the topics that we have learned in this book, as listed here:

- Defining the CISO role and what the role entails
- How a CISO ensures **end-to-end** (**E2E**) security operations are in place in an organization
- The compliance factor and how a CISO addresses the issue
- The role of **human resources** (**HR**) management in cybersecurity issues
- How documentation plays a huge role in effective security leadership
- **Disaster recovery** (**DR**) and **business continuity** (**BC**) factors in cybersecurity
- Understanding the role of various stakeholders in an organization
- Other CISO roles in an organization

- Getting hired as a CISO
- What security leadership entails

Defining the CISO role and what the role entails

The first chapter in the book defines the CISO role as a cybersecurity requirement for every organization. It introduces the concept of security threats to organizations that target the informational assets in an organization. To ensure the security posture of a business, it has increasingly become a basic requirement to have an individual in the organization in charge of the security situation, given the fact that the threat landscape is an ever-present threat. Security breaches have become the order of the day, with many businesses being destroyed by security incidents. A CISO executive thus needs to ensure that every aspect of the organization is taken care of and that the organization has measures in place to mitigate such security incidents. If a security incident does occur, the CISO should also have plans in place to address the aftermath of the security incident. The CISO role has also been evolving with the changing cybersecurity landscape, with executives playing an increasingly critical management role in businesses.

How a CISO ensures E2E security operations are in place in an organization

A CISO ensures E2E security operations are in place in an organization by engaging in actions such as evaluation of the threat landscape, devising policies that control and reduce risk, leading in auditing and compliance initiatives, managing information security initiatives, and establishing partnerships—both internally and externally. The evaluation of threats is a continuous process that entails reviewing all digital assets in an organization to determine weaknesses that could be exploited by potential attackers. It also entails consideration of the external threat landscape in terms of the abilities of attackers to carry out attacks and the kind of attacks a business is likely to face. After this consideration, the CISO then develops various security policies that the business follows internally to keep attackers out and to keep internal users in check as well. The CISO also ensures that the systems comply with all standards and regulations to avoid fines and increase the organization's security posture in the process. Establishing partnerships with people such as vendors helps the CISO obtain the required tools for system review and effectively implement security initiatives.

The compliance factor and how a CISO addresses the issue

Compliance with government and other regulatory bodies is a critical aspect of cybersecurity, and a CISO ensures that their organization's systems comply with these regulations. Non-compliance with regulations attracts fines and could lead to issues such as suspension of business operations. Regulations are developed mostly to protect the users of an organization's systems both from attackers and from the organization potentially misusing the data they collect from their users. Some of the popular statutes discussed in the book include **General Data Protection Regulation (GDPR)**, **Health Insurance Portability and Accountability Act (HIPAA)**, **California Consumer Privacy Act (CCPA)**, and **Children's Online Privacy Protection Act (COPPA)**, among others. These regulations ensure that businesses put in place security measures that will enhance the protection of the data they collect from consumers and users of their systems. By ensuring regulatory compliance, organizations also benefit from more secure systems and increased abilities to keep attackers at bay.

The role of HR management in cybersecurity issues

It is the primary role of a CISO to ensure an organization maintains a good security posture. The users of a system—in this case, the employees of the organization—pose a huge security threat to the organization. A CISO needs to protect the system and the organization both from external threats and from internal security compromises. The HR department aids the CISO in this case by enabling the CISO to play an important role during recruitment and in the management of the employees. The CISO ensures that background checks are done for all employees, especially ones being recruited into the organization, and for employees that have access to sensitive data. Access to sensitive data in an organization makes the user a potential security threat, and it's the CISO's responsibility to ensure that individuals posing a potential threat pass verification tests and have enough training to appreciate the security policies in place and uphold security initiatives.

How documentation plays a huge role in effective security leadership

Documentation enables a CISO to implement the many security initiatives they develop to keep their organization safe from threats. Firstly, documentation is a regulatory requirement, and organizations are required to keep documentation of their systems and the security aspects of these systems for ease of evaluation and maintenance. Secondly, it enables governance of various aspects of an organization as well as management of HR by providing guidelines on the various security policies and initiatives in place. Thirdly, documentation is critical during security incidents and in the aftermath of a security incident as it offers a step-by-step guideline on the handling of various business aspects. This helps increase the chances of recovery and BC following a security incident. Without documentation, employees would not have the direction needed to handle the aftermath of an incident, and this could majorly impact an organization's prospects of surviving the incident.

DR and BC factors in cybersecurity

The cybersecurity situation globally is such that attacks are a guarantee. It is not a matter of *whether* a business will be attacked but rather *when* it will be attacked. In such an environment, a business needs to plan for these security incidents when they do occur. Major security incidents threaten the survival of a business. Statistics show that many businesses do not survive major data breaches and those that do survive end up closing shop within 2 years of a security incident. DR entails procedures being put in place to handle security incidents, and BC encompasses processes in the aftermath of a security incident that ensure that a business survives such an attack. A CISO develops these processes in anticipation of security attacks and creates guidelines on how the business will handle security incidents when they do occur to minimize the impact of the incident and to ensure the business survives attacks with the least negative impact.

Understanding the role of various stakeholders in an organization

Various stakeholders in an organization play a role that affects the security situation within the organization, therefore a CISO needs to have processes in place that ensure interactions with various stakeholders help in upholding the security posture of the organization—for instance, the employees in an organization pose a security threat to the organization. The CISO develops security policies to keep their actions in check and to ensure they manage threats. Shareholders need to be convinced to release funds to implement various security initiatives. The CISO needs to convince them to support security initiatives by communicating all aspects of the business, the risks involved, and the strategy the CISO and the security team will need to address the various risks. Even the community around the business location plays a role in the security situation and having them on board will help them report any suspected security incidents that may affect the business's security posture.

Other CISO roles in an organization

A CISO plays many roles in an organization. The evolving roles of a CISO have seen them take on more responsibilities in a business. Some of the other less highlighted—but still important—roles include contributing to technical projects, partnering with both internal and external providers, evaluating employee behavior, financial reporting, and addressing cybersecurity as a business problem. Technical projects such as developing an information system for an organization have a direct impact on the security situation of a business, therefore a CISO needs to contribute during the development of such projects to guide their development in order to ensure that the finished product has minimal security risks. This will reduce initiatives that will later be needed to protect the system during production. Partnering with internal and external security players ensures that the CISO remains in charge of the security situation. All security initiatives need funding, and this calls for the CISO to contribute toward financial reporting of the various aspects of security initiatives and the financial impact on an organization.

Getting hired as a CISO executive

Getting hired as a CISO executive is a huge accomplishment for an individual in the cybersecurity world as it represents the pinnacle of a career in the **information technology (IT)** arena. However, before getting hired as a CISO, it requires years of experience for an individual to gain the necessary credentials. A CISO requires both technical and managerial expertise. While schooling and certification will get a potential CISO executive the theoretical knowledge to handle the role, an individual will need several years of experience to master their craft and be able to lead other people in an organization. Excellent organizational and communication skills are essential as well to communicate with both the security team and with other management executives, including the board of directors. During the first 90 days of getting hired, a CISO needs to ensure they develop and communicate their security strategy and develop relationships internally with key internal staff that will help in the execution of security initiatives.

What security leadership entails

Security leadership is the basic role of a CISO executive in an organization. As a CISO, all aspects of an organization that affect the security situation of the organization concern you. To play this role effectively, the CISO needs to create and build security awareness in the organization among all staff because they pose one of the biggest threats to the organization's digital assets. Building security awareness entails training and ensuring employees understand the security policies in place and why they need to be there. This will enable them to uphold these policies, hence reducing potential internal threats. The CISO then needs to build a cybersecurity strategy that the security team will follow and on which all security initiatives will be anchored. The strategy will act as a blueprint that determines how security policies are developed and how the business will address security threats and incidents affecting the organization. Finally, the CISO needs to play a leadership role within the security team effectively. Without effective leadership, even with individual technical experts, implementing a security strategy may not be as effective as it could be. An effective leader communicates well with the team and ensures that team members remain on track with their duties and responsibilities to the organization.

Summary

With that, we have come to the end of this book. Congratulations on successfully completing the lessons! You are now ready to explore the world and become a CISO executive. I tried to share my experience from the field as a previous CISO advisor and current CISO at **Comodo Cybersecurity**. Next, you will find a **bonus** chapter called *Ask the Expert*, where you will read some industry experts' opinions and recommendations that I hope will add great value to your CISO journey.

12
Ask the Experts

You have finally reached the last chapter of the book. This chapter has not been written by me, but instead by a selection of very well-known **cybersecurity experts**, some of whom protect the world's biggest organizations with their services and products, and some of whom are trainers who teach **chief information security officer (CISO)** classes as well as advanced security classes.

In this chapter, they have shared their perspectives with you as guest authors in my book. With more than 300 years' experience between them, I am sure you will enjoy reading and learning from this chapter as much as I did.

So that you can navigate this chapter in an order of your choosing, we have divided the contributions into four broad topics.

We will cover the following expert insights in this chapter:

- Protecting and defending your organization from cyberattacks—by Marcus Murray
- Path to becoming a successful CISO—by Adel Abdel Moneim
- Recommendations for cybersecurity professionals who want to be CISOs—by Mert Sarica
- How a modern CISO could work on improving security within their organization and maintain a good cybersecurity posture—by Dr. Mike Jankowski-Lorek and Paula Januszkiewicz
- Advice for a CISO—by Raif Sarica and Şükrü Durmaz

- Cybersecurity leadership demystified—Pave your way to becoming a world-class modern-day cybersecurity expert and a global CISO—by Dr. Timothy C. Summers

- The future of cybersecurity leadership—by Timothy C. Summers, Ph.D.

- Working with security experts—by Vladimir Meloski

- A CISO's communication with the board on three critical subjects—by Dr. Süleyman Özarslan

- Crush the triangle—by Raymond Comvalius

Protecting and defending your organization from cyberattacks – by Marcus Murray

In 2005, I founded the cybersecurity specialist firm Truesec. At the time, I already had 10 years of experience in penetration testing, system hardening, and other technical aspects of cybersecurity. In addition to that, I was frequently speaking at large international events demonstrating novel hacking techniques to raise awareness around cyber threats. A long time has passed since then, and the Truesec team and I—consisting of around 200 cyber experts—have engaged in a massive number of advanced cybersecurity projects over the years.

Looking back, the cyber landscape has changed dramatically. As a society, our information, our monetary instruments, and most of our business processes have become digital and, as a natural reaction to that, a criminal universe has grown up and is active within the cyber domain. 10 to 15 years ago, we wanted to generate awareness around future cyber threats; today, organized threat actor groups are inflicting more damage to targeted organizations than we ever wanted to imagine a few years ago. Cyber criminals are now making billions of dollars from destroying, robbing, and extorting organizations across the globe.

This year alone, my team has conducted more than 100 complex cyber **incident response (IR)** engagements related to full-scale ransomware attacks, massive data theft, and espionage activities.

Our deep experience in providing IR to targeted organizations has given us priceless insights into not only how to perform rapid and accurate incident management, forensics investigations, and recovery, but also how to build defenses that will prevent a breach or at least heavily minimize the business impact from a breach.

The largest challenge when giving advice on these topics is that every organization usually needs advice tailored to them based on various factors, such as which technology they are currently using, current security controls already in place, industry, size, legislations, and so on. Since this book is intended for a larger audience, I will focus on some more holistic insights that will be valuable to most organizations.

1 – Include cyber risks in your risk catalog

One thing that is striking to me is that most of the organizations we proactively protect on a continuous basis have defined cyber risks as the number-one risk to their business today. At the same time, the organizations that made their first contact with our IR team because of a severe ransomware incident had cyber risks listed either very far down the list or, in most cases, not at all. It also differs a lot depending on the sector; banks, for example, typically list cyber risks the highest, while industrial companies list them very low, if at all. Ironically, in recent years, we have responded to many more incidents targeting industrial companies than banks.

Most corporate risk managers know very little about cyber threats. Understanding the threat landscape, relevant risks, and how they could affect your business is an absolute must to make the right decisions over time. If cyber is not in your risk catalog, though computing is an important part of your business processes, I highly recommend that you take action. There are many experts today that can help an organization identify its relevant cyber risks.

2 – Define the greater goal of your cybersecurity efforts

As obvious as it may sound, most organizations are implementing security tools, functions, and controls without having a larger understanding of what they really want to accomplish.

Even a simple, non-quantified goal such as "*The goal of our cybersecurity efforts is to prevent and minimize the impact from breaches that will have a negative effect on our business*" can be very helpful.

By having such a goal, you can, for example, have a sanity check for any investment by simply asking how this investment will—directly or indirectly—contribute to achieving the goal.

Another positive effect is that it will contribute to internal acceptance and, hopefully, support when implementing security controls.

When employees have to use **multi-factor authentication** (**MFA**) to access your **information technology** (**IT**) platform from home, you can inform them that it's one of the mandatory controls for the organization to maintain its capability to prevent a breach or minimize the impact of a breach according to the goal.

In addition to the holistic goal, I also recommend adding sub-goals that are quantifiable, much like traditional business **key performance indicators** (**KPIs**). They should all be designed to meet the business needs and to ensure a sustainable business.

As a simplistic example, several banks have identified that if their IT platform is taken completely offline for more than 3 days, there will be consequences that can potentially bring them out of business. A sub-goal could be: "*Maintain a capability to secure and restore our IT platform to normal operation within 48 hours in case of a cyberattack.*" As you can imagine, a simple sub-goal such as that will shape everything from defense to detection capabilities and backup/restore strategies. If you cannot accept more than 48 hours of downtime, you will probably not invest in a **security operations center** (**SOC**) solution that is limited to operating 9 a.m.-5 p.m. on weekdays.

3 – Design a pragmatic cybersecurity program and choose an advisor wisely

Cyber is becoming **top of mind** (**TOM**) for top-level management in many organizations today. The recent rise in ransomware attacks and data leak operations has instigated fear in both boardrooms and **chief experience officers** (**CXOs**), especially since news outlets are increasing their coverage of cyberattacks.

A natural step when an organization fears cyber threats and C-level managers want to take action is that they contact one of the larger international management firms and order a **National Institute of Standards and Technology** (**NIST**) assessment. NIST is a good framework for cybersecurity; however, it seems most of the management consultants delivering NIST assessments lack a true understanding of the threat landscape and what is really needed to protect an organization today. Make sure that the individuals who run such assessments have real-world experience of both cybersecurity and incidents and a good understanding of, and experience from working with, enterprise IT. A clean-cut management consultant without such knowledge will simply follow a questionnaire, and the result may well reflect your own perception of what you need but the recommendations will usually not be optimized to what's best for your organization.

The five functions in the NIST framework are *Identify*, *Protect*, *Detect*, *Respond*, and *Recover*, and the typical idea of management consultancy firms is that you assess the business by asking your organization a large number of questions related to categories and subcategories within each function. After that is done, they will compile the results into a score that will later become the basis for designing a cybersecurity maturity program. This is where the problem usually begins. For some reason, every program built by management firms basically seems to believe that the program must be built from left to right. The assumption is that you cannot run a security program unless you have implemented a perfect IT asset management system (**configuration management database**, or **CMDB**) for identifying every system and application in your environment. So, only after the *Identity* function in the NIST framework is at a satisfactory level should you move on to the next function, *Protect*. In theory, you could argue that this is the perfect approach. The big problem is that it assumes that the threat actors will wait until you are done with the whole program before they attack. 10 years ago, that could be true, but today, your organization risks getting breached every day; therefore, I would not recommend any organization to approach the NIST model from left to right. For most organizations today with a large number of servers and workstations, I would strongly recommend that a strong detection and response capability should be implemented first. If a ransomware actor breaches your organization 3 months into your *Identity* project, you may lack any capability to detect the attack and mitigate it before your IT environment gets encrypted and the business becomes totally disrupted. If you instead had focused on implementing a quality **endpoint detection and response** (**EDR**) tool and connected it to a capable and efficient 24/7 SOC service, the threat would have been managed and mitigated long before any real damage was done. To extend the example, a capable backup solution would also make most organizations sleep better at night than a full inventory in today's threat landscape. Experienced cyber specialists that truly understand the threat landscape, cybersecurity, and enterprise IT should be used to design a pragmatic cybersecurity program for your organization.

4 – Use threat intelligence as a tool for strategic cybersecurity

Over the years, my team and I have performed many red team assignments to measure the organization's capability to prevent, detect, and respond to cyberattacks. A red team assignment is a full-scale realistic attack simulation, testing various attack vectors to mimic real threat-actor campaigns. The biggest value appears for organizations that run these tests on a regular basis. After each assignment, they start to shape their defense and detection capabilities to make it impossible to attack them the same way again. After a few years, these organizations become very challenging to breach, even for our most skilled experts.

There is an additional and more efficient way of shaping your defenses—**threat intelligence** (**TI**). The concept is very straightforward. If you have accurate intel on the threat actors and the **modus operandi** (**MO**) they use, then you can shape your defenses much more surgically. In fact, for most large organizations today, this is a necessity since their IT environments are so complex and the number of potential vulnerabilities is so large that they must prioritize which vulnerabilities to mitigate and what action to take. We provide two services that are very helpful to most organizations.

The first service is to create a threat profile that will define exactly which threat actors would be likely to target the assessed organization. In the threat profile, we detail the known attack methods that they are expected to use and provide detailed information on how the threats can be mitigated. A threat profile is an excellent input to everything, from strategic cybersecurity maturity programs to immediate actions.

The other service is a subscription service whereby you get tailored updates on the threat landscape on a regular basis.

Typically, you get a quarterly tailored update on your threat profile. Monthly updates on the threat landscape and relevant threat campaign information alerts are pushed in real time.

Services such as these will be more and more important for setting up defenses that will prevent or minimize the impacts of a breach. There is nothing that frustrates me more than witnessing organizations investing large amounts of money in security solutions that will mitigate very unlikely threats while they lack protection from likely ones.

5 – Invest in a detection and response capability

Most large organizations have some kind of external SOC. The general idea is to use a **security, information, and event management** (**SIEM**) tool such as Splunk, QRadar ArcSight, or NetWitness for log collection, feed logs from security products, network devices, systems, and applications to the SIEM solution, and then define so-called use cases to define what to look for. I have several issues with this approach. I like SIEMs, and I believe that they play an important role in the security ecosystem. They are great for statistics, structured log storage, event correlation, and various types of analysis and investigations. However, as a one-stop tool for detecting and responding to breaches, there is better tooling for most scenarios.

The most common and straightforward example is a ransomware attack where a top-tier EDR tool would be a much better tool for detection and response.

I'll explain why by presenting an example ransomware attack. A typical attack flow is that a threat actor compromises an internet-exposed service or successfully tricks a user to execute code delivered as an email attachment or a link. The code installs an implant for remote control, typically a cobalt strike agent or some custom implant executed on compromised systems. Next comes a series of events including, but not limited to, lateral movement, deletion of backups and disabling of security features, data exfiltration, and—last but not least—encryption of servers and workstations. An SOC that solely relies on an SIEM would have very limited visibility into what was really going on inside the systems, and therefore maybe missed the attack entirely. In addition to that, an SIEM does not normally have any capability to go live on affected systems or isolate them to contain and eradicate threats.

A top-tier EDR managed 24/7 by specialists would not just provide better visibility into what's happening on the systems—it would also provide response capabilities so that the threat could get contaminated and eradicated before systems got encrypted.

I believe an SOC today should rely heavily on a top-tier EDR for most types of threats targeting your servers and workstations. SOC staff should also have the ambition and competence to tailor and optimize the detection of the EDR to a specific customer; they should have the knowledge and ambition to analyze every alert and be able to distinguish between false positives that should be logged and discarded and harmful true positives that should be rapidly reported and disarmed.

6 – Implement the most important controls as quickly as possible

There are some features that should be implemented in basically every organization.

Here is a basic list:

- In no circumstance should a threat actor be able to destroy or manipulate backups, one thing a threat actor does after they obtain complete control of the IT environment. Make sure that your backup solutions are protected from a compromised environment. If that's not possible, then make offline backups.

- Make sure that internet-exposed services are always hardened and patched. This year, there have been countless attacks exploiting vulnerabilities in exposed services. For example, many organizations were breached earlier this year because of a vulnerability in Microsoft's on-prem mail server exchange. Some organizations had already migrated to Office 365, and the on-prem exchange server was forgotten and not patched. Mistakes such as this can have a huge impact if the vulnerability is used as a stepping stone for a ransomware attack.

Implement an EDR-based detection and response capability. I have mentioned this earlier; see *5 – Invest in a detection and response capability* for details.

- Require MFA on internet-exposed services. Tricking users to expose their passwords is often easier than most people believe. All it takes is usually a well-crafted phishing email tricking a user to enter their credentials into a form controlled by a threat actor. Many users also create weak passwords, and requiring MFA will limit the attack surface. A common mistake is also in the form of some **system administrator** (**sysadmin**) configuring MFA to be allowed but not required; that way, a great actor can still execute attacks on the service. Enforce MFA on every internet-exposed service if possible.

- Minimize the exposure of high-privilege credentials and dependencies. During the lateral movement phase, a threat actor will try to harvest credentials from every system they compromise and reuse them to access other systems of higher importance. The best way to prevent lateral movement is to limit exposure and follow the **principle of least privilege** (**POLP**). Expose high-privilege accounts on as few systems as possible.

- Protect high-value targets. Protect your most important systems, assets, data, and identities. Make sure you know what is important and take measures to protect these systems. You may not need a complete inventory of every system but you need to protect the high-value targets. Also, remember that some systems hold and have the capability to prove access to other high-value targets, so make sure that you also protect these. Examples are domain controllers, virtual hosts, and **storage area network** (**SAN**) systems.

There are always more things that would be relevant to this chapter, so look at this as inspiration, and please add relevant controls and advice to your own programs within your own organization. Good luck and stay safe!

About Marcus Murray

Marcus Murray is the founder of Truesec and an internationally recognized cyber expert with 20+ years of experience in enabling organizations to predict, protect, detect, and respond to cyber threats.

Marcus is frequently interviewed on national television and in the news press and media. He is also a top-rated keynote speaker at cybersecurity and tech events worldwide, raising awareness about cyber threats, vulnerabilities, and how to prevent cyber breaches.

Marcus is the creator of **state-of-the-art (SOTA)** cyber programs at Truesec and is a frontrunner in advanced TI and breach detection and response. He also orchestrates large red team assignments, cyber IR efforts, and other cyber operations for global enterprise customers, government agencies, banks, and military organizations.

Path to becoming a successful CISO – by Adel Abdel Moneim

Nowadays, IT has become an essential part of our daily life. We are surrounded by tens and hundreds of smart devices: smart TVs, smart watches, wearable electronics, smart home appliances, **internet of things (IoT)** home sensors, and more. Furthermore, at the business level, all sectors are affected by this as well. Technologies such as **industrial IoT (IIoT)**, **operational technology (OT)**, and **financial technology (FinTech)** are affecting the financial sector, smart cities and real estate, critical infrastructure, energy, manufacturing, and industrial sectors, in addition to a wide range of digital transformation services. In other words, *everyone* is affected.

Based on this great expansion in technology everywhere, cybersecurity has become a crucial factor that affects almost everything and everyone. Hence, the importance of cybersecurity became very clear in sustaining IT ecosystems and, therefore, the role of CISO obviously became extremely critical, not only to manage information security risks but also to manage any business risks that may arise through cyberattacks.

Within this section, I will highlight the main areas any CISO should focus on, along with some advice and guidelines for those who hold the position of CISO or who are aiming to reach that position.

Business context understanding

A CISO must understand that information security is a tool to secure and protect critical IT assets. Security is not a target in itself, therefore before implementing any security controls, the first step for any CISO to start with is to understand the business context, including but not limited to the following:

- Understanding the corporate vision, mission, and strategy
- Identifying internal (audit/IT/**human resources (HR)**/legal) and external (vendors/suppliers/customers/regulators) stakeholders
- Understanding the role of information security (how information security acts as a business enabler)

- Understanding compliance requirements (contractual obligations/industry standards/regulations and laws)

- Understanding the sourcing model (insourcing/outsourcing/hybrid)

- Defining if the company is working within a highly regulated industry (such as the financial sector) and if the company is collecting, processing, or storing regulated data

After gaining a deep understanding of the business context, a CISO has to apply security governance practices in order to ensure that the security strategy is aligned with the business strategy, security resources are optimized to best fit the business needs, information security risks are managed within the accepted risk level, and, finally, deliver value through implementing a proper security program that supports and enables the achievement of business goals.

Governance, risk, and compliance

A CISO's role is mainly a leadership role; simply, it is a C-level position. This position does not require strong technical knowledge; being a successful CISO depends mainly on the ability to effectively employ security as an enabler of business goals' achievement. A CISO should work to understand security challenges that face the business in order to provide a proper solution to overcome such challenges through implementing an information security program that has an adequate level of protection for the company's digital assets yet is flexible enough to adapt to the dynamic nature of risks.

Based on the previous information, the CISO's approach will be a top-down approach (holistic view) by managing and integrating the three main aspects of any successful information security program, outlined as follows:

- **Governance**: To ensure that the security strategy and program are aligned with strategic business goals and resources are optimized for best serving the business goals, and, finally, to ensure effective implementation of the security program, realizing the **return on security investment (ROSI)**.

- **Risk**: Risk management is a crucial function in building and implementing an information security program. The CISO has to periodically conduct risk assessments to identify new risks (if any), as well as update the risk register with new risks or new information for existing risks (updates in probability or impact for existing risks). The function of risk management within this context includes—but is not limited to—confidentiality risk, integrity risk, availability risk, or compliance risk. The ultimate goal for this function is to manage all risks within the risk management scope at the accepted level of risk in accordance with top management's risk appetite.

- **Compliance**: Nowadays, compliance has become a big challenge given the presence of a wide diversity of compliance requirements. Compliance requirements may include the following:

  - **Baseline**—An information security program must achieve the minimum requirements (baseline) needed to protect the company's assets as defined by the security program objectives.

  - **Contractual obligation**—The CISO must ensure compliance with all contractual obligations such as **service-level agreements** (**SLAs**), IR requirements, or data protection measures.

  - **Industry/international standards**—Numerous industry-specific standards/requirements such as the **Payment Card Industry Data Security Standard** (**PCI DSS**), the **Health Insurance Portability and Accountability Act** (**HIPAA**), and the **North American Electric Reliability Corporation** (**NERC**), for the finance, health, and critical infrastructure sectors respectively, exist, and the CISO must define the applicable industry standards to comply with.

  - **Regulation and laws**—These requirements are obligatory to fulfill, and the CISO has a diversity of laws that must be abided by, covering—but not limited to—the following: data protection laws, **intellectual property** (**IP**) laws, record management laws, cybercrime laws, data privacy and protection laws (for example, the **General Data Protection Regulation** (**GDPR**)). Noncompliance thereof may involve huge financial fines or the revocation of business licenses.

In conclusion, the CISO acts as an orchestrator to manage and integrate all requirements in order to ensure that the information security program runs properly to fulfill the organization's IT asset protection requirements. Here are some excellent references for **governance, risk, and compliance** (**GRC**) aspects:

- **International Organization for Standardization/International Electrotechnical Commission** (**ISO/IEC**) *27005:2018*—Information technology/Security techniques—Information security risk management

- ISO *37301:2021*—Compliance management systems—Requirements with guidance for use

- ISO *31000:2018*—Risk management—Guidelines

- NIST **Risk Management Framework** (**RMF**)

- ISO/IEC *38500*—Information technology—Governance of IT for the organization

- **Control Objectives for Information and Related Technologies** (**COBIT**)

Security domains

The following diagram shows the different security domains:

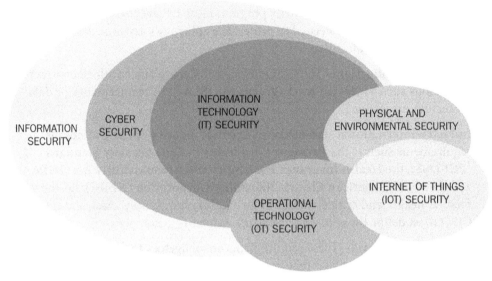

Figure 12.1 – Security domains

In the information age, information security no longer remains a single domain; rather, as in the preceding screenshot, it can be divided into various subdomains, each focusing on a specific area of security implementation. Information security still represents a wide umbrella covering all other subcategories as it covers both digital and non-digital information, such as printed reports. On the other hand, cybersecurity is mainly focused on digitized information or electronic systems, which are usually connected to the internet cyberspace. Cybersecurity in itself is divided into two subcomponents, these being IT security (email systems, web servers, file servers, databases, and so on) and OT security, which covers the area of **industrial control systems (ICS)** such as **programmable logic controllers (PLCs)**, **distributed control systems (DCSes)**, and **supervisory control and data acquisition (SCADA)**, in addition to hundreds of **cyber-physical systems (CPSes)**. With technological evolution, we also have to deal with IoT security to cover a very wide range of devices including home appliances, wearable electronics, industrial sensors, and many more. Finally, we cannot ignore the importance of physical security for any of the mentioned systems since physical security represents a non-dividable part of the ecosystem of information security.

Here are some proposed definitions for each domain, along with the security scope of implementation:

- (Reference: `https://www.sans.org/information-security/`)
  "Information Security refers to the processes and methodologies which are designed and implemented to protect print, electronic, or any other form of confidential, private and sensitive information or data from unauthorized access, use, misuse, disclosure, destruction, modification, or disruption."

- (Reference: `https://www.itu.int/en/ITU-T/studygroups/com17/Pages/cybersecurity.aspx`) *"Cybersecurity is the collection of tools, policies, security concepts, security safeguards, guidelines, risk management approaches, actions, training, best practices, assurance and technologies that can be used to protect the cyber environment and organization and user's assets. Organization and user's assets include connected computing devices, personnel, infrastructure, applications, services, telecommunications systems, and the totality of transmitted and/or stored information in the cyber environment. Cybersecurity strives to ensure the attainment and maintenance of the security properties of the organization and user's assets against relevant security risks in the cyber environment. The general security objectives comprise the following:*

  - *Availability*

  - *Integrity, which may include authenticity and non-repudiation*

  - *Confidentiality"*

- (Reference: `https://www.myrasecurity.com/en/it-security-in-practice/`) *"IT security has to do with guaranteeing the security of all information techniques and technologies (IT) used, i.e., all hardware and software systems and all computer and network systems. The primary objective of these techniques is to ensure the security of information processing and communication, which requires the proper hardware operation processes as well as software and program system processes."*

- (Reference: `https://www.forcepoint.com/cyber-edu/ot-operational-technology-security`) *"Operational Technology (OT) is hardware and software that detects or causes a change through the direct monitoring and/or control of physical devices, processes and events in the enterprise, according to Gartner. OT is common in Industrial Control Systems (ICS) such as a SCADA System. In the world of critical infrastructure, OT may be used to control power stations or public transportation. As this technology advances and converges with networked tech the need for OT security grows exponentially."*

- (Reference: `https://internetofthingsagenda.techtarget.com/definition/IoT-security-Internet-of-Things-security`) *"IoT security is the technology segment focused on safeguarding connected devices and networks in the internet of things (IoT). IoT involves adding internet connectivity to a system of interrelated computing devices, mechanical and digital machines, objects, animals and/or people. Each "thing" is provided a unique identifier and the ability to automatically transfer data over a network. Allowing devices to connect to the internet opens them up to a number of serious vulnerabilities if they are not properly protected."*

- (Reference: `https://www.csoonline.com/article/3324614/what-is-physical-security-how-to-keep-your-facilities-and-devices-safe-from-on-site-attackers.html`) *"Physical security is the protection of people, property, and physical assets from actions and events that could cause damage or loss. Though often overlooked in favor of cybersecurity, physical security is equally important. All the firewalls in the world can't help you if an attacker removes your storage media from the storage room."*

Cybersecurity frameworks, standards, and best practices

A professional CISO should master one or more security enterprise architecture frameworks in addition to global/industry standards and best practices relevant for their industry. Based on my practical experience, I would recommend the following frameworks as a base to build successful information security management capabilities.

NIST Cybersecurity Framework

NIST **Cybersecurity Framework (CSF)** is a brilliant, mind-shaping framework that provides great support for any CISO to build the information security program life cycle, starting from identifying key business functions and accordingly protecting the relevant critical business assets, then applying appropriate controls, detecting and responding to incidents, and finally recovering business operations back to normal after any high-severity incident. NIST CSF does not dictate following any specific standard; however, NIST CSF can provide the necessary guidance to build a robust security framework/architecture to adopt any relevant standard adapting to business security requirements such as ISO *27001*, PCI, NERC, and GDPR.

At a very high level, NIST CSF consists of 5 main functions (*Identify/Protect/Detect Respond/Recover*), 23 categories, 108 subcategories, and a vast number of informative references that can adapt to a diversity of global standards. For further details on the categories, please refer to the following screenshot:

Function	Category	ID
Identify	Asset Management	ID.AM
	Business Environment	ID.BE
	Governance	ID.GV
	Risk Assessment	ID.RA
	Risk Management Strategy	ID.RM
	Supply Chain Risk Management	ID.SC
Protect	Identity Management and Access Control	PR.AC
	Awareness and Training	PR.AT
	Data Security	PR.DS
	Information Protection Processes & Procedures	PR.IP
	Maintenance	PR.MA
	Protective Technology	PR.PT
Detect	Anomalies and Events	DE.AE
	Security Continuous Monitoring	DE.CM
	Detection Processes	DE.DP
Respond	Response Planning	RS.RP
	Communications	RS.CO
	Analysis	RS.AN
	Mitigation	RS.MI
	Improvements	RS.IM
Recover	Recovery Planning	RC.RP
	Improvements	RC.IM
	Communications	RC.CO

Subcategory	Informative References
ID.BE-1: The organization's role in the supply chain is identified and communicated	COBIT 5 APO08.01, APO08.04, APO08.05, APO10.03, APO10.04, APO10.05 ISO/IEC 27001:2013 A.15.1.1, A.15.1.2, A.15.1.3, A.15.2.1, A.15.2.2 NIST SP 800-53 Rev. 4 CP-2, SA-12
ID.BE-2: The organization's place in critical infrastructure and its industry sector is identified and communicated	COBIT 5 APO02.06, APO03.01 ISO/IEC 27001:2013 Clause 4.1 NIST SP 800-53 Rev. 4 PM-8
ID.BE-3: Priorities for organizational mission, objectives, and activities are established and communicated	COBIT 5 APO02.01, APO02.06, APO03.01 ISA 62443-2-1:2009 4.2.2.1, 4.2.3.6 NIST SP 800-53 Rev. 4 PM-11, SA-14
ID.BE-4: Dependencies and critical functions for delivery of critical services are established	COBIT 5 APO10.01, BAI04.02, BAI09.02 ISO/IEC 27001:2013 A.11.2.2, A.11.2.3, A.12.1.3 NIST SP 800-53 Rev. 4 CP-8, PE-9, PE-11, PM-8, SA-14
ID.BE-5: Resilience requirements to support delivery of critical services are established for all operating states (e.g. under duress/attack, during recovery, normal operations)	COBIT 5 DSS04.02 ISO/IEC 27001:2013 A.11.1.4, A.17.1.1, A.17.1.2, A.17.2.1 NIST SP 800-53 Rev. 4 CP-2, CP-11, SA-14

Figure 12.2 – NIST domain and categories

ISO 27001 Information Security Management Standard

One of the highly recommended and widely recognized information security standards is ISO *27001*. If you are about to build a new **information security management system** (**ISMS**) or you need to have a mature security management framework to be applied within your organization, ISO *27001* might be the best option to use. Based on my practical experience throughout more than 25 years, implementing ISO *27001* represents a very solid base for establishing an ISMS covering almost all information security aspects. At a high level, ISO *27001* (*annex A*) comprises 14 clauses, covering 35 control objectives through implementing 114 controls. It is worth mentioning that one of the new ISO *27000* family members is ISO *27701* (**privacy information management system** or **PIMS**), which is an extension to ISO *27001*, an excellent tool to manage all privacy aspects for controllers, processors, or organizations in general. Thus, implementing both standards will support achieving information security and privacy protection goals.

Other relevant frameworks and standards

In addition to NIST CSF and ISO *27001*, there are many other great frameworks and standards, such as the following:

- **Sherwood Applied Business Security Architecture** (**SABSA**), which is one of the best enterprise security architectures

- COBIT

- **Information Security and Assurance (ISA)/IEC** *62443*: Security for industrial automation and control systems

- **Cloud Security Alliance Cloud Controls Matrix (CSA-CCM)**: A cloud control matrix that represents an excellent cybersecurity framework for cloud computing

Business continuity, disaster recovery, and resilience

In today's world, where almost everything is dependent on technology, the availability of systems—or, in other words, supporting **business continuity** (**BC**)—has become a crucial issue for a majority of organizations. It has become a more and more complex challenge to ensure BC within a complex technology environment, ranging from traditional systems to hybrid complex systems mixing between on-premises solutions, cloud computing, IoT devices, or OT solutions. One of the critical tasks every CISO has to understand is how to ensure BC not only through having a deep understanding of all fundamental aspects of supporting BC (including, but not limited to) IR, **disaster recovery (DR)**, and contingency plans but also by mastering how to deal with the diversity of technical terminologies such as **recovery time objective (RTO)**, **recovery point objective (RPO)**, **maximum interruptible window (MIW)**, or **maximum tolerable downtime (MTD)**. A clear understanding of different virtual/physical systems is something very important to develop any BC plan, including all relevant plans, selecting your service sourcing model in addition to having a proper way for selecting which technologies, vendors, or suppliers to work with in relevance to this subject.

The following screenshot illustrates the different stages of a BC plan:

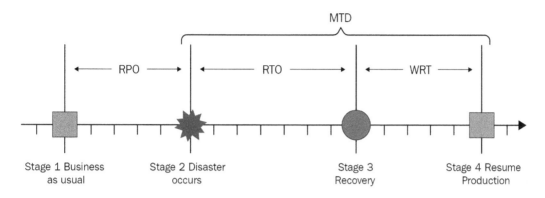

Figure 12.3 – BC stages for CISOs

When it comes to BC, we cannot ignore ISO *22301*, the globally recognized standard for supporting BC and resilience. However, many other excellent related references are available, as outlined here:

- ISO *22301* Security and resilience—Business continuity management systems—Requirements

- ISO/**Technical Specification** (**TS**) *22317*—Security and resilience—Business continuity management systems—Guidelines for **business impact analysis** (**BIA**)

- ISO *27035* Information security incident management—Part 1: Principles of incident management

- ISO *27035* Information security incident management—Part 2: Guidelines to plan and prepare for incident response

- ISO *27035* Information security incident management—Part 3: Guidelines for ICT incident response operations

- **Special Publication** (**SP**) *800-61 Rev. 2*—Computer Security Incident Handling Guide

Cybersecurity workforce skills development and security awareness

Any successful information security program has three main pillars: *people*, *process*, and *technology*. However, within the context of cybersecurity, it is critical to consider the human factor. This could be presented in the form of competencies. A successful CISO has to pay special attention to cybersecurity HR competencies, which are essential for achieving cybersecurity program goals—developing the proper job description for each member of the cybersecurity team, along with linking each job description with the needed competencies for the employee to successfully fulfill their own job, developing a complete career path (technical/managerial), in addition to following the proper capacity building and training plan. On the other hand, security awareness for all organizations' employees is something that is very important and required by all global security standards, such as ISO 27001 and PCI. A successful awareness program must target changing people's culture to be aligned with cybersecurity hygiene guidelines. Today, a successful security awareness program is an innovative one, where awareness content is not delivered in the form of a direct message to the employees but could be through **virtual reality** (**VR**) games or in the form of competition between different teams of employees, or by attracting employees' interest through a reward program or best employee behavior in detecting and reporting potential incidents, phishing emails, or social engineering attempts.

When it comes to professional skills for cybersecurity human resources, we cannot ignore the importance of the NIST–SP workforce framework for cybersecurity (**National Initiative for Cybersecurity Education** (**NICE**) framework), which lists all needed competencies for a cybersecurity workforce, providing a great linkage between each job and relevant competencies (skills/knowledge/abilities).

The **NICE Cybersecurity Workforce Framework** (**NCWF**) consists of various components. The first tier comprises seven categories, each containing a number of specialty areas—33 in total. Each specialty includes a number of work roles, totaling 52 roles, with the specific aspects required to perform them by integrating **knowledge, skills, and abilities** (**KSAs**). For more details, kindly refer to `https://niccs.cisa.gov/about-niccs/workforce-framework-cybersecurity-nice-framework-work-roles`.

In regard to how to develop a successful security awareness program for the organization's employees, NIST SP *800-50*, *Building an Information Technology Security Awareness and Training Program*, is an excellent resource to do so.

Here are some recommended professional/industry certifications for CISOs:

- **Information Systems Audit and Control Association (ISACA)**

  - **Certified in Risk and Information Systems Control (CRISC)**

  - **Certified Information Security Manager (CISM)**

  - **Certified in the Governance of Enterprise IT (CGEIT)**

  - **Certified Information Systems Auditor (CISA)**

  - COBIT

- **International Council of Electronic Commerce Consultants (EC-Council)**

  - **Certified Chief Information Security Officer Program (CCISO)**

  - **EC-Council Certified Incident Handler (ECIH)**

- **International Information System Security Certification Consortium (ISC2)**

  - **Certified Information Systems Security Professional (CISSP)**

  - **CISSP-Information Systems Security Architecture Professional (CISSP-ISSAP)**

  - **CISSP-Information Systems Security Management Professional (CISSP-ISSMP)**

  - **Certified Cloud Security Professional (CCSP)**

- **Professional Evaluation and Certification Board (PECB)**

  - ISO *27001*—Lead Auditor/Lead Implementor

  - ISO *27005*—Lead Risk Manager

  - ISO *22301*—Lead Auditor/Lead Implementor

  - ISO *31000*—Lead Risk Manager

  - ISO *27701*—Lead Auditor/Lead Implementor

  - **Certified Data Protection Officer (CDPO)**

- **International Association for Privacy Professionals (IAPP)**

  - **Certified Information Privacy Professional (CIPP)**

  - **Certified Information Privacy Manager (CIPM)**

- **Association of Project Managers Group (APMG)**

  - **NIST Cyber Security Professional (NCSP)**

- SABSA Institute

  - **SABSA Foundation Certificate (SCF)**—SABSA Chartered Security Architect—Foundation Certificate

- **SysAdmin, Audit, Network and Security (SANS)**

  - *MGT514*: Security Strategic Planning, Policy, and Leadership

  - *MGT525*: IT Project Management and Effective Communication

  - *SEC566*: Implementing and Auditing CIS Critical Controls

Security operations

One of the most challenging responsibilities CISOs face nowadays when handling security issues within a highly complex environment is security operations. Under the umbrella of security operations, we have numerous functions and tasks, such as the following:

- **Building information assets inventory**: A basic step for all upcoming functions/tasks is to create an asset inventory including tangible and non-tangible assets, conducting asset classification based on the three aspects for information security: **confidentiality, integrity, availability (CIA)**. One of the important outputs of this stage is to identify critical business assets to be monitored after conducting BIA.

- **SOC**: Due to today's vast amount of attacks, **continuous monitoring (CM)** has become a necessity, whereby we need to keep an eye on critical business assets along with sensitive business data. Developing an appropriate CM plan including what should be monitored, what kind of data should be collected, and what kind of analysis has to be conducted is a real challenge each CISO faces nowadays. Accordingly, having a SOC has become an important tool in order to serve the complex requirements for CM in large-scale operations. It's worth mentioning that CM could be obtained **as a service (CMAAS)** if it represents a cost-effective solution in addition to providing an acceptable risk level.

  Successful SOC operation definitely depends on a magical mixture between the three main pillars of the SOC: people, process, and technology. Identifying the needed competencies for a SOC workforce is critical for the success of operations, in addition to keeping the SOC team skills constantly up to date for the effective handling of emerging cyber threats.

At the policy and process level, I can confidently say that without having well-developed, detailed, and consistent use cases, policies, and procedures such as incident management policies, communication procedures with all stakeholders, incident escalation criteria, and asset classification policies, in addition to considering all legal or regulatory compliance requirements, the SOC operation will not only look like chaos but may also lead to a complete failure.

Finally, at the technology level, a skilled CISO should implement the most appropriate technology adapting to the organization's business needs, in addition to employing the emerging detection and response technologies such as TI, **artificial intelligence** (**AI**), and **machine learning** (**ML**).

- **Log management**: In large-scale corporations with numerous technologies and thousands of devices, processes of log collection, normalization, correlation, analysis, and archiving (retention) represent yet another challenge. This is why this task should be implemented very carefully to identify what should be monitored, what kind of data should be collected for monitoring and analysis purposes, the criteria of analysis, and how to convert low-level log data into a meaningful and effective cybersecurity operation to protect the organization's digital assets.

Another important dimension when it comes to log management is legal/regulatory compliance since the collected logs should fulfill regulatory requirements from their content, protection, and data retention period.

As a final piece of advice for CISOs, you have to ensure that your organization's security operation is converting all business-related information security domains (IT, OT, IoT… and so on). Modern SOC solutions have the capability to deal with all of them. Also important is being informed of the latest technology updates when it comes to protecting company assets, such as EDR, **endpoint protection platform** (**EPP**), **defense in depth** (**DiD**), **security orchestration, automation, and reporting** (**SOAR**), and the zero-trust model.

Cybersecurity performance metrics and monitoring

A well-developed and mature security management system/program has to have performance metrics or KPIs. We cannot guarantee the performance of our security controls without measuring the effectiveness of controls; developing a well-selected set of assessment criteria, methods, and techniques to assure suitability, sufficiency, and adequacy of security controls is a critical factor not only to measure the performance for our security solution but also to support continuous improvement and detecting any deviation in performance or control deficiencies.

A professional CISO should implement diverse assessment techniques such as vulnerability assessment, red teaming activities, application penetration testing, conducting phishing campaigns, and analyzing IR statistics such as the number of successfully handled incidents or the timeline for incident handling. Reduction in business losses, negative impact after applying specific security solutions. These are all different techniques used to assess the security program's effectiveness.

As a recommendation on how to develop your own information security metrics, I would recommend the following:

- ISO *27004* (Security Techniques—information security management—monitoring, measurement, analysis, and evaluation)
- NIST SP *800-55 Rev.2*—Performance measurement guide for information security
- **Cybersecurity Maturity Model Certification (CMMC)**

Other business-related skills

As mentioned earlier, a CISO is mainly a leadership position; this is why being a professional CISO is not mainly dependent on your technical background, but on having adequate skills in business-related aspects such as financial management. These skills are crucial since a CISO manages budgets, expenses, **capital expenditures (CAPEX)**, and **operational expenses (OPEX)**. Also, CISOs should be part of negotiation processes for security solutions or professional services' pricing. This is why understanding the fundamentals of financial management is highly important for the holder of this position. Moreover, a CISO has to master developing business cases in order to assess the cost of any proposed security solution, assuring the proper ROSI and support to get management approval based on **cost-benefit analysis (CBA)**. Furthermore, the CISO is considered a portfolio manager, where they may be managing multiple programs or projects at a time such as building a new DR site, migrating to a cloud business solution, developing an enterprise-level risk framework, or applying for new certification such as ISO *27001* (ISMS certification) or CMMC. Thus, a successful CISO must be competent enough to manage, monitor, and evaluate project performance, assuring successful implementation and value delivery.

Quotes

Here are some quotes for you to take away from this section:

- *Security is a process, not a product*
- *No physical security is equal to no security at all*
- *Information security is all about risk management*
- *Security is a tool to support and enable the business, not an objective itself*
- *There is no 100% secure system*
- *Security is everyone's responsibility*
- *Information security is not a technical issue*

About Adel Abdel Moneim

Adel Abdel Moneim, a registered **International Telecommunication Union (ITU)/ Arab Regional Cybersecurity Center (ARCC)** cybersecurity expert, has over 25 years of experience in the IT/cybersecurity fields, spending most of his career in information security consultation and training. Adel is globally recognized as a security top influencer in *IFSEC Global influencers in security and fire 2019*, in the *Security thought leadership* category. In 2020 and 2021 Adel was selected top influencer in the *cybersecurity* category, ranking # 3 and # 2 respectively at the global level.

Adel is an international certified trainer from ISC², APMG, EC-Council, ISACA, PECB, CertNexus, and a **Certified Internet Web (CIW)** professional who has delivered hundreds of official training courses and workshops. He maintains an exceptional track record of excellent feedback throughout his course delivery, be it at multinational companies, academic/training entities, or law enforcement/military institutions, in the areas of penetration testing, digital forensics, risk assessment and management, ISO standards implementation/audit, or security governance and compliance.

Capitalizing on his proven expertise and hands-on experience in executing security governance, risk assessments, compliance, conducting security audits, assessing the effectiveness of controls, ISMS, **integrated platform management systems (IPMS)**, **BC management systems (BCMS)**, **learning management systems (LMS)**, data privacy, IR, digital forensics, and cyber operations, Adel successfully provides consultation for large-enterprise security projects in various government/industry verticals, serving many reputable organizations and companies nationally, regionally, and internationally.

In a bid to continually rise cybersecurity awareness, Adel has dedicated hundreds of hours to voluntary work, providing the governmental sector, **non-governmental associations** (**NGOs**), and technical communities with his experience and knowledge in the field. As a public speaker, he is often requested to share his knowledge as a keynote speaker in TV/radio interviews and at conferences, seminars, and workshops. Furthermore, he contributed to preparing many proposals regarding cybercrime and data privacy protection laws in Egypt and the Arab world.

Recommendations for cybersecurity professionals who want to be CISOs – by Mert Sarica

Passing through all of the obstacles one by one in your career path to becoming a CISO is a bit challenging, depending on the industry that you work for, the culture, and the country that you live in. As Erdal Ozkaya articulates, the inner details of how to become a cybersecurity leader are crystal clear; I would like to touch on different aspects of becoming a CISO with a technical background.

In my opinion, some books and articles on being a CISO underestimate the power of technical skills for CISOs and highlight only the soft skills. To become a successful CISO, you must certainly have leadership, communication, presentation, and many more skills, but at a time where cyberattacks are getting much more complicated and threat actors are becoming much more dangerous and persistent, CISOs should be able to lead and assess their teams to combat such kinds of advanced threats. Therefore, soft skills and technical skills should be in balance for CISOs, and technical skills and background should not be seen as a bogeyman.

In my experience, if you are a cybersecurity researcher professional and have a strong technical background in areas such as penetration testing, malware analysis, reverse engineering, and so forth, you will probably have a high chance of hearing *"Isn't he/she too technical?"* from critics when you try to take a step back from management positions such as **vice president** (**VP**) or CISO.

I am a security enthusiast and have been passionate about this field since my childhood. I was therefore really amazed—and still am—with the "technical" parts, the puzzle of cybersecurity. I have read bunches of *technical* articles and books, have published more than 150 *technical* articles, and have spoken at various *technical* cybersecurity conferences. I am 100% confident that you will have noticed how many times I repeated the word *technical*. In consequence, I was negatively stamped by the word *technical* in the middle of my career, and that brought a challenge to overcome in becoming a VP and then a CISO.

My career began by discovering a security vulnerability in the web application of the university that I was studying at in 2003. After sharing my findings with the executives, I was awarded an achievement grant and recruited as an ethical hacker.

After my previous employer, which was a bank, was targeted by an unknown **advanced persistent threat** (**APT**) group and had a security breach, they decided to revise their security organization, established a cyber defense center, and hired me as the VP in 2018. Usually, being a VP means spending little or no time on hands-on technical tasks in your daily business routine but spending much more time on managerial tasks—the ones including people.

When I became a VP, I heard some rumors circulating about me. Many of them had something in common: "*Is he not too technical to be a VP?*" Well, if you manage technical teams that detect and defend the enterprise against the most dangerous threat actors and APT groups, having a strong technical background and leading your team in which steps it should take in an APT attack or a security incident is a blessing. Trust me—that motivates people in teams that you manage, makes them feel safe, and also satisfies executive management who do not want to experience any more security nightmares.

To become a good leader, I added much more stamps besides *technical* by reading many leadership books, listening to audiobooks about management, attending security training, achieving non-technical security certification, improving my soft skills, and keeping both technical and soft skills in balance. Now, I am a CISO in an IT subsidiary of a bank, with a strong technical background and strong managerial and leadership skills. I will continue improving my technical skills for leading and supporting my teams in any emergency situation.

Before ending my contribution to this book, in thinking of transitioning from a technical position to a management position, you will probably hear some advice about the difficulties of managing people. They will tell you some horror stories, but believe me—that does not mean that you will have the same experience. It really depends on how good you are at communication, listening, and empathy. Until you try, you don't know what you can do. Keep in mind that people are like flowers. If you water them enough, they will grow and be a part of your success; otherwise, they will dry up and be part of your failure.

By way of conclusion, becoming a CISO with technical background and skills is a tremendous power, so do not hesitate to become one. Try to keep your soft and technical skills in balance to communicate with your team and also the C-level executives, board members, stakeholders, and business partners.

About Mert Sarica

Mert is a well-known and respected cybersecurity researcher, speaker, and blogger.

In October 2020, Mert became Executive VP/CISO of IT Security & Risk Management Group, which incorporates Cyber Defense Center, Cyber Security Technologies, Cyber Security Architecture, Information Security and Risk Management teams (40 **human capitals – HCs**) at InterTech. InterTech is an IT subsidiary of DenizBank, owned by Emirates NBD.

Between January 2018 and September 2020, as the VP, Mert was responsible for the management of Akbank's **Cyber Defense Center** (**CDC**), which incorporates vulnerability management, threat detection, threat response, intel, and security engineering teams (26 HCs).

From 2007 to 2017, Mert was responsible for performing and managing penetration tests, malware analysis, and security incident detection and response as a technical lead in the Threat and Vulnerability Management team at IBTech (IT subsidiary of QNB Finansbank).

From 2014 to 2016, Mert instructed a Malware Analysis course in the Cyber Security graduate program at Bahçeşehir University.

In 2003, Mert's career began by discovering a security vulnerability in the e-portal web application of Yeditepe University, where he was studying at that time. After sharing his findings with the executives of the university, he was awarded an achievement grant and recruited as an ethical hacker. In 2006, Mert graduated in Information Systems and Technologies from Yeditepe University and completed the Master of Business Administration program at Yeditepe University in 2010.

Since the beginning of 2011, Mert has spoken at more than 30 technical cybersecurity conferences. In addition, he was invited as a guest speaker to more than 40 universities to share with students his cybersecurity career journey and his profession as an ethical hacker, acting as a role model to them.

How a modern CISO could work on improving security within their organizations and maintain a good cybersecurity posture – by Dr. Mike Jankowski-Lorek and Paula Januszkiewicz

Having worked in the cybersecurity and IT industry for over 10 years, I have seen how the perception of the CISO role across many organizations has changed. The CISO role was evolving at the beginning; there was no specific outline of CISO tasks and responsibilities, but as time went on, it became more and more imperative for many organizations.

Now, in the era of cyberattacks and data breaches, the role of a CISO has increased immensely, especially taking into consideration the ever-growing need for an urgent and comprehensive response to emerging threats in the cyber world. Today, CISOs are an integrative part of companies' C-level suite, thus having their resolute word about cybersecurity strategy and resilience. Modern CISOs are not only technical professionals but also great managers, leaders, and mentors. Along with evolving cyber threats and technological advancement, the role of CISO is on the rise as well, becoming more innovative and oriented on the strategy in the business context.

As CQURE experts, we work with many organizations and advise multiple CISOs, and therefore we would like to share our insights on how modern CISOs could work on improving security within their organizations and maintain a good cybersecurity posture. Furthermore, we will also uncover how cybersecurity experts can transform into CISOs.

How could a CISO work on improving security within their organization and stay ahead of the game?

It goes without saying that CISOs are sitting at the forefront in leading cybersecurity strategy from vision into reality, and therefore it is imperative for them to embrace security across many dimensions, including their daily routine. It would be next to impossible, however, to elaborate on and address each and every peculiarity of cybersecurity best practices, but we would still like to provide you with the most important tips on how to stay proactive and be a super-secure CISO.

Tip 1 – Choose a framework

It is generally known how tremendous the importance of an implemented cybersecurity framework is in *ANY* organization. Even more imperative for a CISO would be to choose and adopt their own framework that will take into consideration the company's environment and business context. The base framework could be one of the well-known and tested frameworks, such as NIST CSF, ISO *27001/27002*, or PCI DSS. Of course, it should also ensure it meets compliance aspects that are applicable in a given industry—they should be addressed in the framework as well. Of course, having an implemented cybersecurity framework also implies that the CISO has complete visibility over the organization—this will definitely help in taking decisions adequate to the IT infrastructure and documented procedures. It shouldn't be forgotten that frameworks always require reality checks so that the real cybersecurity posture of an organization can be verified to show what is written on paper or what IT managers are informing the supervisor about.

Tip 2 – Ensure proper communication of your cybersecurity needs across the organization

As mentioned earlier, a CISO is not only technically oriented—they are a manager and a leader who also possesses great soft and organizational skills, such as clear communication and the ability to work with cross-functional teams. It is imperative for any CISO to be able to clearly communicate the need for cybersecurity organization-wise. One of the challenges that we see at CQURE while working with CISOs and cybersecurity teams is that they are constantly struggling with the conviction across their co-workers from non-IT teams that cybersecurity is purely a technical concern with which they have nothing in common. We believe the reason for that is a lack of clear communication and understanding that cybersecurity is an activity for the whole organization on different functional levels. For example, from our experience, there are often no defined cybersecurity requirements for third-party vendors when it comes to application development. A CISO should be a part of the process of security requirements' definition (functional and business) for such applications, and the aforementioned frameworks could be helpful. Quite often, cybersecurity concerns are neglected in this process—as a result, developers create applications without factoring in further penetration tests, which in turn has an impact on the security posture of a developed solution. A CISO should communicate to the business owners the security requirements, including the format of the penetration testing (for example, this should be performed internally or by a third party) and its frequency.

Another important point is to remember about third-party contractors or **managed service providers** (**MSPs**) is that it is crucial to **control whether they are compliant** with cybersecurity standards. A CISO should be sure that such partners have implemented CSFs or performed cybersecurity audits, because the more privileged access to the company's environment they have, the greater the attack surface is. What is also important to mention in this context is that following our own observations as well as the reports from national cybersecurity agencies, we can observe increased activity among APT groups, targeting organizations through MSPs.

Another aspect of proper communication should be considered—the *WAY* it is performed. From our experience of advising CISOs, we see that a key challenge for them is that their employees are often *tired* of a standard approach and repeating the same patterns with regard to communicating about cybersecurity. We advise you to think about that this way: every 3 months, a non-IT person gets a notification from a local IT security team that they should use complex passwords or not click on links. Of course, at a certain point, a user will just start ignoring such campaigns because there will be no novelties there. Therefore, a CISO should try to find a balance between too many similar (often trivial) campaigns and too-simple messages. On the other hand, it is important not to overload co-workers with too much cybersecurity and ask a local marketing team to help with proper framing. We would also advise you to change from time to time the *form* of the communication: for example, to move the focus of secure practices from being oriented on the company to secure practices at home (which, in fact, still relates, in a majority of the aspects, to the company). The colleagues across the whole organization will definitely become more attentive to the topic of cybersecurity if it is more dynamic and not focusing only on daily routine at work.

In this context, it is also important to emphasize the management component of the CISO role—they need to ensure necessary resources (budget and people) to achieve cybersecurity goals. In order to do so, a CISO should be communicating clearly about increasing needs and requirements. One of the ways to persuade a C-level into bringing cybersecurity onto the agenda is to perform a dedicated cybersecurity awareness campaign for **very important persons** (**VIPs**). This is a great way to show C-level people how important it is to invest in the cybersecurity of the organization, and from our experience, such **security awareness training** (**SAT**) campaigns indeed result in more attention and interest being paid to it.

Tip 3 – Build a roadmap step by step

When it comes to roadmaps, we highly recommend CISOs build their cybersecurity roadmaps based on performed audits. Earlier, we mentioned the necessity for a reality check of the cybersecurity posture—this is also necessary for building an effective roadmap that will address existing gaps and issues and will be based on real-world inputs. The prioritization of goals is often not the easiest task to perform. However, we would recommend CISOs have long-term goals but also use in full the potential of small ones. Smaller goals can help gain quick changes that can significantly increase the cybersecurity posture. By making smaller steps, CISOs will see the progress in a more dynamic way, which is also good for reporting on their own activities as a CISO. Of course, it is also important to have big changes in mind in the future, but to achieve them, we advise you to always start with smaller steps or low-hanging fruits that might increase cyber resistance until the readiness for major changes is achieved.

Tip 4 – Improve your cybersecurity arsenal and invest in cyber TI

Our recommendations couldn't help but include this important point—CISOs should constantly enlarge their cybersecurity arsenal. Besides some obvious recommendations such as having implemented EDR, SIEM, log collectors across the whole infrastructure, and **product information management/privileged access management (PIM/PAM)** solutions, we would also recommend considering using **cyber TI**. Such tools/solutions/ services allow staff to be updated about ongoing attacks and incidents and have a clear view of how they might impact the organization's security posture. They provide the IT security team with updated, quick, and constant feeds about new emerging threats, attackers, and techniques. These context-specific insights are imperative if a CISO wants to enhance security controls and improve reactions to ongoing incidents, taking into consideration the organization size, business model, and industry. Cyber TI solutions are a great source of information if a CISO wants to make smart decisions about security and evaluate a potential surface of attack.

Tip 5 – Develop your cybersecurity team

Every CISO should remember that cybersecurity is not only about technical solutions! Cybersecurity is also about people. Even if there are top technical solutions monitoring all events, a CISO still needs to have a professional team to configure them and react to incidents in a more custom way. This is especially true for solutions that are AI-based. Such solutions are indeed great—they learn more over time, recognize patterns, detect anomalies, and can handle huge amounts of data before providing any response. However, such solutions still require someone to fully understand how attackers are acting and how to distinguish false positives from real threats.

Therefore, we consider it paramount to build a cybersecurity team and accelerate its skills and knowledge, especially with regard to proper and systematic reactions to incidents. In order to approach this aspect holistically, we would recommend CISOs develop a detailed hiring plan (of course, with the internal HR team), in which they can set expectations and requirements from potential candidates. Also, internal IT staff shouldn't be forgotten about on a roster of candidates—maybe there'll be those who would like to expand their skills and go into cybersecurity. From our experience at CQURE, such an approach to hiring could be also very beneficial because internal hires already possess a solid knowledge (for example, all ins and outs) of the company's infrastructure and systems, so they won't have to learn it all from zero.

Tip 6 – Embrace table-top exercises

Another aspect we observe is that many organizations, besides implementing cybersecurity solutions, frameworks, and **standard operating procedures** (**SOPs**), *do not practice* scenarios of the most popular attacks and, most importantly, they don't practice how to react to them properly organization-wise. This gives them a false sense of safety and readiness for incidents that is brutally tested at some point, showing real gaps and problems that were not anticipated. Let's take a real-life example when backups are to be reproduced after an incident: in these rather common settings, the IT infrastructure team cannot start the backup procedure globally because the documentation or the credentials needed for the launch have also been encrypted or are simply not available. In a critical situation when a rapid reaction from the cross-functional teams is needed, there's no time for creating procedures and preparing a response team. In order to avoid delays in reaction and improper responses to incidents, we would highly recommend performing **table-top exercises** (**TTXs**). This is a great way to check the organization's critical procedures and verify reactions to incidents across the organization. Any TTX is based on realistic scenarios and resembles a dynamic game in which a facilitator introduces scenario and injects the following the actions taken by the team. Such exercises could be performed on absolutely different levels (global, regional, local) and can involve either focused teams (IT only) or cross-functional (IT, marketing, HR, and so on). TTXs are also helpful when it comes to improving existing SOPs and boosting the team's skills—a CISO will be able to see if utilized procedures are indeed effective and the respective team possesses all the necessary knowledge. In any case, we would highly recommend performing such exercises at least once a year to ensure the organization is all set before an incident occurs.

Tip 7 – Be ready for incidents

As a CISO, you can be definitely sure of one thing—sooner or later, there will be an important cybersecurity incident. It is not the question of *if*, but rather *when*. Therefore, the role of the CISO in this context is extremely important.

First of all, a CISO's primary task is to prepare the organization for incidents—we have already elaborated on ways to do this effectively and what needs to be done prior to an incident. However, we would also like to underscore the importance of having a contract for ad hoc support with a third-party organization if there's no SOC at a given organization. It is of paramount importance to have well-defined terms of a contract, including an SLA and communication channels, so that a CISO won't have to look for immediate support and negotiate rates when the infrastructure has already been hacked. Another point we would like to emphasize is that the partner who is chosen as an IR support should be *reliable*. Those who have already experienced serious incidents in their organization probably know how stressful such situations are, so in order to reduce this stress a little bit, we advise you to find a partner who will be strongly trusted and relied upon.

Secondly, it is the CISO's responsibility to ensure a proper and timely reaction at the moment of an incident—SOPs, playbooks, and IR plans are definitely a CISO's must-have. By the time of an incident, a CISO should already have a real and clear picture of the incident readiness, such as availability of the documentation, logs, contact persons, alternative communication channels, and so on in case of a major incident.

Thirdly, we advise you not to neglect the *lessons-learned phase* after an incident because it is vitally important for avoiding the same type of incident in the future and minimizing its impact on the organization. Also, a CISO should keep track of necessary changes after the IR has been implemented.

Tip 8 – Talk to other CISOs and broaden your knowledge

There is no limit to perfection, they say; it is important to bring your skills and knowledge to the next level. This relates not only to reading a lot about cybersecurity events and news or getting another certificate—it is also about networking and building the CISO community. In our opinion, networking opens up a unique opportunity to exchange experiences with other CISOs and discuss best practices or challenges for the industry. Altogether, CISOs may come up with new solutions or approaches to existing problems, and find new ways of how to deal with them.

In addition to the tips for those who are already CISOs, several recommendations for CISOs-to-be have also been prepared, which will hopefully be inspiring!

One of the primary things for an aspiring CISO is to have a *vision*. You should always stay ahead of the game and be able to forecast how cybersecurity will be progressing in the future. Such a wide and forward-looking perspective will allow a future CISO to learn how to set the right priorities. This is, of course, an important skill that any CISO needs in order to be able to develop a cybersecurity strategy that will be realistic and addresses core issues. Having worked with many CISOs, we have also noticed that all of them are capable of taking a holistic view when it comes to cybersecurity. This ability helps them in taking the right strategic decisions, thus factoring in a wide range of cybersecurity events, updates, and developments. It is also necessary to implement the main CISO's responsibility—for example, developing and overseeing a cybersecurity strategy.

Another aspect that is essential for any cybersecurity professional is to get the skills certified. Our team at CQURE possesses such certificates as CISM, CISSP, CCISO, and many others. Having such certificates is imperative if you want to lead a team of cybersecurity professionals and have a solid understanding of cybersecurity at organizations. Of course, as the role of CISO has a huge managing component, it would be highly advisable to get educated in management as well. At the very beginning, we mentioned that soft skills are also necessary for a *good* CISO, and management skills are definitely number one out there.

That said, in our view, technical experience could be partly compensated if a CISO-to-be is constantly developing their knowledge and looking for external support, especially in the initial phases of being a CISO. At CQURE, we work closely with many CISOs, advising them on building cybersecurity roadmaps, enhancing strategy, and taking the right decisions. In our opinion, it is always good to have an internal CISO with some external support because of the wider knowledge about the organization and its internal processes. Therefore, a CISO should have a deep understanding of the organization they are going to work at. Structure, IT assets, information flow—a CISO needs to know almost everything about the organization in order to be able to come up with "good fits" in terms of decisions, procedures, and approaches.

For those cybersecurity professionals who plan to be CISOs, we would advise you to develop the ability to communicate cybersecurity needs in a transparent and clear way. A CISO won't be talking only to a local IT team or SOC (if there is one); they will also have to deal with the business owners, managers, and executives, who are not always technically skilled. This only contributes to how important it is to keep working on the communication style and approach to the framing of cybersecurity needs. It is important not to forget to be open for the business needs too—you just need to find a resolute way of "injecting" the cybersecurity needs into the strategic agenda.

Of course, networking is another important recommendation for a CISO-to-be. The network that is built before you become a CISO will be made use of afterward. The connections made in the cybersecurity industry will allow you to expand your knowledge in the field, stay up to date with ongoing cybersecurity events, and, of course, it may be useful for the future because you may probably meet other future CISOs as well.

And last but not least, our recommendation for future CISOs is this: remember that a CISO is not only a manager. They are also leaders and mentors for the team that works alongside them. Teammates will come to a CISO with different questions and they will seek the CISO's guidance and support. In our opinion, what makes a great CISO mentor is enthusiasm, an ability to give honest though respectful feedback, and an eagerness to invest in others.

If you are already a CISO, you can always reach out to CQURE—we will be more than happy to support you with building cybersecurity roadmaps, being your advisor in implementing a cybersecurity strategy, and preparing you and your team for incidents, including TTXs. You can also rely on CQURE when it comes to IR services and cybersecurity audits! We perform penetration tests of the highest quality and target everything, starting from web and mobile apps, infrastructure, and even IoT!

The role of the CISO is indeed very complex and demands a lot of work and effort. However, if you follow the preceding tips, work closely with the team, and absorb knowledge (from inside and outside of the organization), you will definitely succeed in being a super-secure CISO.

About Dr. Mike Jankowski-Lorek

Dr. Mike is a security expert, solution architect, and developer with more than 12 years' experience in the field. He specializes in the areas of databases and network and identity management, mainly for the Microsoft ecosystem.

He holds multiple certifications, especially related to security, databases, and software development.

He is passionate about IT and education (he has a Ph.D. degree in computer science).

About Paula Januszkiewicz

Paula Januszkiewicz is a Microsoft Security Enterprise expert specializing in penetration tests, audits, architecture consulting, training, and seminars.

She is the founder of CQURE Academy. Paula likes to share her expertise with the community by blogging, writing articles, and books.

Advice for a CISO – by Raif Sarica and Şükrü Durmaz

After a few hours' hot discussion about the best advice to give to a CISO candidate, we ended up with just one simple word: awareness. We believe that creating and maintaining awareness among employees of an organization must be the number-one priority of a CISO. From the top management to the front desk personnel at the entrance of the organization's building, a cybersecurity culture and behavior model against the probable threats or risks to the organization's IT infrastructure must be established because employee awareness is the first and most risky line of defense against cyber threats. Before delving into the details, we especially want to put an emphasis on upper management because most executives think that cybersecurity is the responsibility of IT personnel only, and they are free to do whatever they want on their computers because IT personnel will protect them regardless of their mistakes. For that reason, a CISO must be very careful about creating awareness among upper management. After giving this first piece of advice, let's delve into the details.

Although the cybersecurity concept is about people, processes, and technology, the industry has been mainly focusing on technology and processes for years. To us, the most important aspect of cybersecurity—people—has, unfortunately, been disregarded or taken for granted. However, we all should understand the fact that people are at the heart of cybersecurity, and the human factor should be prioritized to improve the cyber resiliency of an organization. The industry is generally investing in providing the best cybersecurity tools, but this approach cannot be enough to create a secure infrastructure for protecting information. The human factor of cybersecurity must also be addressed by organizations with a well-informed and proactive workforce.

Organizations may have the best cybersecurity tools in the market or they may have the best practices, policies, and procedures ever documented, but all will share the fate of being void without the human element that is responsible for using or implementing them. The best SIEM, SOAR, **data loss prevention (DLP)** tools, or **intrusion prevention system (IPS)**, no matter how advanced or sophisticated they are, will not provide any benefit if you don't have cyber risk-aware personnel because these tools will always be constrained by the employees of the organization. Simply put, technological tools work with a binary system such as on or off, open or closed, white and black, yes or no. There cannot be a gray area if we are talking about digital technology, and the rules are very simple: one or zero. For example, on a firewall, you can either open a port or just close it. There is no alternative that you can leave the port halfway open. Thus, having 100% control of hardware or software is the easiest part of enforcing cyber resilience. On the other hand, the alternatives are countless when it comes to human beings. We can experience so many different emotions that undeniably affect our behaviors. We can be happy, sad, angry, joyful, disgusted, fearful, surprised, anxious, pessimistic, optimistic, and so on. Emotions, which evolved over millions of years for the survival of our species, are the main source of our behaviors, and almost all of them are in the gray area. You cannot feel 100% happy or sad because there could always be a better or worse situation. There cannot be a level of satisfaction if you are talking about happiness because we are insatiable and always ask for more. Although we declare that we are the most reasonable creatures on the planet, that we use reasoning effectively, and that we always decide based on our logical evaluations or we decide what to do by weighing the anticipated risks against the benefits of our actions, the truth is the exact opposite because our behaviors are mainly under the control of our emotions rather than reasoning. Scientifically speaking, our limbic system has more control over our behaviors, thoughts, and feelings than the frontal cortex. Hormones such as serotonin, endorphin, oxytocin, dopamine, and cortisol that affect the amygdala are the main cause of our thoughts and behaviors. To tell you the truth, the conscious mind—in other words, the frontal cortex—makes up less than 10% of our total brain functions. In reality, we are just one of the mammals with a slightly bigger frontal cortex. Considering the countless states of mind or emotions that we may have, human beings are the most difficult and, at the same time, the most important element for creating cybersecurity resilience in an organization. For these reasons, the main priority of a CISO must be focusing on the human element of cybersecurity, and they should work heavily on creating a culture and behavior model throughout their organization.

If we agree that human factors underlying the cyber risks are the most difficult and important ones to cope with, then we can delve into the strategies that a CISO may think about implementing. First and foremost, we can start with improving the well-known and truly accepted concept of humans being the weakest link in the cybersecurity chain. A CISO should improve upon and rephrase this concept as "*understanding human beings is the weakest link in the cybersecurity chain.*" Along with cybersecurity training on regular basis, a CISO should consider new and better ways of communicating about cybersecurity with employees. They should think about and conceptually understand how employees receive cybersecurity messages during awareness training, how they are reacting, and what positive behavioral changes are created. This approach mostly involves understanding the ways of thinking, making decisions, consequently behaving based on these thoughts and decisions, or—simply put—how our brains are working. For that reason, a CISO should also be knowledgeable about psychology, sociology, and even neuroscience. Considering our brains' processing methods, a CISO should know the phenomenon of "*shortcuts in the brain,*" also called heuristics, which in fact have a significant influence on how we behave. We believe that heuristics or cognitive biases should at least be taken into consideration to positively affect the behavior of employees and create a positive cybersecurity culture in the organization.

Here are some examples of heuristics:

- Social proof

- Fear

- Optimism bias

Let's look at these heuristics, starting from the social proof concept, which causes people to behave like those around them, especially when they don't know how to act. As Robert Cialdini clearly argued in his book *Influence: The Psychology of Persuasion* (*Constantinides, P. (2013). The failure of foresight in crisis management: A secondary analysis of the Mari disaster. Technological Forecasting and Social Change, 80(9), 1657-1673*), people who don't know how to behave in a certain situation will imitate what other people are doing and seek guidance for their actions. The social proof theory makes us figure out the correct behavior through reference to what other people think is correct.

As we all accept, cyber threats and risks are not something that everyone can have detailed information or knowledge about. So, from the perspective of employees, the best or the most guaranteed option for them would be imitating the behaviors of people around them. They will look around and imitate other employees who seem to know or understand the steps to be taken against those cyber threats. Suppose that you conduct a social engineering simulation exercise in your organization and inform employees about the results during one of your training sessions. Do you say that 20% of staff downloaded a malware-infected file or do you say 80% did not download the file? If you are aiming to positively influence the behaviors of staff and encourage them to practice secure behaviors, it would be much more fitting to highlight the positive behaviors of others and promote the percentage of people who did not download the file. You don't have to mention 20% because everybody has basic mathematical knowledge and can subtract 80 from 100. Instead of inadvertently using social proof against yourself, let them do the math and encourage positivity, leading them toward the correct behavior.

Fear that protects us from negative events is the second heuristic to consider when creating a cybersecurity culture in the organization. As the early warning system of the brain for probable unpleasant events, fear plays a crucial role and causes us to be cautious prior to making any decisions. However, it can only be useful when it is optimally matched to actual risk. A disproportionate fear approach always results in problems by causing overestimation or underestimation. On top of that, fear should be handled very carefully to motivate employees toward positive behaviors. Unfortunately, the traditional cybersecurity approach has been to use fear improperly. Delivering scary messages to employees in order to prevent them from making mistakes just does not work because people are mainly drawn more to positive messages than to negative ones. For that reason, a CISO should use clear, non-technical, and positive language while explaining cyber threats, their probable danger, and the recommended behavior to tackle them. Along with probable unwanted results, we must highlight the positive outcomes and benefits that the organization will gain from good cybersecurity. Fear-based or technical messages to non-technical audiences will do nothing more than lead them away from the end goal. Additionally, we should always take into account that human beings' never-ending curiosity always wins. When we ask employees not to click on suspicious-looking links or to use strong passwords for each account, we must clearly make them understand the risks, why these requests are important, and how we will stop cyberattacks with these precautions, ensuring that no stone is left unturned.

Optimism bias is the third heuristic that a CISO should be aware of. We want to start explaining this heuristic with a quote by the Architect from the movie *The Matrix*: "*Hope, it is the quintessential human delusion, simultaneously the source of your greatest strength, and your greatest weakness.*" Hope can be a driving force to achieve the most difficult tasks successfully, but at the same time, overly expected or unbalanced hope can be the sole reason for our failure. Hope is the reason why most of us are optimistic. Actually, our never-ending or insatiable appetite for happiness hormones such as serotonin, endorphin, oxytocin, and dopamine is the main cause of hope and optimism bias. We simply always seek happiness. Unfortunately, hope or optimism bias is a double-edged sword due to our tendency toward overestimating the likelihood of positive outcomes while underestimating the likelihood of bad things happening. As with other areas of our lives, optimism bias is also valid for the cybersecurity area. The training team may explain how big and dangerous threats are or how likely employees are prone to be hacked, but employees will still retain their optimism with underestimated thoughts. They will create excuses such as: "*I am just front desk personnel. Why would hackers want my data? The probability of the finance department being hacked is more likely than my department.*" It won't matter how many cyberattack or data breach statistics you provide, as they will still successfully find excuses to exclude themselves from these dangers until a time when they're actually facing them. To overcome optimism bias before any cyberattack happens, a CISO should find ways to encourage them to follow the organization's cybersecurity policy and procedures. Instead of bombarding employees with lots of probable threats and catastrophic consequences of attacks, a CISO should put themselves in the employees' shoes, take their side, use a more optimistic and empowering tone, and convince them that the threat is real, but there are just a few simple and straightforward steps needed to stop hackers. This approach will definitely be enough to convince employees to change their minds and engage in desired cybersecurity behaviors.

About Şükrü Durmaz

Şükrü is one of the leading experts in the field of cybercrime investigations on a global scale. He is an award-winning speaker and technical expert in worldwide conferences organized by the **International Criminal Police Organization (INTERPOL)**, the **European Union Agency for Law Enforcement Cooperation (Europol)**, the **International Association of Gendarmeries and Police Forces with Military Status (FIEP)**, the **North Atlantic Treaty Organization (NATO)**, and the **Organization for Security and Co-operation in Europe (OSCE)**.

About Sarif Sarica

After serving more than 23 years in the Turkish Gendarmerie, Sarif recently joined **Digital Forensics Services (DIFOSE)** as **chief information officer (CIO)**. DIFOSE provides investigative, consulting, and training services.

Cybersecurity leadership demystified – Pave your way to becoming a world-class modern-day cybersecurity expert and a global CISO – by Dr. Timothy C. Summers

Calling for nothing less than transformative innovation in how cybersecurity is structured, managed, and designed, Summers provides a strategic model for building resilient organizations with a security posture that does the following:

- Welcomes normal chaos
- Establishes resilience
- Uses agility to embrace change
- Seeks innovation where it lives

Building upon the latest research and experience, Summers suggests that innovation in cybersecurity leadership is likely to create a long-term advantage for future companies. Building on insights from his body of work *How Hackers Think*, he describes how cybersecurity leaders, today and tomorrow, can get a head start on the future of building tomorrow's best practices today.

In this section, you will gain an understanding of the following:

- The tremendous challenges that will determine competitive success in an age of normal chaos
- The harmful effects of stagnant, reactive cybersecurity management
- The unconventional cybersecurity leadership principles that must become part of every organization's design
- How disruptive technologies such as AI and blockchain will change traditional cybersecurity roles and the emergence of digital trust
- The strategies for future CISOs to build a 21st-century cyber system.

This section provides essential advice for (1) people interested in becoming a CISO or **Chief Information Security and Digital Trust Officer (CISDTO)**; (2) people who are already as CISOs; and (3) people who want to be cybersecurity leaders in the age of the next-generation internet.

The future of cybersecurity leadership – by Timothy C. Summers, Ph.D.

Defending from unwanted foreign influence and disruption is as old as humanity itself. In 1788, Alexander Hamilton acknowledged that having a massive ocean separating the United States from the rest of the world served as an important factor in America's security. Still, he asserted that improvements in technology would make distant nations into next-door neighbors. In no place or time has his wisdom been more relevant than in the Information Age, which we live in today. To no population is it more accurate than to those in cybersecurity.

To say that we're living in exciting times is an understatement. Over the last 2 decades alone, we've seen catastrophic natural and environmental disasters such as earthquakes and floods (for example, Hurricane Katrina in 2005 and the Haiti earthquake in 2010), mechanical and technological failures (for example, the **British Petroleum (BP)** oil spill in the Gulf of Mexico in 2010), human-induced disasters such as terrorism (for example, 9/11), economic crises (for example, the subprime market collapse), and biological threats such as pandemics (for example, the Coronavirus pandemic in 2020). There is broad recognition that our world is complex—one that is abundant with space-rocket billionaires, human-mimicking AI, and relentless waves of ransomware disrupting entire swathes of logistics and supplies across the world.

To minimize the risk to organizations and make the right decision for the best outcomes, cybersecurity leaders attempt to identify and detect possible vulnerabilities, take action to mitigate them, and, if necessary, contain disruption and finally recover. This approach is not wrong but is disadvantageous, as it assumes that if the organization experiences a cyberattack, it is due to its failure of foresight, with the sentiment that with a little more effort, "*we should have been able to foresee the problem and prevent it.*" It assumes that cybersecurity leaders will produce perfect plans supported by perfect equipment and governed by perfect rules that will be executed by perfectly trained people without any room for error. This perfect worldview perpetuates a culture of imperfection shaming and seeking someone to blame. Implicit to the perfect worldview is the idea of equilibrium (that is, steady-state). Cybersecurity leaders are aware of the following three truths:

1. Culture eats strategy for breakfast.
2. There is no such thing as a steady-state organization.

3. Rules and regulations only work when the environment is stable (*Leveson, N., 2011. Engineering a Safer World, Systems Thinking Applied to Safety. London: MIT Press*; *Thompson, J. D., 1967. Organizations in action. New York: McGraw-Hill*; *Schulman, P. R., 1993. The Negotiated Order of Organizational Reliability. Administration and Society, 25(3): 353-372.*).

As suggested by Taleb (*Taleb, N. N. (2012). Antifragile: Things that gain from disorder* (*Vol. 3). Random House Incorporated*), the most successful and impactful organizations will either adapt or die in the future.

Organizations seek to ensure the protection of their most valued assets and minimize the risk of a cyberattack. These objectives place three particular demands on organizations: appoint a suitable official to head up their information security strategy and operations (a CISO), establish a cyber design inclusive of digital trust, and ensure that stakeholders are appropriately informed of the organization's security posture and status. Organizations need to be very clear on what they want from the CISO role, expectations to perform, and the corresponding attributes that such an incumbent must possess.

The actual fuel for long-term cybersecurity resilience is not just operational excellence, technology breakthroughs, or new business models. These methods provide temporary advantages, and at some point, a competitor will arrive at superior operations, next-generation technology, or more effective business models. Instead, the key to sustained long-term cybersecurity resilience is innovation—more specifically, finding new and better ways to mobilize your people, effectively allocate resources, and formulate forward-thinking strategies.

The current rules of cybersecurity were designed for an earlier era of business and technology—different types of organizations of a different time. Their emphasis on control and efficiency will no longer suffice in the modern cybersecurity landscape where leaning into agility, adaptability, and creativity underpins and drives cyber success.

With this in mind, the time is now to imagine the future of cybersecurity leadership and become an active participant in inventing tomorrow's successful cybersecurity strategies and practices.

Cybersecurity leadership is out of date. As with many classic technologies, it has essentially stopped evolving, and that's not good. Why? Because we've been focused on management—the capacity to organize resources, plan to get things done, lead effectively, and place guardrails to ensure we meet our goals is central to achieving the human purpose. When management is less effective than we need it to be, we all pay the price. That is why cybersecurity leadership is not limited to the CISO—it is everybody's job.

Ultimately, what constrains the cybersecurity performance of your organization is not its operating model but the way it views cybersecurity leadership. The goal of this section is to encourage you to become a 21st-century cybersecurity pioneer; to equip you to reinvent the principles, processes, and practices of cybersecurity leaders for our post-COVID age. Innovative cybersecurity leaders will have the unique capacity to create long-term advantages for their organizations.

Why is innovative cybersecurity leadership important?

Today, cybersecurity is at the heart of everything an organization does and achieves. Therefore, it is reasonable to assume that for organizations to thrive in the disruptive markets of the 21st century, new and better ways of managing cybersecurity posture will be required. The only way to out-think and out-invent the bad guys will be for companies to find more innovative ways to protect themselves, their customers, and their partners while maintaining the integrity of the digital trust established with each. A shift in how we think about cybersecurity leadership is required.

Recent high-profile attacks show how much more needs to be done in the decade ahead. Cyberattacks are one of the top 10 global risks of most significant concern for the next decade, according to the *World Economic Forum Global Risks Report 2019*, with data fraud and theft ranked 4th and cyberattacks 5th (`http://www3.weforum.org/docs/ WEF_Cybersecurity_Guide_for_Leaders.pdf`). This is why corporate leaders are increasingly elevating the importance of cybersecurity to their organizations. But try as they might, there are massive challenges that must be overcome, such as the following (`https://www.weforum.org/agenda/2021/01/top-cybersecurity-challenges-of-2021/`):

- Cybersecurity challenges are more complex than they used to be
- A fragmented and complex regulatory environment
- Dependence on others in a high-risk landscape
- Lack of widely available cybersecurity talent and expertise
- Hard to track cyber criminals for accountability

We need to rethink what cybersecurity leadership means

The role of the CISO is changing. There is a massive opportunity for CISOs to step into a more valuable, high-profile role within the organization. The core skills of cybersecurity professionals—evaluating and mitigating risk—are as essential for designing cyber-resilient organizations associated with product security, privacy, and regulatory compliance as they are for more traditional IT-related threats. It seems that this broader role requires a change in title and scope that more accurately reflects the convergence of risk and digital trust responsibilities, such as CISDTO or **chief trust officer (CTrO)**.

Taking on a more prominent role requires a broader view and a corresponding set of skills. These executives will need to communicate so that business people understand and build relationships to influence people at all levels across the organization. They also require extensive management and innovative leadership skills to operate at an executive level and inspire expanded risk and security teams.

Historically, companies have expected CISOs and security chiefs to focus on technical tasks and haven't expected much more. Cybersecurity leaders have the monstrous and all-important goal of securing an enterprise. Still, when they make big strategic decisions about business models, digital strategy, products, **mergers and acquisitions (M&A)**, cybersecurity is an afterthought, meaning that the enterprise loses out on the value that the cybersecurity function can bring to bear (`https://hbr.org/2019/11/companies-need-to-rethink-what-cybersecurity-leadership-is`). This was acceptable when the threats were slower and less complex, but today's cyber leaders must embed security throughout business processes and operations, rapidly respond to threats, and influence fellow senior leaders. In short, cybersecurity leaders must be able to lead, and that means organizations need to hire and develop security executives who have the skills to do so.

The CISO must be the enterprise digital trust champion

The CISO must be the digital trust leader and have the capacity to reach out and engage partners across the enterprise, leveraging excellent communication skills and organizational knowledge to home in on strategic assets and review cyber scenarios and outcomes (`https://securityintelligence.com/articles/what-leadership-qualities-for-cisos-are-most-important-in-2020/`). In some cases, the enterprise may implement improved security controls; however, in other instances, the CISO will have to lead negotiations around organizational risk appetite and map it back to the cybersecurity governance and management processes in place.

Strong cybersecurity leaders recognize the importance of strategy

Strategy is a cornerstone of cybersecurity leadership, explicitly identifying and implementing the best practices for protecting enterprise networks from cyber adversaries. Laying the solid ground for enterprise security, developing contingency plans for when things go sideways, and thinking dynamically to solve problems are essential to being an effective cybersecurity leader. As suggested by Veltsos (2020), an effective cybersecurity leader will develop a strategy that will "*shine a light on risk and bring it out into the open*" (`https://securityintelligence.com/articles/what-leadership-qualities-for-cisos-are-most-important-in-2020/`).

Imagining the future of cybersecurity

To come up with breakthrough cybersecurity innovation, you need to have a sound methodology and approach. While the opportunity for ad hoc breakthroughs is there, the enterprise can substantially increase the chances of success by assembling the correct elements, to begin with. In the case of cybersecurity innovation, you should try to gather three key components, as follows:

- A set of principles by which existing cybersecurity norms can be discovered and challenged

- New cybersecurity strategies that have the power to inspire changes in enterprise procedures and practices

- Insights from unexpected places and misbehavior within the enterprise

Cybersecurity leaders must embrace big ideas

For cybersecurity leaders, big ideas should be long-term. But with more disruptive technical innovation happening than ever before, how are cybersecurity leaders supposed to identify strategies that could deliver future growth? Cybersecurity leaders must aim to keep up with the accelerating pace of change to avoid missing out on potential long-term strategic opportunities.

Cybersecurity leaders must seek to understand how their security posture is positively and negatively exposed to AI, **deep learning** (**DL**), big data, cloud computing, and distributed ledger technology. These innovations are changing how the world manages information, analyzes data, purchases and consumes goods, and communicates across the globe.

Successful 21st-century cybersecurity leaders will recognize that disruptive innovation causes rapid cost declines, cuts across sectors, and spawns further innovation. They must look throughout their organization, conducting both top-down and bottom-up research, aiming to identify innovation opportunities early, capitalize on them, and provide long-term value to the enterprise.

Successful cybersecurity leaders must think like business leaders

Nearly every business needs to get transformed by adopting leading technologies and innovative data-driven business models. This is not a simple task but it's a given that cybersecurity operations are a vital element of every business's success. As a cybersecurity leader, you are responsible for educating the board and executive leadership on the importance of cybersecurity management.

It is undeniable that our world is genuinely complex. To establish resilience and cyber dominance, we must accept that heavy reliance on plans and rules is flawed and leaves us vulnerable. This is precisely why in cybersecurity, it is not a question of if, but when. Experience demonstrates that failure happens more frequently than we would like to admit. These failures are often the result of emergent phenomena that overwhelm or shock the organizational system and people. Our current approach to cybersecurity leadership is to produce large and complicated plans, procedures, and behavioral rules to prevent failures (*Lauder, M., Marynissen, H., & Summers, T.* (2017, September). *A study of normal chaos: a new research paradigm. In Seventh International Engaged Management Scholarship Conference; Ashby, W. R., 1956. An Introduction to Cybernetics. London: Chapman & Hall.*). This approach fails to appreciate the point of diminishing returns in cyber-planning exercises. Future cybersecurity leaders will be required to review this and other aspects of failure to better understand the likely consequences and how best to develop cyber programs that establish a culture around coping with new situations within such complexity.

About Dr. Timothy C. Summers

Timothy C. Summers, Ph.D. is a hacker, professor, and consulted cyber and risk strategist specializing in identifying cyber risks and sensitivities within public and private organizations. He is a specialist in understanding the relationship between human thinking and sociotechnical systems. He has served as an executive advisor for one of the world's oldest multinational strategic management firms. He has also been a consultant for *Fortune 500* companies worldwide and is a regularly invited speaker. He's the **chief executive officer** (**CEO**) of Summers & Company, co-founder of Vitazi.ai, and the Executive Director of Digital Trust Initiatives within the University Technology Office at Arizona State University. He leads the development of Pocket, a digital wallet and portfolio for ubiquitous learning. Dr. Summers is one of the world's leading experts in understanding how hackers think.

Working with security experts – by Vladimir Meloski

An organization's strategic goals always include information security as one of the top priorities. In order for this strategic goal to be achieved, expert knowledge is required.

Security experts are people who have dedicated a significant part of their professional career to learning about security and working with security technologies. Security experts are your first line of defense against security threats. Larger organizations can decide to build their own team of security experts. They create departments and invest in a team that will act proactively and defend the organization from different threats. Small and medium organizations might decide to have a smaller security team, working closely with external companies specialized in security technologies. Another option for small and medium organizations is to outsource security services to external companies specialized in security technologies.

Working with security experts will mean having a team that will support and defend the organization in every step. Security experts will analyze the security risks, constantly monitor trends in security threats, and analyze results that are recorded 24/7 from the SOC. They will analyze the security products offered by vendors and decide what is the most appropriate solution for an organization.

No matter which type of decision is made (having an internal security team, an external security team, or a combination of both), working with security experts will ensure that the organization and its business will be protected and secured.

Analyze the risks

In today's world, some organizations think of the necessity of IT security only in cases when they are somehow affected, or when they have read news of some major security breach that has happened at some other organization.

The main topic when thinking about security is: How can potential security threats affect our business and our customers in a way that our business will be at risk? Starting from this point, organizations can analyze the components of the core business that need to be secured, first at a high level, and then going into details.

There is an old saying, "*If you want to stop the hackers, you need to start thinking like hackers.*" Following this statement, pretending that we are hackers, one of the first questions we would ask ourselves is: How can I attack this organization in order to achieve my goals? From here, we could continue with trying to find every possible way that hackers can attack an organization. You would be surprised how many types of attacks hackers commit against our information security.

By identifying and analyzing the risks, organizations make the first important step against any potential threat. They know what kinds of security issues could happen, and they start building a security strategy that will defend them against security threats.

Constantly monitor trends in security threats

In the IT industry, there are many statements that are often misinterpreted. One of them is "*set it and forget it,*" referring to the systems that work reliably and after the initial configuration do not need any additional management and maintenance. This statement is very wrongly transferred to information security systems as well.

Here is one example: "*We have bought this great expensive firewall, which is a set-it-and-forget-it device, very easy to configure, and we do not need to worry about it anymore, because we are now protected and secure.*" Totally wrong! No matter how expensive the security technology is, hackers never sleep, so they always invent something new that might be challenging for any security technology. Any security technology, no matter whether it is a firewall, anti-malware software, or a cloud security appliance, must be constantly monitored. All logs and information that those technologies collect must be parsed and analyzed in detail, conclusions must be defined by security experts, and the appropriate defensive action should be performed. Organizations' security experts should regularly meet with security device/software vendors in order to discuss questions related to device/software usage and feed back on its functionalities.

The security device/software must be constantly monitored, updated, and tuned in order to use its full potential and to meet the organizations' security and business requirements.

Apply security best practices

For any product or solution that is implemented in an organization, the vendor of that product recommends so-called best practices, which are settings and procedures that will achieve the optimal results with that specific product. For example, *Vendor A* recommends that one of the best practices is to configure their email anti-malware product to block executable attachments.

Every security technology vendor has their own best practices for how to configure, manage, and maintain their product. Security experts should follow these guidelines and apply them so that optimal results are achieved. However, as we mentioned in previous sections, best practices are never set-it-and-forget-it settings. It has been proven over the years that vendors tend to change their best practices because they have found that settings that were best practices in the past are now obsolete, and that best practices should be updated with new settings and procedures.

Best practices should be applied for any security solution. They usually originate from the solution vendor; however, best practices might also be developed by the security team as well, according to team members' experience with specific security technology.

Correlate information from different security products

No matter if you work for a smaller organization or a multinational enterprise, chances are that there are security technologies deployed in your organization that are produced by different vendors—for example, an endpoint protection solution is from *Vendor A*, an email anti-spam and anti-malware solution is from *Vendor B*, and a **cloud access security broker** (**CASB**) solution is from *Vendor C*. In other organizations, you might find that all security technologies deployed are produced from the same vendor.

In both scenarios, it is important that information from the security product, such as logs and reports, is correlated to information from another security product. For example, a CASB collects logs from a firewall and displays security-related information on the central dashboard. If the CASB and the firewall are produced by the same vendor, the information between both products flows between the devices, which are natively integrated. However, every vendor wants to be interoperable with other vendors' security solutions, and therefore most security products have options to connect to another vendor's product with some standard protocol.

Once the products are connected, they will be able to exchange information, correlate the information received, and act accordingly in order to protect the organization's environment.

Deliver regular security training for IT employees

IT departments in organizations are pretty heterogeneous. Depending on the size of organizations, they consist of networking experts, workplace experts, messaging experts, voice experts, developers, and so on.

In an IT department, security is important for each IT employee, and therefore regular security training is essential for strengthening the security of all aspects of the IT infrastructure. For example, after the security training, messaging experts would consider additional security measures related to protection from malware and phishing attacks that have recently been launched on the internet. Developers would analyze their code in order to deploy stronger authentication for apps. Some organizations consider security training as an expensive investment. However, the reality has proved that damage arising from security attacks and breaches can have a far higher cost than the security training itself.

Security threats arise every day, and because of that, knowledge of the security threat received today must be updated tomorrow. Therefore, security training and briefings within the IT department should be regularly scheduled, and IT employees should receive updated security training.

Deliver regular security training for business employees

Business employees in an organization do not have in-depth knowledge of IT or security technologies. They perform their work tasks by using the environment provided by the IT department.

It is very important that business employees are trained on not just how to use the IT environment such as hardware and software, but also on how to secure devices and data they work with. For example, the IT department should deploy MFA to strengthen the security of user identities and their credentials. In this example, it is essential that business employees are trained about what is the purpose of MFA, why it is important to use it, and how to protect their identities and credentials.

The same as for IT employees, business employees should be regularly trained on what are the latest security threats and how to respond to those threats. For example, if there is a new phishing outbreak, they should be trained on how to react to it, and who to inform from the security department regarding any email they suspect might be a phishing attack.

Perform ethical hacking procedures

Many organizations ask themselves this: "*We have invested heavily in security equipment, software, and services. But how do we know if we are prepared to respond to a hacker attack or any other kind of security threat?*"

Ethical hacking procedures involve activities by security experts named ethical hackers, who aim to simulate hacker attacks, phishing attacks, or any other security threat in the organization environment. After the procedures are completed, ethical hackers will deliver a report to the organization that contains a list of all attacks performed and vulnerabilities found (if any). The report also contains recommendations on what steps need to be taken in order to eliminate any potential vulnerabilities.

Ethical hacking should be performed on a regular basis—for example, once per year—because hacker techniques evolve, and organizations need to be assured that their security equipment and procedures can defend against any latest hacker threat.

Implement a security standard

There are organizations that, due to their specific type of work, need to be compliant with different security standards, such as ISO/IEC *27000:2018*, which provides the model of ISMS.

Standards help organizations to verify that they have fulfilled the requirements for securing their data and services. Even if the organization is not obliged to implement standards according to the law or industry regulations, being compliant with security standards helps organizations to establish, maintain, and manage a system for information security.

Organizations should perform regular assessments in order to verify that they are compliant with a specific security standard. Being compliant with a security standard not only helps organizations stay secure but also improves the organization's reputation when working with customers and partners.

Prevention is better than cure

There is an old saying used in medicine, "*Prevention is better than cure*," that can be freely applied to information systems security as well.

If organizations work constantly on improving their security and protecting their infrastructure, data, and services, they will stay secure and prevent any potential security threat. Organizations that do not pay much attention to security and see it as an "*expensive investment*" may face a breach that will cost them much more. It will be more difficult for organizations to recover from attacks that result in security breaches because, in these situations, it is not only data and services that are at risk but also company reputation and trust from customers and partners.

Organizations need to carefully plan and implement a strategy for how to prevent any type of security risk. The security strategy should be regularly assessed and improved upon so that it will address the latest security developments and will use the best security technologies. Having secure information systems is the biggest asset that builds an organization's reputation and helps in its business success.

About Vladimir Meloski

Vladimir Meloski is a Microsoft **Most Valuable Professional** (**MVP**) on Office Server and Services, and a Microsoft Certified Trainer and Consultant, providing unified communications and infrastructure solutions based on Microsoft Exchange Server, Skype for Business, Office 365, and Windows Server.

With a bachelor's degree in computer science, Vladimir has devoted more than 20 years of professional experience in IT. Vladimir has been involved in Microsoft conferences in Europe and the US as a speaker, moderator, proctor for hands-on labs, and technical expert. He has been also involved as an author and technical reviewer for Microsoft official courses, including Exchange Server 2016, 2013, 2010, 2007, Office 365, and Windows Server 2016 and 2012, and is one of the authors of *Mastering Microsoft Exchange Server 2016*.

As a skilled IT professional and trainer, Vladimir shares his best practices, real-world experiences, and knowledge with his students and colleagues, and devotes himself to IT community development by collaborating with IT Pro and developer user groups worldwide.

He enjoys spending his spare time in the country with his son and wife.

A CISO's communication with the board on three critical subjects – by Dr. Süleyman Özarslan

Without a doubt, communicating with the board has become a necessary skill for a CISO. I want to explain three critical subjects of this communication: security posture management, security investment rationalization and compliance, and how the **continuous security validation** (**CSV**) approach helps you with these subjects.

The first subject is security posture management. How do you explain the overall state of your organization's cybersecurity readiness to the board? As a CISO, you need to measure your security posture to answer this question. But the boardroom is not the only reason.

The rapid evolution of cyber threats continues to present substantial security challenges, making it difficult for CISOs to answer critical questions such as "*How secure is my organization right now?*". So, you need to achieve a clear understanding of your security status. You must understand the full scope of your security posture and correctly prioritize areas of relevant risk to protect your organization against breaches, and it is crucial to have an understanding of the effectiveness of each control in reducing your cyber risk. Besides these reasons, you sometimes need to prove the strength of your organization's security posture to third parties—for example, during a cyber insurance assessment process, you will need to show how well your organization is prepared for cyberattacks and can defend itself against attackers. Security posture assessments may also be required during M&As. You can assess the cybersecurity controls of onboarding organizations to establish the level of risk and recommend areas for improvement before a deal is finalized.

How can you measure your organization's security posture? There are five key measures to do this, as outlined here:

- The first measure is **the visibility of your asset inventory and attack surface**. An accurate inventory of all your assets is at the heart of your security posture. Then, you should identify your organization's attack surface, which includes all the ways an attacker can gain unauthorized access to any of your assets through any attack technique.

- In order to identify your security posture, it is crucial to understand the effectiveness of security controls that you use to protect your organization against cyberattacks. Accordingly, the second measure is **security control effectiveness**.

- The next aspect that influences an organization's security posture is **the ability to detect attacks**. It is impossible to prevent all cyberattacks. We need to operate under the *assume breach* mindset, and we cannot fully understand our cybersecurity posture without knowing the current state of compromise.

- A swift and effective response to attacks that we have detected is also crucial for cyber resilience. So, the fourth critical aspect of maintaining a strong security posture is **our ability to react and recover from incidents**.

- **The degree of automation** is a significant factor for your security posture. Attackers use automated tools and techniques to conduct cyberattacks. You need to automate all possible parts of security posture management to keep up to date and stay protected. Automated tools such as asset managers, vulnerability scanners, detection and response solutions, and CSV platforms are crucial for increasing your level of automation and cyber resilience.

The second subject is **security investment rationalization**. How do you explain to the board that the security products you buy really work and your security investments are not wasted?

Organizations run 50 separate security tools on average. However, more tools does not always equate to better security. Moreover, it's worth noting that only 30% of organizations evaluate a security solution based on its impact on decreasing cyber risk. According to a research report of *Ponemon Institute*, only less than half a percent of IT professionals state they have an idea of how well the cybersecurity tools they've deployed are performing, and only 39% of respondents admit they are getting the most out of their security investments.

These statistics show that organizations struggle to rationalize their security investments. However, with most boardrooms now recognizing the importance of investing in cybersecurity, there is an increasing need for security leaders to demonstrate the effectiveness of their security controls, deliver continual improvements, and achieve the best return from budgets. For a CISO, it is vital to rationalize security controls to spend in the right areas since it can be easy to make bad decisions, prioritize the wrong areas, and waste money on disparate tools without quantitative data.

Accordingly, security investment rationalization is a data-driven approach to facilitate strategic decisions about security controls, maximize their effectiveness and efficiency, and achieve the best ROSIs by obtaining a holistic view of how security controls are functioning.

How can you perform a data-driven assessment of your existing security controls to make strategic decisions about cybersecurity investments, such as deciding whether to invest or divest in a specific area or security control? How can you assess the capabilities of security products and **managed security service providers** (MSSPs) in the pre-sales stage? Bear in mind that it is crucial to evaluate the security controls in the production environment.

In order to rationalize investments in security controls, you need to quantify the individual and overall effectiveness of security controls and identify gaps and overlaps in the security control stack, and a CSV approach is the most effective way to provide data and insights to rationalize security controls. For example, the overall effectiveness level of your security controls provided by the Picus Security Control Validation Platform helps a CISO's decisions and communication with the board.

The third critical concern of a CISO and board is **compliance**. As we all know, compliance is the process of adhering to policies. Although the terms *compliance* and *security* are sometimes confused, there are substantial differences between them. For example, compliance is mainly used to meet external requirements and to protect business activities. Legislations, industry regulations, standards, and agreements are examples of external requirements. However, security is focused on internal technical requirements. Compliance is driven by business requirements instead of technical ones. Most importantly, compliance criteria should be regarded as *minimum acceptable practice*, not strictly *best practice*.

For which areas is compliance a significant business concern? For example, you may need to comply with privacy regulations in the country or countries where your organization is located, such as GDPR for **European Union (EU)** countries and the **California Consumer Privacy Act (CCPA)** for the US. Moreover, some industries have heavy regulations. For instance, the payment card industry mandates PCI DSS, and HIPAA is mandated for healthcare organizations in the US. Some clients with high-security maturity also push compliance with some frameworks and standards as contractual terms, such as the MITRE **Adversarial Tactics, Techniques, and Common Knowledge (ATT&CK)** framework, the ISO *27001* standard, and the NIST *800-53* document.

Briefly, your organization may have to comply with some standards and laws to operate in some countries and sectors or acquire new customers. Accordingly, lack of compliance may result in legal and financial consequences that could result in your organization paying hefty fees or being barred from working in a specific geography or industry. Moreover, it may also result in loss of trust and reputational damage.

By continuously testing and helping to improve the effectiveness of security controls, the CSV approach allows organizations to comply with a wide range of regulations and standards. For example, Picus simulates attacks across the cyber kill chain, helping security and risk leaders to understand whether critical assets are protected and whether threats could lead to breaches and the loss or encryption of sensitive personal and financial data.

Picus also provides quickly accessible reports and dashboards that help CISOs to quantify risks, make tactical and strategic decisions, and demonstrate compliance to business leaders and auditors.

About Dr. Süleyman Özarslan

Süleyman is the co-founder and VP of Picus Labs at Picus Security, which develops innovative cybersecurity software that assesses and validates the effectiveness of security controls. He has a Ph.D. in information systems from Middle East Technical University. He has received several academic and professional awards and medals throughout his career, such as the SANS Institute RSA 2016 NetWars Global Interactive Cyber Range Award and a medal from the Centre of Excellence Defense Against Terrorism. He trained security experts from 10 different countries as part of NATO Advanced Cyber Defence training courses. He has 19 years of experience in IT security, with a special focus on cyber threats, malware analysis, penetration testing, application security, and security controls. Süleyman has several professional certificates, such as **Certified Ethical Hacker (CEH)**, **Open Source Security Testing Methodology Manual (OSSTMM) Professional Security Analyst (OPSA)**, and **OSSTMM Professional Security Tester (OPST)**.

Crush the triangle – by Raymond Comvalius

I once wrote a book in 2009. The security chapter started with the famous triangle consisting of three focus areas: security, usability, and cost. The message at the time was to choose two because it was impossible to create a secure and user-friendly solution without adding a significant cost component. What has changed since then?

Well, the security landscape has changed a lot, especially because of the potential cost involved with a breach. In recent years, we have seen many organizations being seriously hurt by ransomware gangs who base their ransom on the profitability of the company in question. The higher the profits or revenues, the higher the ransoms to be paid. This is where chances are for the CISO that it is no longer a theoretical idea that the business might get hurt from an attack. The threat is real, and defense comes at a cost. Today, it is easier than ever before to calculate the cost of a breach.

The first three scenarios that come to my mind are these:

- The core business comes to a halt when critical parts of the assets get encrypted. What is the cost for each day that there is no business? How long does it take to restore, either from a backup or using the keys required to decrypt? Time is what you pay for, anyway.

- Criminals charge a certain amount of money to allow for decryption, usually a (small) percentage of the annual revenues. Will you pay or is there a chance for you to get out without the sacrifice of paying the criminals?

- Data is extracted from the company. Publication of the data may lead to public damage and/or claims from customers, vendors, and business partners. Will you pay, and hope that the other party will keep their word and not ask for more, or—even worse—still go public after you paid?

Conclusion: when your time has come, you're going to pay.

Back to the triangle. Let's visualize cost as the vertical.

Now, look for that point where you pay enough to not get hacked and still allow enough to make a profitable business, as illustrated in the following diagram:

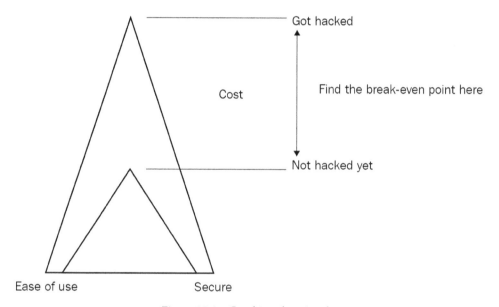

Figure 12.4 – Crushing the triangle

Continuous life-cycle management

Too many organizations rely on old technologies to run their business. These days, legacy equals insecurity. Don't stick to the old stuff because it still works. This can be a recipe for disaster to happen to any company, no matter how large or small the victim may be—be reminded that only one weak spot is required for a hacker to successfully attack your business.

Continuous patch management

The rat race is real. Whenever a new vulnerability becomes public, it's time to patch. It's quite common that a patch is used as the key to develop an exploit if the exploit wasn't already in the wild. A zero-day bug has become a very common phenomenon. This is when a vulnerability is misused before a patch is available. A zero-day bug may sound scary as it may be used to attack the target while the target has no patch and may even have no alternative defense in place. What's even more scary is when the process keeps you from implementing the patch when it's readily available or when a lengthy testing procedure stands in the way.

Once a month may just not be enough for every patch.

Cloud focus

For a long time, the cloud was seen as the more vulnerable option for implementing infrastructure and services. Sometimes, things may still be like this, but those cases are becoming less frequent over time. Flexibility, as well as the scale and agility of the cloud, has become a strength that is currently essentially helping many on-prem implementations to become more secure by providing extra services that are hard or impossible to implement in the relatively small scale of an enterprise data center. Many EDR solutions currently rely on the cloud as it's the fastest way to respond to the ever-changing security landscape.

When your organization shifts toward the cloud, there is usually very little reason not to shift along with it.

Zero trust

It is not because you are on my network that I trust you, and it's not because you're logged on to one of my systems that I trust you. It is not because you have my username and password that I trust you. With zero trust, there is no such thing as implicit trust.

You are only trusted when everything that has to be checked is under control. This may mean that you will only be trusted when you are the right users with the required multi-factor credentials working on a certain endpoint that is compliant and operating from a credible location. Then, I may trust you to access the jewels.

Retention policies

We are living in an era where storage is almost for free. This makes us less willing to clean up. Why should we worry? There is no financial impact in keeping all that data, but what you don't have cannot be stolen. If you keep that in mind, it may become a lot easier to clean up on a regular basis. Many recent data leakage incidents became much worse because the data involved was not supposed to be there in the first place. Lots of information, especially **personally identifiable information** (**PII**), is only supposed to last for a limited time. If you don't clean up, you're not compliant, and you are keeping stuff that you're not supposed to have stored as your assets. Especially when the information contains lots of PII, such as resumes, an organization is supposed to clean things up after the selection procedures. If you didn't and the information is stolen and misused, it's not only the hacker that did wrong, and the fact that you didn't do a proper cleanup can backfire for your organization.

The biggest risk factor – your colleagues

Word has it that the biggest risk of getting hacked is between the keyboard and the chair.

Don't forget about the people while you're taking care of the technology!

About Raymond Comvalius

Raymond is a multi-focused **information and communications technology** (**ICT**) specialist/architect with broad experience in designing and implementing Microsoft-centric IT infrastructures. He has direct experience with companies ranging from small businesses to multinational banks and governments. He is known as an inspiring speaker on a wide range of ICT subjects. He is also active as a Microsoft Certified Trainer, author, and ICT journalist. Raymond specializes in Windows Modern Workplace, cloud transition, security, **public key infrastructure** (**PKI**), clustering, and Windows-based infrastructure design and implementation.

Index

A

access control 101
advanced persistent threat (APT) 201
Adversarial Tactics, Techniques,
    and Common Knowledge
    (ATT&CK) 231
advice, for CISO 211-215
annual general meetings (AGMs) 132
anti-malware programs 19
anti-spyware software 19
artificial intelligence (AI)
  about 197
  strategies, implementing 119
  using, for BC processes 119
  using, for DR processes 119
attack surface 62
attack vectors 17, 61
Automated Teller Machines (ATMs) 46

B

BC landscape
  emerging technologies 120
BC processes
  artificial intelligence (AI), using 119

best cyber-attack strategies
  blind testing strategies 99
  external testing strategies 98
  internal testing strategies 99
  targeted testing strategies 99
best cyber defense strategies
  about 99
  defense in breadth 102
  defense in depth 100, 101
blind testing strategy 99
board of directors
  reporting to 129
business continuity (BC) 192, 193
business continuity plan (BCP)
  about 90
  documenting 90
  key components 116
  risks, identifying 117
  versus disaster recovery
    (DR) plan 118, 119
business impact analysis (BIA)
  about 107, 108, 193
  data classification 108
business opportunities
  considerations, for evaluating 124, 125
  versus security risks 124

business requirements
  knowing 96

C

California Consumer Privacy Act (CCPA)
  about 40, 41, 173
  consequences, of failing to comply
      with regulations 42
  personal information 42
  rights 41, 42
California Insurance Information and
      Privacy Protection Act 41
capital expenditures (CAPEX) 198
CCISO program 13
certified and skilled cybersecurity
      workforce 121
Certified CISO (CCISO) certificate 12
certified CISO programs 10
Certified Ethical Hacker (CEH) 232
Certified Information Security
      Manager (CISM) 13
Certified Information Systems
      Auditor (CISA) 13
Certified Information Systems Security
      Professional (CISSP) 13
Certified in Risk and Information
      Systems Control (CRISC) 13
chief executive officers (CEOs) 6, 52, 127
chief experience officers (CXOs) 180
chief financial officer (CFO) 52
Children's Online Privacy
      Protection Act (COPPA)
  about 48, 173
  compliance 50
  violations 49
CIO 6

CISO
  about 1, 7, 56, 80, 107, 172
  auditing and compliance
      initiatives, leading 19
  becoming 9, 10
  business context 185
  change agent 5
  changing role 8, 9
  compliance 187
  compliance factor 173
  compliance, with international
      regulations 20
  consequences, of non-compliance 20
  defining 2
  ensuring, E2E security operations
      place in organization 172
  governance 186
  influencer 5
  issues, solving 91
  leader 4
  modern marketer 4
  recruitment role 138, 139
  regulations and regulatory
      bodies, examples 20
  responsibilities 3, 11
  risk 186
  role, expanding 8
  role, in organization 175
  security domains 188
  security planning 138
  security policies implementation 137
  strategist 4
  successful, becoming 185
  technical projects 136
  trusted security advisor 4
CISO certification 12

CISO, communication with board
  compliance 231
  security investment rationalization 230
  security posture management 229, 230
CISO, employee behavior evaluating
  about 140
  employee motivation 141
  employee skill level 141
  remuneration schemes 141
  rewarding schemes 141
CISO executive
  hiring 176
CISO, external providers
  partnering with 137
CISO functions, in risk management
  about 125
  business continuity (BC) 126
  continuous monitoring (CM) 125
  critical systems and data, reviewing 125
  external threats management 125
  incident response (IR) 126
  internal threat management 126
  vendor risk management 126
CISO, internal providers
  partnering with 137
CISO role
  about 150, 151
  aspects 154, 155
  challenges 167
  communication ability 149
  defining, in organization 156
  handling 167
  hiring 148
  information, presenting to
    board of directors 168
  job description 152, 153
  job experience 149

leadership skills 149
leadership style, signaling 157
leadership support, securing 156
professional relationships, building 156
qualifications 148
security strategy for organization,
    developing 156
skills requirements 151, 152
trust, establishing with
    security team 157
CISOs, cybersecurity professionals
  recommendations 200, 201
CISO, security consultants
  partnering with 139, 140
CISO, security tool providers
  partnering with 139, 140
CISOs partnerships
  communication channels,
    establishing 25
  customer advisory groups 25, 26
  establishing 23
  establishing, with security experts 22
  establishing, with vendors 22
  long-term working relationships,
    creating with vendors 24
  security experts, as knowledge
    resource 23
  system security evaluation tools 24
CISOs, risk management
  business continuity and
    incident response 91
  continuous monitoring 91
  critical systems and data 90
  external threat management 90
  internal threat management 90
  vendor risk management 91

cloud access security broker (CASB) 225
cloud focus 234
Cloud Security Alliance Cloud Controls
　　Matrix (CSA-CCM) 192
communication 127
community
　onboarding 133, 134
company policies 18, 19
compliance requirements
　understanding, with security
　　documentation 85
compromised credentials 61
Comvalius, Raymond 235
confidentiality, integrity,
　　availability (CIA) 196
configuration management
　　database (CMDB) 181
consultants procedures 74
Consumer Financial Protection
　　Bureau (CFPB) 47
continuous life-cycle management 233
continuous monitoring (CM) 196
continuous patch management 234
continuous security validation (CSV) 229
contractors procedures 74
core duties, of top management
　internal controls, ensuring 128
　regulations and laws, abiding 128
　safe business community, creating
　　for stakeholders 128
corporate governance 127
cost-benefit analysis (CBA) 126, 198
CSO, and CISO
　differences 5
　similarities 5
CTO 6

customers
　onboarding 131
　security initiatives, for
　　onboarding 131, 132
cyberattacks
　organization, defending from 178-184
　organization, protecting from 178-184
cyber-physical systems (CPS) 188
cyber risk
　about 64
　factors, considerations 65
cybersecurity
　addressing, as business problem 144
　BC factors 174
　DR factors 174
　integrating, with DPP 107
　performance metrics 197, 198
　performance monitoring 197, 198
　security awareness 194-196
　workforce skills development 194-196
cybersecurity and business
　　continuity (BC)
　DoS attacks, planning for 114
　objectives 113
　quality backups, using 114
　ransomware, planning for 114
　relationship between 112, 113
　user training and education 115
cybersecurity awareness
　bigger budget, obtaining 164
　building 162
　cybersecurity issues,
　　communicating 163, 164
　organization leading, by example 165
　security policies, developing 163
　training conferences and seminars,
　　organizing for employees 166

cybersecurity documents, examples
  about 86
  business continuity plan (BCP) 90-92
  disaster recovery (DR) 90-92
  incident management plan (IMP) 87
  information security policy (ISP) 86
  risk management 87, 89
cybersecurity leadership
  about 216, 217
  future 217-222
cybersecurity posture
  maintaining 203-210
cybersecurity strategy
  building 166, 167
cyber strategy
  about 93
  approaches 95
cyber strategy, building
  business, knowing 96
  documentation 97, 98
  reasons 94
  risks, knowing 96
  threats, knowing 96
cyber strategy plan
  building 93

D

data compliance
  defining 30, 31
data loss prevention (DLP) 212
Data Protection Officer (DPO) 35
data protection plan (DPP) 107
  used, for integrating cybersecurity 107
deep neural networks (DNNs) 119
defense in breadth 102

defense in depth approaches
  about 100
  components 100, 101
defense in depth (DiD) 197
disaster recovery (DR)
  about 90, 192, 193
  documenting 90
disaster recovery (DR) plan
  building tips 120
  versus business continuity
    (BC) plan 118, 119
disaster recovery (DR) types
  about 118
  cloud-based DR 118
  data center DR 118
  network DR 118
  virtualization DR 118
distributed control systems (DCS) 188
documentation process
  considering, areas 82
  innovation 82
  need for 82
DR as a service (DRaaS)
  about 109
  automated testing processes 110
  communication plan,
    developing 109, 110
  continuous updates 111
  data reuse 111
  immutable data backups 110
  long-term planning 112
DR landscape
  emerging technologies 120
DR processes
  artificial intelligence (AI), using 119
Durmaz, Şükrü 215

E

EC-Council CISO program 12
edge services 107
E-Government Act 53
Electronic Fund Transfer Act (EFTA)
    about 46, 47
    history 47
    requirements for service providers 47
emerging technologies
    in BC landscape 120
    in DR landscape 120
employees
    onboarding 130, 131
encryption 100
endpoint antivirus system 100
endpoint detection and
        response (EDR) 181
endpoint protection platform (EPP) 197
European Data Protection Directive 33
external communication plan 109
external testing strategies 98
external threat 165

F

Federal Bureau of Investigation (FBI) 65
Federal Information Security
        Management Act (FISMA)
    about 53
    compliance 53
    non-compliance penalties 54, 55
    reasons, for creating 53
Federal Reserve Bureau (FRB) 47
Federal Trade Commission (FTC) 48
financial reporting 143
financial technology (FinTech) 185
function categorization 61

G

GDPR compliant 32
General Data Protection
        Regulation (GDPR)
    about 20, 32, 139, 173, 187
    CISO role 35
    data controller 33
    data processing 33
    data processor 33
    data protection principles 34
    data subject 33
    history 32, 33
    personal data 33
governance, risk, and compliance (GRC)
    aspects 187

H

Health and Human Services (HHS) 39
Health Information Technology
        for Economic and Clinical
        Health Act (HITECH Act)
    about 43
    amendments 44
    goals 45
    provisions 44
Health Insurance Portability and
        Accountability Act (HIPAA)
    about 20, 36, 64, 173, 187
    privacy rule 36
    right, to access PHI 37
    rules 38-40
HIPAA title II 36
hiring procedures
    about 67
    anomalous activities, investigating 75
    background check 74

employment procedures 73
general safety procedures 72
identity and access management
    (IAM) policies 70
internet access, securing 75
misuse of assets, monitoring 76
organizational culture 69
perimeter strategies and
    tools, refocusing 76
security education and training 68
security risk awareness 69
strong authentication
    mechanisms, using 75
verification checks, performing
    for job candidates 68
HR management
  role, in cybersecurity issues 173
human resources (HR) 162
hyper-scale clouds 107

I

identifier (ID) 73
incident management plan (IMP) 87
incident response (IR) 60, 178
industrial control systems (ICS) 188
industrial IoT (IIoT) 185
information and communications
    technology (ICT) 235
Information Security and
    Assurance (ISA)/IEC 192
information security documentation
  about 80
  examples 81
information security initiatives
  managing 21
  security team, hiring 22
  strategic security, planning 21

Information Security Management
    System (ISMS) 85, 191
information security policy (ISP)
  about 86
  creating, best practices 86
information system documentation
  guidelines, by ISO 83
  security, need for 80
Information Systems Audit and Control
    Association (ISACA) 13
Information Technology Infrastructure
    Library (ITIL) 13
information technology (IT) 61,
    109, 129, 176, 180
infrastructure as a service (IaaS) 118
insider security threats, preventing
  about 66
  examples 66, 67
intellectual property (IP) 187
internal staff policies 18
internal testing strategies 99
internal threat 165
International Information System Security
    Certification Consortium (ISC²) 13
International Organization for
    Standardization (ISO)
  guidelines, for information
    system documentation 83
international regulations
  compliance with 20
  examples 20
Internet of Things (IoT) 162, 185
intrusion prevention system (IPS) 212
ISO 27001
  about 85
  planning process 85, 86
  security specification 85

IT assets inventory 61
IT compliance 56
IT threat landscape
  assessment tools 16
  company operations 16
  evaluating 16
  trends, in cyber threats 17

J

Jankowski-Lorek, Mike 210

K

Kennedy-Kassebaum Act 36
key performance indicators (KPIs) 180
knowledge, skills, and abilities (KSAs) 194

L

leadership
  issue 169
local area network (LAN) 75

M

machine learning (ML) 119, 197
malware 61
managed security service
    providers (MSSPs) 230
man-in-the-middle (MitM) 61
maximum interruptible
    window (MIW) 192
maximum tolerable downtime
    (MTD) 192
Meloski, Vladimir 228
mitigation 89

modern CISO
  working, on improving security
      within organizations 203-210
modus operandi (MO) 182
Moneim, Adel Abdel 199
multi-factor authentication
    (MFA) 66, 126, 180
Murray, Marcus 184, 185

N

National Initiative for Cybersecurity
    Education (NICE) 194
National Institute of Standards and
    Technology (NIST) 53, 180
network security 100
New Technology (NT)/Windows
    2000 (Win2K) 75
NICE Cybersecurity Workforce
    Framework (NCWF) 194
NIST Cybersecurity Framework
    (CSF) 190
non-disclosure agreements (NDAs) 73
North American Electric Reliability
    Corporation (NERC) 187

O

Open Web Application Security
    Project (OWASP) 102
operational expenses (OPEX) 198
operational security (OPSEC) 73
operational technology (OT) 185
optimal budgeting 126
organization
  defending, from cyberattacks 178-184
  protecting, from cyberattacks 178-184

organizational culture 69
organization's security posture
  assessing 63
  improving, methods 62
Özarslan, Süleyman 232

P

Payment Card Industry Data Security
    Standard (PCI DSS) 187
Payment Card Industry (PCI) 64
penetration testing 24
Personal Information Protection and
    Electronic Documents Act 55
personally identifiable
    information (PII) 235
phishing 61
physical security
  about 71
  biometric authentication 71
  lock and key 72
  Two-factor authentication (2FA) 71
policies
  devising, to reduce risk 17
principle of least privilege (POLP) 184
privacy information management
    system (PIMS) 191
programmable logic controllers
    (PLCs) 188
project document 81
Protected Healthcare
    Information (PHI) 36
public key infrastructure (PKI) 235
public relations (PR) team 109

R

ransomware 61
recovery point objective (RPO) 192
recovery time objective (RTO) 192
regulatory bodies
  examples 20
remediation 89
resilience 192, 193
retention policies 235
return on security investment (ROSI) 186
risk 96
risk acceptance 89
risk avoidance 89
risk management
  about 87, 89, 125
  functions, CISO 125
risk management, data security
  assessment 89
  identification 89
  treatment 89
Risk Management Framework (RMF) 187
risks transference 89

S

Sarbanes-Oxley Act
  about 51
  history 51
  key provisions 52
Sarica, Mert 202
Sarica, Sarif 216
Securities and Exchange
    Commission (SEC) 51
security awareness training (SAT) 205
security consultants 139

security controls
  about 61
  devising, to reduce risk 17
  function categorization 61
  type categorization 61
security documentation
  approving 84
  communicating 84, 85
  maintaining 84
  tips, for better security 92, 93
  used for understanding compliance
    requirements 85
security education and training 68
security experts
  ethical hacking procedures,
    performing 227
  information, correlating from
    different security products 225
  risks, analyzing 224
  security best practices, applying 225
  security standard, implementing 227
  security training, delivering for
    business employees 226
  security training, delivering
    for IT employees 226
  trends, monitoring in
    security threats 224
  working with 223
security, information, and event
  management (SIEM) 182
security initiatives, for customers
  onboarding 131, 132
security leadership
  about 176
  documentation impact 174
security leadership role
  designing 7

security operations
  about 196
  functions 196, 197
security operations center (SOC) 180
security orchestration, automation,
    and reporting (SOAR) 197
security policies
  about 163
  developing 163
  implementing 70
security posture
  about 60
  automating 62
  features 60
security posture assessment
  attack surfaces, mapping 64
  cyber risk 64
  IT asset inventory, determining 64
  steps 63
security team
  issue 169
senior management executives
    (SMEs) 127
service-level agreements (SLAs) 187
service providers (SPs) 107
shareholders
  methods, for onboarding 133
  onboarding 132, 133
Sherwood Applied Business Security
    Architecture (SABSA) 192
software-as-a-service (SaaS) 107
Special Publication (SP) 193
stakeholder onboarding 123
stakeholders
  role, in organization 175
  security documentation,
    communicating to 84

standard operating procedures (SOPs) 207
state-of-the-art (SOTA) 185
storage area network (SAN) 184
Summers, Timothy C 223
supervisory control and data
    acquisition (SCADA) 188
supply-chain continuity
  learning 116
SysAdmin, Audit, Network, and Security
    Institute (SANS Institute) 13
system administrator (sysadmin) 184
system development documents 81
system documentation 81

T

targeted testing strategy 99
Technical Specification (TS) 193
threat intelligence (TI) 182
top management, in organization
  core duties 128, 129
top of mind (TOM) 180
training conferences and seminars
  organizing, for employees 165, 166
type categorization 61

U

User and entity behavior analytics (UEBA)
  about 142
  advantages 142, 143

V

vendors procedures 74
virtual private networks (VPNs) 107
virtual reality (VR) 194

W

Web Application Firewalls (WAFs) 102
Whistleblower Protection Act 52

Z

zero trust 234

Packt.com

Subscribe to our online digital library for full access to over 7,000 books and videos, as well as industry leading tools to help you plan your personal development and advance your career. For more information, please visit our website.

Why subscribe?

- Spend less time learning and more time coding with practical eBooks and Videos from over 4,000 industry professionals
- Improve your learning with Skill Plans built especially for you
- Get a free eBook or video every month
- Fully searchable for easy access to vital information
- Copy and paste, print, and bookmark content

Did you know that Packt offers eBook versions of every book published, with PDF and ePub files available? You can upgrade to the eBook version at packt.com and as a print book customer, you are entitled to a discount on the eBook copy. Get in touch with us at customercare@packtpub.com for more details.

At www.packt.com, you can also read a collection of free technical articles, sign up for a range of free newsletters, and receive exclusive discounts and offers on Packt books and eBooks.

Another Book You May Enjoy

If you enjoyed this book, you may be interested in these other books by Packt:

Incident Response in the Age of Cloud

Dr. Erdal Ozkaya

ISBN: 9781800569218

- Understand IR and its significance
- Organize an IR team
- Explore best practices for managing attack situations with your IR team
- Form, organize, and operate a product security team to deal with product vulnerabilities and assess their severity
- Organize all the entities involved in product security response
- Respond to security vulnerabilities using tools developed by Keepnet Labs and Binalyze
- Adapt all the above learnings for the cloud

Packt is searching for authors like you

If you're interested in becoming an author for Packt, please visit `authors.packtpub.com` and apply today. We have worked with thousands of developers and tech professionals, just like you, to help them share their insight with the global tech community. You can make a general application, apply for a specific hot topic that we are recruiting an author for, or submit your own idea.

Share Your Thoughts

Now you've finished *Cybersecurity Leadership Demystified*, we'd love to hear your thoughts! Scan the QR code below to go straight to the Amazon review page for this book and share your feedback or leave a review on the site that you purchased it from.

https://packt.link/r/1801819289

Your review is important to us and the tech community and will help us make sure we're delivering excellent quality content.